WHAT ARE FRIENDS FOR?

WHAT ARE FRIENDS FOR?

*Feminist Perspectives on
Personal Relationships
and Moral Theory*

MARILYN FRIEDMAN

CORNELL UNIVERSITY PRESS / *Ithaca and London*

First published 1993 by Cornell University Press.

International Standard Book Number 0-8014-2721-5 (cloth)
International Standard Book Number 0-8014-8004-3 (paper)
Library of Congress Catalog Card Number 93-25812

Printed in the United States of America

*Librarians: Library of Congress cataloging information appears on the
last page of the book.*

⊗ The paper in this book meets the minimum requirements of the
American National Standard for Information Sciences–Permanence of
Paper for Printed Library Materials, ANSI Z39.48-1984.

DEDICATED TO
THE MEMORY OF MY PARENTS,
FLORENCE KATZ SOTZKY
EDWARD SOTZKY

CONTENTS

Acknowledgments   ix

Introduction   1

Part I. Partiality and Impartiality

1. The Impracticality of Impartiality   9

2. The Practice of Partiality   35

3. The Social Self and the Partiality Debates   62

Part II. Care and Justice

4. Care and Context in Moral Reasoning   91

5. Gendered Morality   117

6. Liberating Care   142

Part III. Friendship

7. Friendship and Moral Growth   187

8. Friendship, Choice, and Change   207

9. Feminism and Modern Friendship: Dislocating the
    Community   231

Selected Bibliography   257

Index   271

ACKNOWLEDGMENTS

What *are* friends for? I owe an immeasurable debt to the many friends, students, and colleagues who stimulated my explorations of the themes and topics in this book. Some of those colleagues provided formal commentaries on earlier versions of these chapters which I presented at professional meetings. For both the formal and the informal, for the provocative challenges as well as the gratifying encouragement, for the many wise, witty, and wonderful ideas that helped me out, I am happy to thank Thomas Attig, Sandra Bartky, Marcia Baron, Lawrence Becker, Lawrence Blum, Claudia Card, Anne Donchin, James Fishkin, Owen Flanagan, Carol Harding, Helen Haste, Virginia Held, Kathryn Jackson, Alison Jaggar, Eva Kittay, Dorothy Leland, Angela McBride, William McBride, Howard McGary, Larry May, Diana Meyers, Christopher Morris, Vikki Patraka, Bill Puka, David Solomon, Joan Straumanis, Robert Strikwerda, L. W. Sumner, Cass Sunstein, Laurence Thomas, Margaret Walker, Penny Weiss, Tom Wren, and Iris Young.

Diana Meyers, who read the entire manuscript, and Eva Feder Kittay, who read most of it, each made detailed and crucial recommendations toward its improvement. The resulting work profited immensely from their advice. I am deeply indebted to both of them for this and for many other professional and personal generosities. My editor at Cornell, Kathleen Kearns, has been a treasure, efficient and flexible, as she shepherded the manuscript through the publication process.

Academic audiences in five countries (the United States, Canada, Mexico, England, and Ireland) have heard earlier versions of most of the chapters, and their responses prompted my reconsideration of many points. The students who explored feminist ethics with me in a spring 1992 graduate course on the subject helped me to clarify my latest thoughts about care ethics; thanks are due especially to Joanne Bronson, Peggy DesAutels, Virginia Ingram, Patrick Hopkins, Shari Sharratt, and Leona Warner. The Society for Women in Philosophy provided an especially receptive and stimulating forum for dialogue on several occasions. In addition, the members have given me one of the warmest tributes of all: they laughed at my jokes.

Some of this book was written with research support. In particular, I am grateful to have received a National Endowment for the Humanities Summer Stipend for 1987, a Major Grant from the Faculty Research Committee of Bowling Green State University (where I was then teaching) for the fall of 1987, and a National Endowment for the Humanities Research Fellowship for 1988–89. The project has changed substantially since those early years, when it struggled (and was happily funded) under the title "Justice Among Friends." Justice among friends remains a theme of the middle chapter of the book, where it is now one element in a richer and more comprehensive array of concerns.

Parts of this book have been published elsewhere. I thank the relevant editors and publishers for permission to reprint with revisions all of the following: Chapter 1, which appeared in *The Journal of Philosophy* 86 (November 1989): 645–56; Chapter 2, which appeared in *Ethics* 101 (July 1991): 818–35, published by the University of Chicago Press (©1991 by the University of Chicago. All rights reserved.); Chapter 3, which appeared in *Feminist Ethics*, edited by Claudia Card (Lawrence: University of Kansas Press, 1991), pp. 161–79; Chapter 4, which appeared as MOSAIC monograph no. 1 (Bath, England: University of Bath Press, 1985), and as a chapter entitled "Abraham, Socrates, and Heinz: Where Are the Women? (Care and Context in Women's Moral Reasoning)," in *Moral Dilemmas: Philosophical and Psychological Issues in the Development of Moral Reasoning,* edited by Carol Harding (Chicago: Precedent, 1985), pp. 25–42; Chapter 5, which appeared under the title "Beyond Caring: The De-Moralization of Gender," in *Science, Morality, and Feminist Theory,* edited by Marsha Hanen and Kai Nielsen as *The Canadian Journal of Philosophy* suppl. vol. 13 (1987): 87–110; Chapter 7, which appeared in *Journal of Value Inquiry* 23 (1989): 3–13, ©1989 Kluwer Academic Publishers, reprinted by permission of Kluwer Academic Publishers; and Chapter 9, which appeared in *Ethics* 99 (January 1989): 275–90, published by the University of Chicago Press (©1989 by the University of Chicago. All rights reserved.).

My deepest gratitude is owed to Larry May and to Elizabeth. Always cheerfully contentious and unstintingly supportive, Larry has been a constant professional and personal companion to me through all my recent projects. Elizabeth's "whys" are a continual source of renewal for my own curiosity and wonder; may that wellspring never run dry. Together, they strive with me to realize our highest ideals for a family life of devoted tenderness and mutual inspiration. This book owes an incalculable debt to them.

For whatever insights I have achieved, for whatever wisdom gained, I am deeply beholden to all those friends whose perceptiveness, audacity, candor, and spirit have aroused my feminist moral imagination.

M. F.

St. Louis, Missouri

WHAT ARE FRIENDS FOR?

INTRODUCTION

Modern Anglo-American moral theory, as a whole, has represented "the moral life" in a severely diminished and distorted form. Until very recently, modern ethical theory neglected the moral importance of friendship and familial ties the so-called special relationships. Although a few modern moral philosophers, Kant, Sidgwick, and, most notably, Mill, for example, gave some philosophical attention to personal relationships, these investigations have not figured among the canonical texts or textual passages that have dominated Anglo-American moral theorizing over the past several centuries. The prevailing theoretical developments and research priorities of modern Anglo-American ethics have substantially ignored all intimate and special human affiliations.

In addition to neglecting close personal relationships, Anglo-American moral philosophy, like most of the Western academic tradition, has, until recent decades, almost entirely omitted the voices of women. The marked absence of women's voices, concerns, and perspectives has contributed to a near-total philosophical silence about the gender hierarchies of social life and the gender-specific nature of many norm-governed social roles and practices (again, with the notable exception of writings by Mill).

Since the 1970s, feminist philosophers have sought to rectify these deficiencies and enrich the scope of philosophical theorizing. From the outset, feminist philosophical thought focused on the nature and quality of personal relationships, including their tendencies toward gender hierarchy and the subordination of women. In the early 1980s, Carol Gilligan's research into the moral orientations of women added new directions to feminist philosophical thought. Gilligan's work helped to uncover an ethic of care, a perspective on moral matters and on the self as moral agent that both diverges from traditional moral theory and appears to be closely associated with women's traditional role as nurturer. Out of the philosophical revisions inspired by this and tandem feminist developments, a new subspeciality crystallized: feminist ethics.

At the same time that feminists began to direct ethical attention toward the moral significance of personal relationships, virtue theorists were raising related concerns. Virtue theorists, however, have ignored a number of matters that are of great interest to feminists. These include the quality of close personal relationships, the heavily female responsibilities for the intimate labors of sustaining those relationships, and the need to transform our relationship practices in order more fully to promote women's flourishing. Feminist reflections on personal relationships, thus, represent a distinctly illuminating and invigorating contribution to modern moral theory.

The aim of this book is to continue the feminist reconsideration of moral theory in light of the moral importance and complexity of personal relationships. I proceed by drawing together three topic areas of lively current discussion which bear on our philosophical understanding of personal relationships. In Part I of the book I deal with the debate between defenders of moral impartiality and critics who challenge this principle in the name of the partiality that characterizes personal relationships. In Part II, I investigate the ethic of care, including the interconnections between care and justice, and some complications in our gender-asymmetric practices of caring. The subject of Part III is friendship in particular, a relationship that is, perhaps now more than ever, crucial to moral life. Indisputably, friendship exemplifies justified partiality and care. In addition, it is becoming a preeminent intimate relationship in this era of widespread decline in both the role of extended families and the cohesion of nuclear families.

The book opens with a consideration, in Part I, of the moral requirement of impartiality and the challenge posed to it by close relationships. The principle of moral impartiality calls upon the moral agent to give equal consideration to the morally relevant interests of all persons. Like many of the critics of moral impartialism, I believe that the impartial standpoint is humanly impossible; my arguments against that standpoint take a specifically practical turn (Chapter 1). Nevertheless, I endorse the impartialist's goal of eliminating bias from moral reasoning. Toward that end, I propose a more practicable method for achieving unbiased moral thinking. This method focuses not on an unrecognizable ideal of impartiality, but rather on the elimination of recognizable biases. Biases are best discerned in intersubjective dialogue among persons of different standpoints, including those who are the victims of bias and are therefore likely to be best situated to discern the biases against them in the thinking and practices of others.

Although I challenge the requirement of moral impartiality, I also explore the moral complications in our practices of partiality (Chapter 2). Partiality is only as good, morally speaking, as the relationships it helps to sustain. The critical assessment of personal relationships must take account of the historical circumstances that form the contexts for personal relationship practices. One of the most important of these circumstances is the vastly unequal social distribution of the means for favoring loved ones. Because of this inequality, our conventional relationship practices of partiality can, for some persons, fail to realize the very integrity and fulfillment to which many partialists appeal to justify those practices.

I conclude my discussion of partiality (Chapter 3) by noting some ways in which the partiality debates bear on a conception of the self that has recently gained wide philosophical attention, namely, a conception of the self as inherently social. The conception of the social self, an invaluable contribution to our understanding of the metaphysical foundations of morality and a cornerstone of much feminist philosophy, needs to be reconsidered in the light of several issues raised by the partiality debates. One such issue is the problem of accounting for the possibility of social criticism and resistance on the part of a self who is constituted by the very social relationships and cultural traditions that would be the targets of her resistance. Another problem is that of locating a basis, in the very nature and identity of the self, for global moral concern,

concern for those others who are either not known in any particular detail or for whom no affection is felt. I reconsider the social conception of the self in relation to these two concerns.

In Part II, I turn to the ethics of care and its implications for moral theory. Carol Gilligan's pioneering work in this area, as noted earlier, has explored some of the differences between two distinct and by now well-known moral orientations. One orientation is focused on justice and rights and is formally structured by abstract principles; this perspective has been regarded by some theorists as being paradigmatic of the moral domain. The other orientation focuses on care and personal relationships and is highly attentive to contextual moral details. The two orientations have seemed to be associated with the moral perspectives of men and women, respectively (a gender dichotomy I question below). I defend the view (Chapter 4) that matters of care are not merely reducible to, or comprehensible in terms of, justice, and that justice does not, by itself, define the moral domain. I also explore the role played by contextual detail in reasoning about matters of both care and justice.

A radical dichotomy between reasoning about care and justice however, is implausible. I suggest that gender stereotypes may be at work to promote the appearance that care and justice are mutually exclusive moral concerns, stereotypes that influence both ordinary perceptual judgments and empirical research into moral reasoning (Chapter 5). I also argue that an integration of considerations of care with those of justice is necessary for a fully adequate moral perspective. At the same time, I suggest that the difference in moral perspectives that Gilligan labeled a "care-justice" dichotomy does indeed relate to noteworthy dichotomies of moral thinking. I end Chapter 5 by proposing that one such dichotomy is manifested in a dialectical interplay between two different sorts of moral commitments: on the one hand, commitments to abstract, general values and principles, and, on the other hand, what I construe as commitments to persons in their unique particularity. I sketch an account of commitments to particular persons, a type of commitment the moral value of which is unrecognized by the theories predominant in modern ethics.

In Chapter 6 I investigate some of the ways current formulations of care ethics have not sufficiently attended to the cultural subordination of women. To deal with certain aspects of this vast problem, I call for introducing into care ethics a cautiously individualistic strain of thought, one that is consistent with a care-ethical conception of persons as inherently social beings. This cautious individualism will provide a grounding in the ethics of care for regarding the well-being of individual care givers as intrinsically valuable. I develop this line of thought by considering some of the caretaking responsibilities imposed more heavily on women than on men. Finally, I explore some differences between typical forms of care provided by women and those provided by men, in order to disclose some of the ways caring practices themselves contribute to women's cultural subordination.

In Part III, I turn from the theoretical significance of personal relationships in general to an investigation of friendship in particular. Here, I seek out some of the less frequently noticed values and dimensions of friendship. The capacity of friendships to afford us vicarious participation in moral standpoints other than our own is my first theme here. This capacity enriches the experiential base of our moral understandings and thereby contributes to our moral growth (Chapter 7). In this discussion of friendship as a source of moral transformation, I emphasize the role of friends as potential "moral witnesses" on whose moral attitudes and responses we sometimes rely. This reliance is fostered by a kind of little-understood moral commitment first noted in Chapter 5. This is the commitment to particular persons as such, in their unique particularity, a sort of commitment that supplements and counterbalances our commitments to generalized moral abstractions.

The special responsibilities owed to friends seem best grounded on the voluntary nature of that relationship (in cultures in which this is one of the features of friendship). This voluntariness contributes to the potential of friendship to provide support for persons with unconventional values. With the support of friends, such persons are more able than they would be otherwise to challenge and alter existing traditions and practices (Chapter 8). Friendship thus has importance as a relational practice with socially transformative potential. The voluntariness of such relationships, however, could harbor certain moral hazards, or so it might seem to those feminist theorists who worry that the voluntarist strain of, say, contractarian theory makes it inhospitable to genuine caring and personal relationships. I try to deflect such concerns by differentiating the voluntarism of friendship from that of contractarian theory.

The theme of friendship's voluntary basis is reiterated in my concluding chapter. There I develop a critique of certain versions of recent communitarian theory—in particular, of their seeming bent toward social conservatism, as reflected in the communitarian tendency to be uncritical of traditional practices and to regard traditional "communities," such as family and nation, as paradigmatic of community per se. These "communities of place," whose role in our lives is typically given rather than created, should be supplemented, I contend, by "communities of choice," such as friendship in the modern sense and urban voluntary associations. The voluntary basis of these alternative communities offers steadier grounding than do traditional relationships for the questioning of custom and resistance to oppressive traditions. I argue for the specifically feminist importance of this option.

With cautious and guarded optimism, I believe that modern moral philosophy can surmount its past limitations and move forward to meet the challenges of feminist ethics. To do so, modern moral theories must incorporate the perspectives of diverse women (not to mention various other excluded perspectives that exceed the scope of this book). In addition, moral theories must aim for no less than a thoroughgoing grasp of the moral significance and the complications of personal relationships, including their gender structures and asymmetries. On the basis of such efforts, moral philosophy may yet prove adequate for representing the moral richness, variety, and complexity of personal relationships in our lives. Such, at any rate, is the larger project toward which this book in feminist ethics is aimed.

PART I

Partiality and Impartiality

1

The Impracticality
of Impartiality

*M*oral and political theorists have shared with many ordinary folk a presumption that our everyday moral thinking is often biased and prejudiced. The bias which has most disturbed moral theorists is that of self-regard, a favoring of one's own interests. Other biases, however, may be no less familiar and no less well entrenched: the favoring of one's relatives, for example, or friends, members of one's ethnic group, or co-nationals. It is a familiar view that bias distorts moral thinking and obscures the search for sound moral judgment. That assumption will not be challenged in this chapter.

Eliminating bias and prejudice from at least certain levels of moral thinking has long been a goal of moral theory. As many moral theorists would put it, bias interferes with the equal consideration of all persons which defines the "moral point of view." Some theorists propose various constraints upon moral thinking in order to achieve that end. The result may be characterized as a kind of "standpoint" that one is required to adopt. An unbiased standpoint is widely regarded as the privileged standpoint for critically reflecting[1] on normative matters ranging from basic principles

1. In my usage, critical moral thinking is a type of substantive moral thinking in which moral views are debated and good reasons are sought to support substantive moral conclusions. Critical moral thinking is a kind of

of morality, politics, even rationality itself, to particular and detailed moral situations.

Referred to as "impartiality" by some, as "objectivity" by others, and as "impersonality" by still others, the unbiased standpoint has, unfortunately, proved to be as elusive as it is alluring. The thesis of this chapter is that moral and political theorists who invoke an unbiased, or *impartial*, standpoint, as I shall refer to it, typically do not develop an epistemic or psychological account of how it is to be attained by a person who is, to begin with, biased—that is, who is any one of us. Such theorists provide no independent criteria for recognizing whether or not impartiality has really been achieved by the specified method. One is left with no way to confirm, in practice, that moral thought is genuinely impartial, that is, genuinely free of bias or prejudice.

I begin by sketching the elusive impartiality that still challenges moral theory. Section 2 briefly outlines two contemporary theoretical models of critical moral reflection which have been proposed as yielding impartial normative thought: Rawls's contractual model and Hare's method of universalization. In the third section, I argue that these methods of normative thinking represent psychological and epistemic feats the achievement of which we have no independent way to confirm.

Section 4 discusses an alternative approach to impartiality which does not focus on methods of critical moral reflection or attempt to define an impartial standpoint. Instead, this approach involves an analysis of impartial propositions or impartial reasons in terms of requirements of universality and neutrality. I argue that this analysis also fails to capture what is involved in the notion of full impartiality in moral thinking.

Rather than trying to save either the modeling of an impartial standpoint or the analysis of impartial reasons, I adopt yet a different approach. In Section 5, I recommend that we replace the

"second" level of moral thinking in which we engage when we open ourselves up to questions and challenges and when we consider alternative views and viewpoints. My conception of this level of thinking differs in certain respects from that of R. M. Hare (*Moral Thinking* [Oxford: Clarendon Press, 1981]). For instance, I admit appeals to substantive moral intuition (although I do not regard such appeals as necessarily decisive); on this point, see Hare, p. 40.

single definitive notion of an abstract (and, if my argument is sound, impracticable) ideal of impartiality with concrete notions of specific partialities, that is, specific biases, which are to be eliminated from everyday moral thought. My proposal is that the only practicable route to impartiality is an indirect route, namely, via the elimination of particular nameable biases, whose manifestations in normative thinking can be specifically identified and corrected. Coupled with the empirical assumption that people in general lack privileged access to their own biases, this approach, I suggest, invites us to appreciate the crucial role played by moral dialogue in the recognition of bias and, in this respect, the practical intersubjectivity of the enterprise of critical moral thinking.

1. Delineation of the Problem

First, some terminological clarification. A variety of terms have been used somewhat interchangeably to identify the unbiased normative standpoint which is privileged by moral theory. "Impartial" is most common[2] but "impersonal"[3] and "objective"[4] are also used. "Impartiality" is the term I will use to refer to the unbiased standpoint privileged by normative theories. Impartiality typically means an absence of bias or prejudice.[5] Bias is the unduly favoring of one

2. This term is used, among others, by John Rawls, *A Theory of Justice* (Cambridge: Harvard University Press, 1971), e.g., pp. 187–90; Hare, *Moral Thinking*, e.g., p. 129; and Stephen Darwall, *Impartial Reason* (Ithaca, N.Y.: Cornell University Press, 1984), e.g., chap. 15.
3. This term is used, among others, by Darwall, *Impartial Reason*, e.g., chap. 11.
4. This term is used by, among others, David A. J. Richards, *A Theory of Reasons for Action* (Oxford: Clarendon Press, 1971), e.g., pp. 84–88; and Thomas Nagel, *The View from Nowhere* (Oxford: Oxford University Press, 1986), e.g., pp. 3–9. It should be noted that Nagel leaves a significant place in moral thinking for reasons and values that can be apprehended only subjectively, thus eluding the objective standpoint.
5. Contra theorists such as Roderick Firth ("Ethical Absolutism and the Ideal Observer," *Philosophy and Phenomenological Research* 12 [March 1952]: 340), we do not need to, and should not, define the impartial standpoint as dis-

party, person, or group of persons when disputes arise or interests compete. "Prejudice" can also be used to refer to bias, although it, used more carefully, means prejudgment, a judgment formed prior to due consideration. These two notions are combined in my discussion, which assumes that one goal of moral theory is to determine how to rid critical moral thinking of any favoritism that is not based on due consideration or supported by good reasons.[6]

I will avoid the term "objective" to refer to the lack of bias or prejudice. This term has a history of usage which includes its reference to what is external to mind, consciousness, or subjective awareness, notions that are not pertinent to my discussion. Thus, Thomas Nagel, when using this term to refer to the privileged normative standpoint I am calling "impartial," must explain that he is not thereby committed to the external existence of moral values,[7] that he is *not* using the term in this more familiar sense.[8]

"Impersonal" is a less ambiguous term than "objective," but still not fully satisfactory. Some theorists differentiate impersonality from impartiality. For John Rawls, a moral theory or method is impersonal if it fails to take seriously the distinction between persons, for example, by conflating the desires of all involved persons into one system for the purposes of determining one conglomerated outcome. Rawls faults utilitarianism for having this feature. For Rawls, impartiality, as an absence of bias or prejudice, does not require impersonality, and impersonality is undesirable in a moral theory.[9]

An impersonal standpoint, as distinct from an impersonal the-

---

passionate or unemotional in order to construe it as unbiased. Reason and passion do not necessarily bias normative thinking; whether they actually do so in any given case is a contingent matter.

6. In this chapter I leave the core notions of "due consideration" and "good reasons" undeveloped. I acknowledge, however, the risk of circularity in their further specification, a point recognized by Philosophy Department members at Kansas State University when I presented this chapter there as a Philosophy Colloquium on April 19, 1989.

7. Nagel, *View from Nowhere*, p. 144.

8. Hare discusses different meanings of the term 'objective'; *Moral Thinking*, pp. 206–14.

9. Rawls, *Theory of Justice*, pp. 187–88.

ory, is simply the standpoint of no one in particular; it is Thomas Nagel's "nowhere."[10] Even in regard to standpoints, however, impersonality should not be equated with impartiality, that is, with an absence of bias. Such an equation would require certain debatable assumptions. First, one would have to assume that a personal standpoint is necessarily biased. An unbiased standpoint, however, might be feasible, for all we know, as the standpoint of some person in particular. Second, one would have to assume the conceivability and meaningfulness of a standpoint, a point of view, a *view*, which was not the view of some personal being, yet was nevertheless both accessible to our understanding (else how could its determinations influence our moral reasonings?) and, most important, authoritative with respect to our moral judgments. Rather than undertake the formidable task of trying to justify such an assumption, I shall avoid the notion of an impersonal standpoint or theory and use only the terms "impartiality" and the "impartial standpoint" to refer to that absence of bias which is taken by moral theory to define the moral point of view.

At the same time, the notion of impartiality itself admits of at least two distinct applications, only one of which is of concern here. Besides defining the privileged standpoint we are supposed to adopt when critically reflecting on moral matters, impartiality also identifies a duty we are sometimes to incorporate into our daily activities and practices. In this other application, impartiality is a specific duty, for example, of those who fill roles of public trust which involve the dispensing of goods or services among competing applicants. One is not to show bias toward or against any of the particular parties competing for whatever is to be dispensed.

As a specific duty, impartiality is not always morally obligatory. Partiality, or favoritism, in daily life is regarded by many moral philosophers as morally permissible and, sometimes, even morally obligatory.[11] Biases in daily life, tendencies to favor certain others,

10. Nagel, *View from Nowhere*, passim.
11. For a defense of the view that impartiality is not morally required of all persons at all times, see Lawrence Blum, *Friendship, Altruism, and Morality* (London: Routledge & Kegan Paul, 1980), pp. 46–57.

such as family members and friends, in one's care, assistance, attentiveness, loyalty, and so on, may well receive the imprimatur of unbiased critical moral reflection and so may constitute matters of moral duty under certain circumstances.[12] But this issue will not concern us here. My focus is on impartiality as a privileged standpoint for critical moral thinking, and not on impartiality as a specific moral duty.

2. "If I Were You. . . . "

The various contemporary theoretical models of impartial moral thinking include methods of universalization and models of social contract. While the details of these accounts of impartiality differ in important ways, and while there are profound differences among the normative conclusions that theorists justify by appeal to these devices, nevertheless, there are important commonalities as well.

The requirement of universalizability is well exemplified in the work of R. M. Hare.[13] In Hare's view, moral prescriptions and moral principles have to be universal; it is required by the logical properties of moral concepts.[14] To determine whether a proposed principle or prescription has this feature, one attempts to universalize it: that is, one attempts to determine if one would make the same judgment about any other situation, real or hypothetical, which was identical in its "universal descriptive properties" to the one under consideration.[15]

12. Hare, among many other contemporary moral philosophers, has defended this view: *Moral Thinking*, pp. 135–40.

13. Hare has developed his views in numerous writings, including his earlier books, *The Language of Morals* (Oxford: Clarendon Press, 1952) and *Freedom and Reason* (Oxford: Clarendon Press, 1963). My discussion concentrates on the version presented in his latest book, *Moral Thinking*. The selective focus ·of this chapter involves bypassing the approaches to universalizing presented by other philosophers. Among contemporary theorists, these include Marcus Singer, *Generalization in Ethics* (New York: Alfred A. Knopf, 1961) and Alan Gewirth, *Reason and Morality* (Chicago: University of Chicago Press, 1978).

14. Hare, *Moral Thinking*, p. 191.

15. Ibid., p. 21.

Since the range of all cases identical to this one includes those situations, real or hypothetical, in which one would occupy each of the different positions involved in this situation, one needs to imagine what it is like to be affected as each person in this situation would be by the action under consideration. One is required to understand what the situation means from each distinct standpoint of identity, preferences, and so on.[16] One is not to project oneself imaginatively into the situations of others retaining one's own distinctive identity or preferences. Rather, one is both to project oneself imaginatively into the *perspectives* of others and to attempt to comprehend their situations from their own respective points of view. It is this method for achieving impartiality which Lawrence Kohlberg called "reversibility," or, more colorfully, "moral musical chairs."[17]

The contractual model operates rather differently from the method of universalization. It begins by requiring unanimous consent among the members of the relevant community to a set of basic principles for arranging fundamental moral or social institutions. Consenting parties are to reach their unanimous choice of basic principles by means of thinking which is constrained or augmented in certain ways. According to the familiar Rawlsian contractual model for determining basic principles of justice, normative reasoners are, first, to suppress knowledge of their own subjective particulars; second, to suppose themselves possessed of all necessary general knowledge about persons and society; and, third, to abide by certain motivational constraints, most notably, mutual disinterest and lack of envy.[18] The choices sought from this original position must be ones to which everyone reasoning under the same constraints would consent. Unanimous agreement is the sign that no partial interests have been favored by the conclusions. (Of course, the unanimity and subsequent contract are hypothetical only.)

16. Ibid., pp. 91–95.
17. Lawrence Kohlberg, "The Claim to Adequacy of a Highest Stage of Moral Judgment," *Journal of Philosophy* 70 (1973): 641; reprinted as "Justice as Reversibility: The Claim to Moral Adequacy of a Highest State of Moral Judgment," in *The Philosophy of Moral Development* (San Francisco: Harper & Row, 1981), p. 199.
18. Rawls, *Theory of Justice*, pp. 136–42, 538–41.

Rawls's contractual model and Hare's method of universalization contrast in noteworthy ways.[19] The contractual model requires one to diminish one's motivations by eliminating concern for others; by contrast, universalization requires one to comprehend the motivations of others so that one becomes equally concerned with the interests of others as one is with one's own. The contractual model requires one to ignore all particular knowledge about oneself; universalization, instead, requires one to acquire and take account of all relevant particular knowledge about all other involved participants. Both methods suppose that one's relevant general knowledge is comprehensive. And both methods share one theoretically crucial aim: in their different modifications of motive and knowledge, these two methods aim to enable one person's thinking to represent the theoretically relevant interests of all involved persons.

The method of universalization presupposes that impartiality results from the incorporation of all perspectives into one standpoint. That is, the universalizing reasoner must somehow compile the views of all standpoints in reaching her normative conclusions. By contrast, the contractual model leaves self-interested motivation in place and excludes any motivational regard for other persons. This model seeks impartiality by denying the self any self-identifying information that she might use to privilege herself in her calculations. On a contractual model, there is supposed to be no alternative but to choose as would anyone whose motivation and knowledge were equivalently modified. The contractual reasoner is what I call a "stripped down" person, deprived of any individuating self-knowledge, who thereby represents all particular involved standpoints by modeling only what they share in common.[20]

19. The subsequent comparison owes a debt to a similar discussion by Richards, *A Theory of Reasons for Action*, pp. 87–88.

20. Susan Moller Okin argues that the original position is best interpreted as requiring us each to think from, and care about, the position of *"everybody, in the sense of each in turn"* ("Reason and Feeling in Thinking about Justice," *Ethics* 99 [January 1989]: 244–46). This interpretation likens Rawls's method to Hare's. An alternative and, in my view, more accurate reading of *A Theory of*

Both contract and universalization define a reconstructed standpoint for moral reflection which is supposed to eliminate bias and prejudice. In each case, the reconstructed standpoint is supposed to make it impossible for an ordinary person who adopts that standpoint to justify her moral judgment by exclusive appeal to any of the particulars which differentiate her interests or attachments from those of other persons. Her conclusions and supporting reasons may not refer to her specific identity, circumstances, experiences, background, family, friends, community, group, or history, except insofar as these particulars are described so generally as, in those general terms, to be shared by all persons.

Both these methods exemplify what Jürgen Habermas has called a "monological" approach to the privileged normative standpoint, the moral point of view.[21] They describe a discipline of thought that may be practiced by an individual moral reasoner in isolation. The features which make for a privileged normative standpoint are theorized to be formal or methodological features of what could be one person's isolated normative reflections. Of course, no individual begins such an exercise ex nihilo; a background of interpersonal experience, including dialogue with others about moral matters, is a practical necessity in order for someone to have the ability to engage in isolated moral thinking. And professional philosophers employing "monological" methods for seeking impartiality are nonetheless certainly talking to each other.

However, monological theories overlook the possibilities for achieving impartiality that inhere in interpersonal dialogue. In dialogue, persons can together self-consciously seek to eliminate the

---

Justice is that of Seyla Benhabib, who charges the original position with lacking any "real *plurality* of perspectives" ("The Generalized and the Concrete Other: The Kohlberg-Gilligan Controversy and Moral Theory," in Eva Feder Kittay and Diana T. Meyers, eds., *Women and Moral Theory* [Totowa, N.J.: Rowman and Littlefield, 1987], p. 166). At most, Rawls (p. 151) differentiates only the "standpoint of the least advantaged representative man."

21. Cf. Jürgen Habermas, "Moral Development and Ego Identity," in *Communication and the Evolution of Society*, trans. Thomas McCarthy (Boston: Beacon Press, 1979), p. 90; and Benhabib, "The Generalized and the Concrete Other," p. 167.

biases in each other's moral thinking and to reconcile their initially differing moral perspectives. By contrast, according to the models of both universalization and contract, intersubjective communication makes no theoretically significant contribution to the quest for impartiality.

It is beyond the scope of the present work to consider in detail alternatives to the "monological" models of impartiality.[22] On the basis of my criticisms of those models, however, I suggest in the final section of this chapter that real dialogue is crucial in practice for eliminating or minimizing bias in normative thinking and should be theoretically acknowledged as a practically necessary method toward that end.[23]

In the next section, I argue that the modified forms of thought required by either the contractual model or the method of universalizing represent excessively demanding cognitive feats and, as such, are not confirmably attainable. Hence, neither of these theoretical approaches provides us with practical guidance in achieving thinking that is genuinely impartial, that is, genuinely free of bias or prejudice.

3. The Impracticality of Impartiality

To summarize: Rawls's well-known contractual method for achieving impartiality calls for someone, first, to ignore some of her preexisting motivations; second, to ignore all the particular knowledge about herself that reveals her conception of the good or the particular ways in which she might be affected by social arrangements; and, third, to know much more in general than any person actually knows. Hare's method of universalization calls for a moral reasoner, first, to view the world from the standpoint of

22. Cf. Habermas, "Moral Development"; Benhabib, "The Generalized and the Concrete Other"; and Iris Marion Young, "Impartiality and the Civic Public: Some Implications of Feminist Critiques of Moral and Political Theory," *Praxis International* 5 (January 1986): 381–401.

23. For reservations about the "dialogical" approach, see Bruce Ackerman, "Why Dialogue?" *Journal of Philosophy* 86 (January 1989): 5–22.

the motives, preferences, and so on of all other parties in any situation under critical moral scrutiny; second, to know each particular situation fully in its "universal descriptive properties" as it is apprehended from each of those other standpoints; and, third, to know much more in general than any person actually knows. These methods of moral thinking constitute extraordinary cognitive feats. My primary objection to these methods is that we cannot even be reasonably sure in practice that we have met such requirements. Neither Rawls's nor Hare's theoretical approach suggests how we might determine whether or not the resulting thinking is genuinely impartial, that is, genuinely free of bias.[24]

It is true that these methods are presented as "hypothetical" or "fictional" in some sense or other. If such forms of thinking were thoroughly hypothetical or fictional, however, they could provide no substantive normative illumination whatsoever, not even to the theorists who author these methodological devices. If these methods for representing impartial normative thought are to provide us with genuine substantive insights into matters of morality or politics, then they must outline methods of reflection that are within the capacities of human beings to adopt.

Some of the methods specified to yield impartiality are obviously beyond the capacity of any person to achieve simply as an exercise of thought. It is not within anyone's capacity to alter her isolated thoughts so as to encompass general or particular knowledge that she does not, in fact, possess. Instructions of this sort urge us to cultivate a valuable habit for daily life, namely, the habit of expanding our knowledge of moral matters which concern us. Such instructions also help us to identify a presupposition held by those moral reasoners who claim impartiality, namely, the presupposition that all relevant knowledge has been canvased. But being more knowledgeable is not, in itself, an exercise one could perform simply "at will" in reflecting on a moral problem immediately at hand. This limitation already diminishes the practical

24. Whether or not any of those conditions (altered motivation, altered knowledge, or imaginative projection) is *necessary* for the absence of bias is an issue I will bypass.

value of our two models. Let us, however, charitably ignore that fact by supposing that the requirement of augmented knowledge is not critical to either model. We may then examine what remains without this requirement.

We are now left with two modified models of exercises which we might be able to implement "at will" in order to achieve impartiality: first, imaginative projection into the standpoints of others plus compilation of the results (modified universalizing); and, second, disregard of particular information about oneself and certain of one's motives so as to reason only from what is shared with others (modified contracting). Unfortunately, the problem remains that the moral theories from which I have derived these modified methods offer no criteria or guidelines for determining whether any of the correspondingly modified feats have been achieved by a person's normative thinking. It is not clear how a real person, motivated to begin with in the complex ways of ordinary folks, can be sure that she really has either adopted someone else's motivational orientation or disregarded some of her own motivations. Nor is it clear how a person can be sure that she has disregarded her own self-identifying particular information.

Let us examine the requirement to consider matters from someone else's point of view, the linchpin of Hare's method of universalization. This requirement calls, in effect, for empathy with others. Under everyday circumstances, many of us do empathize with others to varying extents. When we understand someone's sorrow over a death in her family, or her depression after the breakup of an intimate relationship, it is often because we have had similar experiences, or because the person herself is so familiar to us that we can participate vicariously in her reactions, her attitudes. However, when we lack personal familiarity or detailed understanding of similar situations, then empathy has little foothold. Even the experience of similar situations may be of no help. One's own understandings and reactions manifest one's own complex of motivational and cognitive attitudes—attitudes not necessarily shared with others, whose reactions will differ accordingly.

Thus, imagine the plight of a single mother of four who has no income other than welfare benefits. What attitude will she have toward proposed government decreases in welfare support? She might welcome decreased welfare payments as an incentive to find a job, or she might rue them as an unwarranted penalty on herself and her children for economic circumstances beyond their control. In order to know whether she will adopt either of these attitudes, or some other attitude, we must know something of what she presupposes about current economic conditions and about individual responsibility within and for those conditions. We must also know her attitudes regarding the entitlement of dependent children to certain minimal material conditions for growth and development and regarding the role of the state in assuring that those conditions are met. In general, one needs to grasp the conceptual organization and framework of presuppositions that she brings to her experience. Someone's view of her own moral situations is shaped by normative presuppositions about, for example, economics, politics, and social life—presuppositions pertaining to profound matters of guilt or innocence, legitimacy or illegitimacy, entitlement or its lack.

In general, there are at least two practical problems in implementing the method of universalization. First: what we know about the standpoints of most other persons *underdescribes* those standpoints. The reference points of being on welfare and contemplating decreased support payments, for example, do not sufficiently define a personal standpoint for moral reflection. An underspecified description of someone else's standpoint does not, by itself, allow one to reason from it to determinate conclusions. Without knowing the motivational complex, basic presumptions, conceptual organization, and so on, in terms of which someone regards her circumstances—without knowing someone's particular point of view in substantive detail—it is simply not possible to consider matters from her point of view. Most of the people whose standpoints we have to consider for the purposes of normative thinking are strangers or mere acquaintances known to us only under limited circumstantial descriptions that underdescribe their personal standpoints.

A second practical problem with the requirement to comprehend a situation from someone else's point of view (one which is a matter of degree only and not an absolute limitation) is that someone's motives or preferences, even if known, might be very unfamiliar, alien, even despised from the standpoint of the would-be impartial reasoner. It is not clear that one can really think from the standpoint of motives with which one is unsympathetic or whose subjective force one has never felt. Can I really adopt a point of view characterized by the motivation to molest children sexually? Or to sacrifice German shepherds in Satanic cult rituals? Or to exterminate Jews in a "final solution"? How does one imagine all the subtleties and extrapolations of motives or attitudes that one despises or simply does not understand? Without a comprehending familiarity, one can hardly think from the standpoint of alien motives and attitudes except in truncated parody. Most, if not all, of us are individually unable to grasp the compelling force of every motivational attitude that has ever moved a human being.

The extremely limited nature of human experience and intersubjective familiarity poses problems for any theory which sets universalizing, by means of thinking from the perspectives of others, as a condition of attaining the appropriate standpoint for moral reasoning. Hare discusses this experiential limitation but considers it to be a practical, and not a theoretical, difficulty.[25] Such an attitude seems to presuppose that practical difficulties in implementing a moral theory have no bearing on the substance of the theory. This would be an unduly narrow view of the proper role of moral theory. A moral theory which sets out an ideal method of reasoning should also provide practical guidelines for implementing that method, or, at the very least, for relating that method to everyday moral thought. If no such practical guidelines accompany a moral theory, this should alert us to the possible practical uselessness of the theory in question. A moral theory that calls for extraordinary—often impossible—feats of imaginative projection into the standpoints of others does not illuminate a practicable notion of impartiality.

To be sure, there is an important difference between those

---

25. Hare, *Moral Thinking*, pp. 126–27. Some "theoretical" problems in determining the preferences of others which Hare discusses (chap. 5) are the problem of other minds and the problem of interpersonal utility comparisons.

motives which are merely unfamiliar and those motives which seem corrupt or despicable. It is clear what would be required to solve the problem of grasping unfamiliar motives: seek out information about the motives in question. It is more difficult, however, to say how much of one's own perspective to modify, and to what extent, so as to take up without prejudice the perspective of motives that seem appalling or despicable. In particular, should the victims of egregious harms also have to adopt the standpoints of those who harmed them as a precondition for taking up the moral point of view? Should the victim of a brutal rape be, thus, required to adopt the standpoint of the rapist? A concentration camp survivor the standpoint of a camp commandant? The requirement of empathic projection seems particularly disturbing when considered in such contexts. Such a requirement calls upon a victim to regard herself as, perhaps, worthless and deserving to be hurt—hardly a healing insight. Must critical moral thinking really require such psychologically troubling maneuvers?

This objection to Hare's method of universalization presupposes that some people really have been gravely harmed by others. To a moral impartialist, such a presupposition seems to beg the questions at issue. It was precisely the impartial moral point of view which was, with equal consideration for all persons, to have *grounded* such judgments. If a judgment that someone has been seriously harmed is not based on impartial critical moral thinking, then it must reflect ordinary biases, the very overcoming of which was the aim of impartial thinking. From the standpoint of impartial moral theory, the project of critical moral thinking demands that all pretheoretical moral judgments be held in abeyance pending an impartial critical review of the cases in question. But how realistic is this imperative?

In the final section of this chapter, I begin to sketch a method of critical moral thinking which does not require us to jettison our precritical moral views as a precondition of taking up a morally reflective standpoint. To anticipate, I construe critical moral thinking as an essentially intersubjective enterprise and consider dialogue to be central to it. Dialogue allows us each the opportunity to strive to correct the biases of others by expressing our own points of view. However arduous and plodding this alternative method may be in practice, it does not possess the disturbing feature of requiring someone who was gravely harmed by another to adopt the perspective of the wrongdoer as a condition for engaging in critical moral thinking. My alternative, intersubjective method allows us to enter the project of critical moral thinking as the complex beings we are, complete with our distinctive histories and limitations. The dilemma for such a *practicable* moral theory is to show how, à la Otto Neurath, to rebuild the ship afloat. I return to this point in the last section of this chapter.

The contractual model bypasses the universalization method's unrealistic requirement of extensive empathy by not requiring imaginative projection into anyone else's standpoint. The contractual model requires, instead, that one consider moral matters from one's own standpoint, but "stripped down" so as to exclude particular information about oneself and some of one's own motivations, for instance, envy, or concern for the interests of others. Does this alternative approach fare any better than Hare's universalizing? For different reasons, I believe that it does not.

The major difficulty with achieving impartiality on the contractual model has to do with the requirement to *ignore* certain of one's motivations and all particular knowledge about how one would be affected by the moral arrangements under consideration. The problem with this requirement is that there is no way to ensure that one's normative thinking is not being *tacitly* affected by one's own subjective particulars or debarred motivations. Stephen Darwall has pointed out that it is not enough to require that there be no *reference* to self-identifying particular information by the reasoners in a Rawlsian-type original position. In addition, such information must not carry any implicit *motive force*.[26]

Darwall has discerned that the veil of "ignorance" must also be what we might call a veil of "influence," in order to achieve

---

26. Darwall, *Impartial Reason*, p. 231. On this point, Darwall cites Margarita Levin, "The Problem of Knowledge in the Original Position," *Auslegung* 5 (1978).

genuine impartiality. In order to avoid the biasing effect of one's own particular identity and place in social arrangements, one's critical moral thinking has to avoid the motivational influence of one's particular education, training, background experiences, history, community, gender, social class, and so forth. The problem is that these factors can have motivational influence on one's normative thinking even when those particulars are not specifically referred to by one's reasons or one's conclusions. Beliefs about the legitimacy of subsidized day care at professional meetings may reflect the motive force of one's parental status. Beliefs about the causes of poverty and about society-wide responsibilities to the poor may well reflect the motive force of one's own class background. Beliefs about the degree of societal responsibility for eliminating employment discrimination may reflect the motive force of one's gender or ethnicity. One's degree of tolerance for sexual and other sorts of social violence may reflect the motive force of one's gender. In general, one's basic concepts, tendencies to attend to certain features of social arrangements and ignore certain others, attitudes toward risk, willingness to trust or not in the benevolence and good will of others, and so on are particulars about oneself the motive forces of which may be unavoidable in practical deliberation.[27]

In *A Theory of Justice*, Rawls notes this problem. There, he admits that, in everyday practical reasoning, real human beings may have difficulty taking up the standpoint of the original position, due to the influence of inclinations and so on. Nevertheless, Rawls maintains that "none of this affects the contention that in

---

27. Rawls's notion of the veil of ignorance drew the early criticism that it was possible to get substantive conclusions from behind the veil only because certain particularistic assumptions or attitudes played a tacit role in determining what counted as good reasons; See Thomas Nagel, "Rawls on Justice," in Norman Daniels, ed., *Reading Rawls* (New York: Basic Books, 1976), pp. 9–10, and R. M. Hare, "Rawls' Theory of Justice," in the same volume, pp. 102–6.

As indicated in the text at notes 29 and 30, Rawls has recently acknowledged that his original position is indeed framed by allegiance to the traditions of constitutional democracy.

the original position rational persons so characterized would make a certain decision."[28] This response, however, does not resolve the difficulty. How would one know for sure just what decision a rational person would make in the original position unless one could adopt that standpoint?

Rawls's recent writings have moderated in substantial ways the original claim of impartiality on behalf of the original position. Rawls now interprets the original position and veil of ignorance as a device for representing legitimate public dialogue in a society with traditions of constitutional democracy. Thus, he now avowedly restricts the application of his theory of justice to people whose particulars of historical tradition pre-commit them to allegiance to a certain conception of society, namely, to "society as a system of fair social cooperation between free and equal persons."[29] Gone is the argument that choice behind the veil of ignorance constitutes rational choice by a self-interested chooser whose identifying particulars are entirely unknown to her.[30] Her choice, as now characterized by Rawls, is historically and culturally specific. In that regard, choice behind the veil of ignorance is biased toward the ideals of a particular political culture; to that extent, it is no longer the model of genuine impartiality.

Although Rawls no longer justifies his principles of justice by appeal to the reasoning of a "stripped down" chooser deprived of all self-identifying particular knowledge, this device for representing privileged moral thinking still lives on in the work of other philosophers. What I am calling stripped down thinking approximates what Nagel calls the "objective standpoint." It is the standpoint of no one in particular, the "view from nowhere." Nagel makes some attempt to explicate how such thinking is achieved by ordinary folk who begin with particular self-identifying knowledge and complex motivations. The process is said to involve "stepping outside of ourselves," "transcending the appearances," transcend-

---

28. Rawls, *Theory of Justice*, p. 147.

29. "Justice as Fairness: Political not Metaphysical," *Philosophy and Public Affairs* 14 (Summer 1985): 225–31; quote is from p. 229.

30. Ibid., p. 237.

ing "one's time and place," and escaping "the specific contingencies of one's creaturely point of view."[31] Nagel's explications are
clearly metaphorical; unfortunately, the metaphors do not illuminate the mode of thinking involved.

If we are to constrain our thinking by ignoring all self-
identifying personal particulars, then we need some way to determine whether or not those personal particulars are exerting any
tacit motive force on our conclusions. Otherwise we cannot know
whether the conclusions we have reached are genuinely impartial.
Ironically, Darwall, who noticed the need for this requirement,
does not himself provide any criteria for determining whether such
motive force is present in a process of thought. He simply lists, as
a condition of impartial reasoning, a requirement that one avoid
the motive force of particular information about oneself,[32] with no
account of how to accomplish this psychologically demanding feat.

These problems with the contractual model and with universalization are "practical" problems, in an important sense. They
are not, strictly speaking, problems in the conceptual nature of the
requirements that have been set out by either model for achieving
impartiality. But even supposing that the concept of impartial reasoning is properly represented theoretically by means of either the
method of universalization or the contractual model, if neither of
these methods can be *implemented*, then moral theory has failed to
illuminate the critical thinking which we need for substantive guidance in our moral practices.

4. Impartiality as Universality plus Neutrality

We have been considering whether or not impartiality can be
attained by methods of thought that require one imaginatively
either to adopt the standpoints of others or to reason from a constrained version of one's own standpoint. My argument has been
that without criteria by which to ascertain whether the results of

31. Nagel, *View from Nowhere*, respectively, pp. 140, 139, 187, 9.
32. Darwall, *Impartial Reason*, p. 231.

such disciplined thinking are wholly free of bias and prejudice, these models are insufficient to ensure that our thinking is genuinely impartial.

A different approach to impartiality is taken by theorists who, instead of trying to define impartial methods of thought, present an analysis of what would count as impartial propositions, reasons, preferences, or understanding. This sort of analysis, if successful, might provide us with just the criteria we need in order to determine whether or not the outcomes of methods such as universalization and contract were genuinely impartial. A typical contemporary analysis involves two requirements: first, reasons must apply to all persons falling within the relevant domain, and second, reasons must lack essential reference to particular or specifiable persons. The second condition is of special concern here. I will call it the "neutrality condition."

The neutrality condition is formulated in various ways by different theorists. Nagel,[33] borrowing Derek Parfit's term "agent-neutral,"[34] calls for the absence of any essential reference to the person whose reasons are under consideration. Darwall, using the term "impersonal," similarly calls for preferences the objects of which "can be expressed without free agent variables."[35] Echoing Rawls, Darwall emphasizes that what is important about this condition is that certain information be lacking, in particular, who one is and how one is related to whatever is under consideration.[36]

Unfortunately, the Nagel and Darwall formulations of the neutrality requirement do not screen out all possible biases. Both formulations prohibit reference only to the person whose reasons or preferences are under consideration. However, biases toward persons other than the agent, including favoritism for one's children, friends, and so forth, may influence moral thinking no less than

33. Nagel, *View from Nowhere*, pp. 152–53.
34. Derek Parfit, *Reasons and Persons* (Oxford: Clarendon Press, 1984), p. 143.
35. Darwall, *Impartial Reason*, p. 133.
36. Ibid. Darwall seems, on this point, to be ignoring his own insight that not only information but also its motive force must be suppressed in the quest for impartial reasoning.

self-regard. Also, out of deference or servility, people may favor the interests of persons other than themselves, perhaps even when those interests compete with their own. The neutrality condition must be expanded so as to prohibit reference to any particular persons at all.

Adrian Piper's formulation of the neutrality condition, which she calls "generality," accomplishes this task more effectively than the previous alternatives. Her formulation calls for the complete absence of proper names and definite descriptions, so that *no* one may be particularly identified by genuinely impartial reasons or judgments.[37] Neither the moral reasoner herself nor any other individual moral agent—indeed, nor any other individual—may be essentially referred to by reasons which are to count as impartial.

But a different sort of bias survives Piper's formulation. Of great contemporary social interest are biases toward or against whole groups of persons, biases such as misogyny, white supremacism, homophobia.[38] To foreclose the possibility of these biases, which transcend partiality toward or against particular individual persons, we need a formulation of the neutrality condition that requires the absence of any reference to social groups.

This sort of formulation would still, however, face at least one remaining difficulty. Even if a moral reason were neutral on the face of it, that is, lacking in any essential reference to any individual persons *or* social groups, it would still be possible for the acceptance or advocacy of such a reason to manifest covert or tacit biases. Reasons can be couched in terms that are universal and neutral, yet still advance special interests. Certain "facts" make this possible, for example, facts about the traits which correlate highly with certain types of persons, facts about preexisting social inequalities, and facts about the ambiguities of terms that merely seem, but are not genuinely, neutral.

37. Adrian M. S. Piper, "Moral Theory and Moral Alienation," *Journal of Philosophy* 84 (February 1987): 102.
38. Nagel's requirement, specified as "agent-neutrality," would handle this problem better than Piper's if groups were moral agents. However, this point is controversial. See Larry May, *The Morality of Groups* (Notre Dame, Ind.: Notre Dame University Press, 1987).

One could try to argue, for instance, that only tall people or only light-skinned people should hold certain privileged jobs or social positions. The "facts" are such that a minimum height requirement will benefit more men than women and a light skin color requirement would exclude mainly people "of color."[39] Or one could try to advocate legal racial segregation in seemingly unbiased terms, for instance, by defending "state's rights," the right of individual states to pass whatever legislation is supported by a majority of their voting citizens and is not explicitly forbidden by the federal constitution. Again, the "facts" of preexisting and entrenched inequalities of resources and power among different racial groups in the various states would combine with such a policy to favor the interests of already advantaged racial majorities over those of minority racial groups. Or one can use male nouns and pronouns as if they were gender-neutral terms. This sadly persistent linguistic convention permits the users of natural languages to mask covert misogynist or male-oriented biases under the guise of a purported gender neutrality.

Recall Darwall's insight that to be genuinely impartial, reasons and conclusions must not only not *refer* to subjective particulars; they must also not be influenced by the *motive force* of those subjective particulars. A preference for racial segregation or for light skin, for example, can be expressed with no essential references to any individuals or social groups, yet still manifest the covert motive force of racial hostility.

We could try to remove this limitation from the analysis of impartial reasons by adding a third condition, namely, a requirement that all "facts" about who would benefit and who would suffer from a moral action or practice be disregarded. This proviso would, however, create a practical problem similar to the one exhibited by the contractual model: there is no way to ensure, in any given case, that someone's moral reasoning has genuinely disre-

39. This is the kind of discrimination which, in law, is called "disparate impact." It contrasts with explicitly intentional discrimination, known as "disparate treatment." See Claire Sherman, *Sex Discrimination in a Nutshell* (St. Paul, Minn.: West Publishing Co., 1982), pp. 220–53.

garded all available information about which persons or groups of persons are favored or not by a moral action or practice.

Rather than attempting to modify the analysis of impartial reasons any further, I briefly propose, in the next and final section, a different approach to the elimination of bias from critical moral thinking.

5. ELIMINATING BIASES

My proposal is that the abstract ideal of impartiality should not be the primary reference point around which to orient methods for eliminating bias from moral thinking. Instead, our reference points should be particular forms of *partiality*, that is, nameable biases whose distorting effects on moral thinking we recognize and whose manifestations in moral attitudes and behavior can be specifically identified. Our methods for improving moral thinking should then involve whatever is needed to eliminate those particular recognized biases.

On this approach, the ideals of moral theory are scaled down so as to coincide with what is practically feasible. People begin their moral thinking with complex motivations, limited information, and entrenched biases. The elimination of all bias seems to be a utopian, impracticable ideal. Instead, impartiality is hereby reconstrued as a matter of degree, probably never fully realizable by human beings, and approachable only incrementally, through the gradual elimination of identifiable partialities, manifestation by manifestation.

Legal practice already strives for limited degrees of impartiality, related to the particular cases at hand. Judges are to excuse themselves from hearing cases in which their judgment might be biased. Various procedures are used by trial lawyers to screen prospective jurors so as to prevent people with biases from sitting in judgment on their peers. In these legal settings, only limited impartiality is sought: those who judge a case involving a conflict of interests among certain particular parties are supposed to be without bias toward or against any of the particular parties in question. The specific biases that might distort thinking about a given case are biases for or against the particular parties to the dispute, or biases for or against the interests and identities which they represent. Full impartiality is not required in each case. In this regard, legal practice seeks to implement the modest approach to impartiality I am recommending.

As for the methods for eliminating recognizable biases from critical moral thinking, foremost emphasis must go to interpersonal, including public, dialogue. For good psychological reasons, each person's unaided thinking cannot be trusted to discern its own biases. One's own thinking—explicit and implicit, avowed and tacit—is not fully transparent to oneself. One's covert racist or anti-Semitic bias, or hostility toward the aged or the disabled, may well be noticeable to others even when invisible to oneself.

The specific moral problems which attract or which escape one's attention can disclose covert biases, for instance, not noticing as a problem the open sexual harassment inflicted by one's colleague on certain students. One's metaphors are often very revealing, for example, "feeding the poor of Africa" as a disparaging reference to the idea of moral concern for distant persons to whom people in general have no personal connection. One's behavioral reactions to different sorts of persons can also expose biases, reactions such as a guarded wariness when approaching black, but not other, men on the street.

The beneficiaries, victims, bystanders, and so on, of one's behavior may often be better situated than oneself to grasp the underlying attitudes revealed by one's actions and practices. Are the persons who are disfavored by a bias, who have the most to lose by the social implementation of that disfavor, more likely than other persons to be sensitive to its presence in moral thinking and practice? On balance, the answer seems to me to be "yes." To be sure, the victims of bias have psychological reasons for not acknowledging its existence;[40] for example, it might well diminish their self-esteem to do so. In addition, if the prospects of successfully

40. Thanks to Diana Meyers for bringing this problem to my attention.

contesting that bias and overcoming its effects are minimal, then its victims have additional motivation to avoid recognizing it. To acknowledge an insurmountable (and damaging) bias against one-self or one's own group is at the same time to acknowledge a dimension of social powerlessness and hopelessness in one's life—not a comfortable admission.

Still, against these considerations must be set certain others. The important question is: who is *best* situated to discern bias in attitudes and practices? The issue is a matter of what might be called "epistemic credentials," in this case, the authority to describe (or "bear witness to")[41] certain oppressive social phenomena. Those with biased attitudes have numerous reasons of their own to avoid recognizing those attitudes; they, after all, gain relative self-esteem and, possibly, other social advantages from the exis-tence and cultural influence of their biases. In addition, the victims of bias, once cognizant of their circumstances, are surely better situated than others to understand and express the experience of being treated according to the attitudes that constitute the particular bias against them.

Furthermore, those who hold positions of cultural power can use that power to shape public debate in the direction of their biases, by, for example, systematically misrepresenting the situa-tions and viewpoints of those against whom they are biased. To counteract this likelihood, the relatively powerless targets of per-vasive cultural biases must, most of all, be specially enabled to participate in public dialogue. Only in that way can they have any hope of challenging the biased direction of public debate and its ensuing impact on social policies and arrangements. It is notorious that certain groups in our culture, for example, certain racial mi-norities, lack the resources and status to influence public dialogue in proportion to their numbers in the population. In accord with my piecemeal and practicable approach to moral impartiality, the

41. In Chapter 7 I make further use of the notion of bearing moral witness when I explore the moral growth we attain through placing trust in (reliable) "moral witnessing" by our friends.

rectification of this political problem takes on singular moral urgency.[42]

In this chapter, I have argued that the abstract ideal of impartiality is an impracticable ideal: not confirmably attainable through the method of universalization nor through that of the contractual model, nor by means of the analysis of impartial reasons into requirements of universality and neutrality. In place of these strategies, I have recommended that impartiality be approached by way of eliminating, from moral thinking, the substantive manifestations of particular nameable biases. I suggested that actual dialogue among diverse persons is a practically necessary forum for this process. On this view, the real social circumstances of different people and different social groups who can or cannot participate in moral dialogue become vital matters for any practicable moral theorizing.

In the next two chapters, I turn from impartiality to partiality. Its philosophical defense will prove to be at least as thorny and challenging as that of impartiality.

42. For an insightful and programmatic discussion of these issues, see Iris Marion Young, "Polity and Group Difference: A Critique of the Ideal of Universal Citizenship," *Ethics* 99 (January 1989): 250–74.

2

The Practice
of Partiality

*H*ardly any moral philosopher, these days, would deny that we are each entitled to favor our loved ones. Some would say, even more strongly, that we ought to favor them, that it is not simply a moral option. This notion of partiality toward loved ones is lately gaining wide philosophical acclaim. (Ordinary people, fortunately, have held this view for quite some time.)

It seems indisputable that intimacy and close relationships require partiality, that is, require special attentiveness, responsiveness, and favoritism between or among those who are to be close.[1] Close relationships, in turn, are among what Bernard Williams has called the "ground projects" that are essential for character, integrity, and flourishing in a human life.[2] Partiality, accordingly, seems instrumentally essential to integrity and the good life. There seems, in addition, to be sheer intrinsic value in the very benefiting of friends and loved ones.[3]

1. See Lawrence Blum, *Friendship, Altruism, and Morality* (London: Routledge & Kegan Paul, 1980), chap. 3; and John Kekes, "Morality and Impartiality," *American Philosophical Quarterly* 18 (October 1981): 299.

2. "Persons, Character, and Morality," in his *Moral Luck* (Cambridge: Cambridge University Press, 1981), p. 13. On the contribution of partiality to integrity and fulfillment, see also John Cottingham, "Ethics and Impartiality," *Philosophical Studies* 43 (1983): 83–99.

3. See Blum, *Friendship, Altruism, and Morality*; and Charles Fried, *Right and Wrong* (Cambridge: Harvard University Press, 1978), pp. 170, 179.

While the appropriateness of partiality toward loved ones is itself uncontested, its theoretical justification is the subject of a lively contemporary debate. The hottest question in this debate is whether partiality can adequately be justified by any of the dominant theoretical traditions of modern moral philosophy, utilitarian consequentialism, or Kantian deontology. The feature of these theories that seems to threaten the legitimacy of partiality is their requirement of moral impartiality—the requirement to be unbiased and to show equal consideration, in some sense, for all persons.[4]

According to critics, impartialist moral theories are not able to account for the moral value of close personal relationships.[5] The impartial standpoint calls for detachment from personal concerns and loyalties, an attitude which Lawrence Blum considers to be inimical to the loving concern and particularized responsiveness that are essential to successful close relationships.[6] The impartial perspective aimed at equal concern for all persons, in John Cottingham's view, radically diminishes or altogether eliminates a person's opportunity to show special attention and concern to her own loved ones.[7]

Each impartialist ethical tradition has its own additional short-

---

4. Of course, the two traditions define very differently the morally relevant interests of persons that are to be considered. In Chapter 1, I characterized impartiality as an absence of bias; I switch in this chapter to construing it as the equal consideration of all persons. This conceptualization is the one most commonly found in the context of the contemporary debates over partiality. For my purposes, there is no significant difference between the two formulations. The two notions diverge in the areas of animal rights and environmental concerns, but those issues are beyond the scope of this book.

5. Some partialists also defend partiality in special relationships other than close personal relationships, for example, relationships among members of the same community, city, or nation. However, there is less agreement about the legitimacy of the partiality shown in these cases. This chapter and the next concentrate only on partiality in close personal relationships, such as those with parents, children, siblings, friends, and lovers. In Chapter 9, I discuss communities.

6. See Blum, *Friendship, Altruism, and Morality*, p. 56.

7. See Cottingham, "Ethics and Impartiality," pp. 89–90.

comings, from the partialist perspective. Bernard Williams charges utilitarianism with failing to recognize the separateness of persons and, therefore, giving no special moral status to personal integrity or to the essential contribution made to personal integrity by relationships and projects which are the agent's own, in some important sense.[8] Kantian deontology, according to Michael Stocker, fails to accord moral value to the motivations, such as loving concern and affectionate inclination, that are necessary ingredients in successful personal relationships, and counts only a depersonalized sense of duty as a genuinely moral motivation.[9]

The recent challenges to impartiality range even more widely. Andrew Oldenquist contends that impartiality calls for equal concern for the whole of humanity, a sentiment which is, in any case, too weak to be effective as moral motivation.[10] Perhaps, the final coup de grace is the claim that genuine impartiality is humanly unachievable, a charge with which I myself concur.[11] In her defense of this view, Iris Young urges, further, that the rhetoric of impartiality[12] be distrusted because it has been used in practice by dominant social groups to disguise their de facto political and cultural hegemony.[13]

Defenders of impartialist moral theories have responded by trying to show that those theories do indeed warrant partiality in special relationships. These rejoinders treat partiality as morally

---

8. See Williams, *Moral Luck,* p. 3 and passim.

9. See Michael Stocker, "The Schizophrenia of Modern Ethical Theories," *Journal of Philosophy* 63 (August 12, 1976): 453–66; and Williams, *Moral Luck,* pp. 3, 15–19.

10. See Andrew Oldenquist, "Loyalties," *Journal of Philosophy* 79 (April 1982): 181.

11. See Alasdair MacIntyre, *After Virtue* (Notre Dame, Ind.: University of Notre Dame Press, 1981); Iris Young, "Impartiality and the Civic Public: Some Implications of Feminist Critiques of Moral and Political Theory," *Praxis International* 5 (January 1986): 384–85; and, for my defense of this view, Chapter 1 of this volume.

12. The rhetorical dimension of uses of the notion of impartiality is insightfully explored by Margaret Walker in "Partial Consideration," *Ethics* 101 (July 1991): 758–74.

13. Young, "Impartiality and the Civic Public," p. 389.

permissible, even obligatory, so long as there is *some* way in which this behavior or the deliberation that justifies it exemplifies an equal consideration of the interests of all. A clarified notion of impartiality has, thus, emerged from these defenses.

Thomas E. Hill, Jr., for example, argues that an impartial perspective is required only when considering basic moral principles, but not when judging the specific moral matters of daily life.[14] Peter Railton draws a distinction between procedures for moral decision making by particular persons in particular situations and the truth conditions of a moral theory: impartiality is part of the latter but need not be part of the former.[15] On Alan Gewirth's view, partiality may be permitted in individual behavior so long as that behavior is regulated by social institutions which themselves give equal consideration to the interests of all persons.[16] Contemporary Kantians, such as Barbara Herman and Marcia Baron, further contend that a sense of duty is necessary only as a second-order limiting condition on our primary, first-order motivations and that partial sentiments are permissible as first-order motivations so long as they do not violate those second-order constraints.[17]

In nearly all of these discussions, both those that favor and those that oppose impartialist defenses of partiality, controversy centers on the notion of *im*partiality and on whether it supports or repudiates the favoring of loved ones. Partialists have generally been on the offensive and impartialists have been compelled to clarify what impartiality really means and what it actually requires. By contrast, the notion of partiality has not been subjected to vig-

14. See Thomas E. Hill, Jr., "The Importance of Autonomy," in Eva Feder Kittay and Diana T. Meyers, eds., *Women and Moral Theory* (Totowa, N.J.: Rowman & Littlefield, 1987), pp. 131–32.

15. See Peter Railton, "Alienation, Consequentialism, and the Demands of Morality," *Philosophy and Public Affairs* 13 (Spring 1984): 153–55.

16. See Alan Gewirth, "Ethical Universalism and Particularism," *Journal of Philosophy* 85, no. 6 (1988): 292–93.

17. See Barbara Herman, "On the Value of Acting from the Motive of Duty," *Philosophical Review* 67 (July 1981): 233–50; and Marcia Baron, "The Alleged Moral Repugnance of Acting from Duty," *Journal of Philosophy* 81 (April 1984): 197–220.

orous critical investigation, except in a few discussions of its un-justified forms.[18]

In this chapter I counteract that trend by taking a closer than usual look at the moral complexity of our social practices of partiality. My adoption of this approach does not represent an endorsement of current notions of impartiality. As I argued in Chapter 1, the concept of impartiality must be substantially reformulated if it is to survive as a practicable ideal of moral thinking. That the concept of impartiality needs reexamination, however, does not mean that the concept of partiality is transparently defensible. In this discussion, I focus on aspects of partiality that complicate the philosophical defense of it.[19]

In the first section of this chapter, I argue that the moral value of partiality depends partly on the moral value of the relationships that it helps to sustain. It matters to the philosophical issues at stake that personal relationships can be abusive, exploitative, and oppressive. I survey some considerations that are relevant to the critical assessment of personal relationships. In section 2 I consider the vastly unequal social distribution of the material means for favoring loved ones. Because many people have inadequate resources for caring for their loved ones, our conventional relationship practices of partiality—practices by which we each care only for our "own"—can be disastrous for many people. This observation seriously complicates the defense of partiality.

1. PARTIALITY AND THE VALUE OF RELATIONSHIPS

Partiality varies widely. It appears in numerous sorts of relationships, is expressed in many forms, and has a correspondingly

18. See Blum, *Friendship, Altruism, and Morality*, pp. 46–47; Marcia Baron, *The Moral Status of Loyalty* (Dubuque, Iowa: Kendall Hunt, 1984); John Cottingham, "Partiality, Favouritism, and Morality," *Philosophical Quarterly* 36, no. 144 (1986): 357–73; and Gewirth, "Ethical Universalism," pp. 295–98.

19. This focus continues in Chapter 3, where I contrast feminist and nonfeminist defenses of partiality. That chapter begins with its own somewhat varied sketch of the partiality debates.

varied moral status. Devoted attention to one's children is a matter of moral duty; loyalty to a distant relative under criminal indictment is morally permissible but not required; white supremacist cults are morally prohibited. Partiality comprises an area of daily moral life about which most people have deeply held convictions.

When partiality is morally required, this is often (if not always) because of what it contributes to the personal relationships of which it is a part. I favor my children, my friends, and so on because such favoring expresses the love I feel for them, promotes their well-being which is of special concern to me (and which, in some cases, is also my personal responsibility), differentiates my close relationships from relationships to people I do not particularly love, and respects the uniqueness of those I love by the specifically appropriate responsiveness I show to them.[20] To the extent that personal relationships are necessary for integrity and fulfillment in life, then, to that extent partiality is instrumentally required as a means to achieving those morally valuable ends.

Even if integrity and fulfillment require close relationships, however, this does not entail that every close relationship contributes to integrity or fulfillment. It depends on the nature of the relationship in question. Personal relationships vary widely in their moral value. The quality of a particular relationship is profoundly important in determining the moral worth of any partiality which is necessary for sustaining that relationship. To the extent that partiality is a duty in close personal relationships, it is a prima facie duty only, to be fully assessed, among other things, in light of the moral worth of the particular relationships it helps to preserve.

Discussions of partiality have, heretofore, largely overlooked the differing moral value of the varied sorts of personal relationships that commonly manifest partiality. Some of these discussions do acknowledge that partiality may be shown in an inappropriate manner, but this is a different issue.[21] Partiality toward loved ones,

20. On the importance of respect for uniqueness in a caring relationship, see Robin Dillon, "Care and Respect," in Eve Browning Cole and Susan Coultrap-McQuin, eds., *Explorations in Feminist Ethics* (Bloomington, Ind.: Indiana University Press, 1992), pp. 69–81.

21. See the references in note 18.

for example, is wrong on the part of someone who holds a public office that calls for impartial treatment of some large number of persons extending beyond the official's loved ones. Also wrong are partial attitudes toward a particular group which unjustly advantage members of that group over other groups, for example, racism and sexism.[22] When partiality is judged to be wrong in those discussions, its wrongness is linked to circumstances other than the nature of the relationship itself. The issue that concerns me, by contrast, is the partialist's apparent underlying presumption that mere relationship with someone who is, in some sense, "one's own" is, all things considered, always morally worth promoting.

In the most general terms, relationships are morally wrong to the extent that they harm people, especially one or more of the participants in the relationship. The relationship between master and slave is the paradigm of a wrongful relationship, and slavery epitomizes immoral relationship practices. Slavery is an extreme form of harmful relationship but by no means the only such form. Even in intimate, "consensual" relationships, people can be subjected to emotional duress, assault and battery, sexual abuse, and economic exploitation.[23] Anything that sustains relationships such as these, including whatever partiality is shown within them, is prima facie morally improper.

Just how bad these sustaining conditions are in any particular case depends partly on the prospects for ending that relationship. If a battered woman, for instance, cannot leave an abusive relationship because she has no viable economic alternative for herself and her dependent children, then, in that case, it is good for her

---

22. The key phrase is "unjustly advantage." Sometimes it is just to favor members of certain groups, most especially in attempts to overcome the persistent untoward effects of their history of unjust treatment and the lingering, unjustified biases against them. This, of course, is the familiar notion of "affirmative action," a topic far afield of the present discussion.

23. Among female homicide victims in the United States, about one-third are slain by a family member or male friend; see Deborah Rhode, *Gender and Justice* (Cambridge: Harvard University Press, 1989), p. 237. See her chapter 7, "Sex and Violence," for a wide-ranging discussion of the abuses to which women in particular are vulnerable in personal relationships.

partner to show the sort of partiality in caring and support that would counterbalance or offset the abuse. To the extent, however, that his partiality diminishes her capacity to recognize her situation for what it is and to pursue any nonoppressive alternatives that are genuinely accessible to her, to the extent that the partiality binds her the more strongly to her still-abusive partner when she could free herself of that tie, then, to that extent, the partiality is insidious and more than simply prima facie bad. In case a troubled relationship can be brought to an end to the betterment of the abused member and her dependents, the morally best option is its dissolution. Sometimes "this marriage" should not be "saved." The current approach to partiality is, thus, incomplete. It fails to take account of the differing moral value of different personal relationships, and it mistakenly presumes that whatever sustains any personal relationship is a moral good without qualification.

Assessing the harm that is done in personal relationships is a complex matter. Intimates and close affiliates can harm each other in a great variety of ways. The harms of a relationship might be a function of its own particularities, or they might be a function of the social conventions for relationships of that sort. A relationship can harm both those who are participants in the relationship and those who are nonparticipants. Nonparticipants can be harmed, for example, if they are unjustifiably excluded from relationship practices which afford some positive value to their participants.[24] My present concern, however, is with the harms to which the participants in a relationship are vulnerable.

Roughly speaking, we may distinguish four levels at which the practice of any particular relationship can be morally evaluated. First, there is the most generic level for defining relationships of a certain sort. The most prominent dictionary definition of "marriage" is wedlock, that is, the relationship between wife and husband; and, by dictionary definition, wives are women while husbands are men. This simple generic meaning covers a variety

24. Here I have in mind such examples as the legal and religious bans against lesbian and gay marriage.

of actual practices in different cultures, for example, monogamy, polyandry, and polygyny.

Second, relationships can be evaluated at the level of the specific cultural formalization of a relationship practice. Historically, American case law considered husbands to be responsible for the economic support of the marriage household while wives were held responsible for child care, domestic work, and the sexual service of their husbands.[25] Any aspect of a relationship on which the law must, at some time or other, pronounce judgment may become a part of its formal social arrangements. Marriage law, in the past, has condoned wife battering by husbands, misconstruing it under a legitimating description: corrective chastisement.[26] Such tolerance made wife battering a formally permissible social practice.

Third, there may be informal practices associated with a relationship tradition which are neither formally codified nor legally enforced, yet which are culturally normative. In our culture, a woman who marries a man is still widely expected to drop her own last name and adopt that of her husband and sometimes to submerge herself entirely under his name ("Mrs. John Doe"). Fourth, and finally, any relationship may have its own specific particularities which do not derive from the generic nature of the relationship or from its formal or informal social conventions. The particular emotional abuse heaped upon one spouse by her partner may be quite idiosyncratic to their interaction.

Marital relationships can be evaluated at all of these levels, from particular marriages on up to the most generic level of marriage practice—and similarly for other relationships. A challenge to the generic notion of marriage as a relationship between a woman and a man may well rely on a related, but even more

25. See Sara Ann Ketchum, "Liberalism and Marriage Law," in Mary Vetterling-Braggin, Frederick A. Elliston, and Jane English, eds., *Feminism and Philosophy* (Totowa, N.J.: Littlefield, Adams, 1977), pp. 264–76.

26. See Dorie Klein, "The Dark Side of Marriage: Battered Wives and the Domination of Women," in Nicole Hahn Rafter and Elizabeth A. Stanko, eds., *Judge, Lawyer, Victim, Thief: Gender Roles and Criminal Justice* (Boston: Northeastern University Press, 1982), pp. 83–107.

generic, meaning of marriage, namely, that of a close or intimate union. Close and intimate unions may form between women and between men. Some lesbian and gay couples are now seeking, for their own close and intimate unions, the formal imprimatur of legally or religiously sanctioned marriage, an innovation which most religious and legal authorities continue to obstruct. Nevertheless, this example reminds us that evaluation of marriage practice can occur even at its most generic level.

In order to decide which close relationships are morally wrong at any level of assessment, we need to consider more than simply the obvious harms its participants inflict on each other. We need as well some sense of what it is that makes close relationships morally right, what it is that determines the moral worth that they have as relationships. Evaluating the worth of relationships in part requires knowing something about the underlying moral basis of the duties of partiality they generate. Robert Goodin has theorized that partiality is morally required in a relationship to the extent that it contributes to the protection of those who are vulnerable.[27] Social conventions assign responsibilities for the care of those who need it to particular others who are (presumed to be) best situated to render care effectively. Such conventions are sensible to the extent that they ensure genuine protection for all at dependent stages of their lives and that, in emergencies, there are guidelines which promote effective help to those in danger.[28]

People are typically held responsible for the well-being of those to whom they are connected in some identifiable way, such as by kinship. Our close friends and relations are especially well placed to offer protection to each of us in virtue of the familiarity, concern, and frequency of interaction which are commonly greater in those

27. *Protecting the Vulnerable* (Chicago: University of Chicago Press, 1985). It is noteworthy that Goodin is particularly concerned to show that the best theoretical account of our responsibilities to loved ones also grounds general duties to strangers, duties that are stronger than is usually allowed by partialists (pp. 9–11). Another perspective on what it is that grounds duties of partiality in personal relationships is offered in Lawrence C. Becker, *Reciprocity* (London: Routledge & Kegan Paul, 1986).

28. Goodin, *Protecting the Vulnerable*, pp. 109–25.

relationships than in others. Immediate family relationships are among our most important social relationships for providing care, nurturance, protection, and support. They are keystones in the social arrangements by which children, in particular, are cared for, and are also centrally important for care of the elderly and of infirm persons at any age. In such relationships, the circumstance of being the one uniquely situated to answer to someone's need derives from an ongoing, publicly recognized connection with her in virtue of which one is held responsible for her well-being.

Goodin recognizes the need to evaluate social conventions themselves. Relationship conventions, on his view, are morally justified to the extent that they are genuinely successful in promoting the protection of the vulnerable.[29] For instance, it is because most people care well enough for their own biological offspring that our social arrangements should and do hold them accountable, as a rule, for that care.[30] Given arrangements of these sorts, the vulnerability of the one who is cared for is especially a vulnerability with regard to the behavior of those persons who are held responsible for her care. A parent's disregard of the needs of her own young child nearly always constitutes neglect; not so someone else's disregard.

On Goodin's view, once caretaking conventions are in place, even if they are not justifiable as the best arrangements for ensuring care of certain sorts of persons (children, the elderly, etc.), they may still create caretaking obligations, since the existence of conventions almost guarantees that no one else will do the required caretaking in any particular case.[31] Knowing that I am related to someone in a specific and close way alerts me to the fact that other people will not likely attend to her needs. On Goodin's view, my duty to care for someone follows from being the one who is conventionally expected to care for her and, because of that expectation, the only one who is likely to do so.

29. Ibid., pp. 124–25.
30. In Chapter 6, section 3, I qualify this view by exploring the gender asymmetry in these practices, particularly the far heavier burden of parental caretaking accountability demanded of women than of men.
31. Goodin, *Protecting the Vulnerable*, p. 125.

Following Goodin's account, we may thus view partiality in close personal relationships as prima facie morally required to the extent that it safeguards those who are vulnerable and to the extent that it accords with social conventions that assign responsibilities for the care of vulnerable persons to certain others who are related to them in particular ways. These responsibilities, to emphasize, constitute prima facie duties only. Their overall moral merit depends on the extent to which the relationships in question really do protect those who are vulnerable without exacting too high a price for such care.

One additional qualification merits special emphasis. Goodin contends that one of the deeper factors which determine whether or not the prima facie duties of partiality constitute duties all things considered is the nature of the vulnerability in question and, in particular, its origin. As Goodin recognizes, some vulnerabilities are socially created. Illness, for example, may result from socially created conditions and be exacerbated by societal hindrances to access to health care. Many socially created vulnerabilities can be directly tied to income levels and employment status, themselves substantially a function of market practices.[32] These reflections on the nature of vulnerability extend Goodin's account in crucially important directions.

It is part of Goodin's enriched account of our responsibilities to protect the vulnerable that we should also be striving to change those alterable social arrangements that foster and perpetuate undesirable human vulnerabilities and dependencies.[33] Susan Moller Okin develops this strand of Goodin's thought into a comprehensive critique of marital practices. In Okin's view, "gender-structured marriage *involves women in a cycle of socially caused and distinctly asymmetric vulnerability.*"[34] The social determinants begin early in a woman's life. Okin's findings are worth quoting at length. In her view, women are:

32. Ibid., pp. 190–91.
33. Ibid., chapter 7.
34. Susan Moller Okin, *Justice, Gender, and the Family* (New York: Basic Books, 1989), p. 138.

first set up for vulnerability during their developing years by their personal (and socially reinforced) expectations that they will be the primary caretakers of children, and that in fulfilling this role they will need to try to attract and to keep the economic support of a man, to whose work life they will be expected to give priority. They are rendered vulnerable by the actual division of labor within almost all current marriages. They are disadvantaged at work by the fact that the world of wage work, including the professions, is still largely structured around the assumption that "workers" have wives at home. They are rendered far more vulnerable if they become the primary caretakers of children, and their vulnerability peaks if their marriages dissolve and they become single parents.[35]

The details that support Okin's account are convincing, yet they are not likely to persuade everyone. The moral value of close personal relationships is a hotly contested matter. In our time, the debates over the nature and value of marital and family relationships are often particularly vitriolic. Many of us have a stake in believing that our family relationships are personally fulfilling. We might, otherwise, feel required to change them—often a daunting prospect. Our evaluations of these relationships may, accordingly, take on idealized and mythic dimensions.

To complicate matters further, family relationships, especially under comfortable material circumstances, are culturally invested with the function of providing emotional nurturance as well as material protection for both their more vulnerable and their less vulnerable members. The modern nuclear family is supposed to be a refuge, a "haven in a heartless world."[36] Such norms are widely appealing. How much better it is to love than to hate one's parents, siblings, and so on. Family members who share mutual affection will care, nurture, help, and support one another out of sponta-

35. Ibid., pp. 138–39. See her chapter 7 for the ample data and persuasive arguments that support her conclusions.

36. The familiar phrase, of course, is the title of Christopher Lasch's book, *Haven in a Heartless World: The Family Besieged* (New York: Basic Books, 1977), a book that bemoans the decline of patriarchal authority in contemporary families.

neous inclination and enthusiasm and will probably do so more attentively and wisely than if the care is begrudged.

Tangentially, let us recall that some critics of impartiality, with an eye toward the partiality they champion for close relationships, have challenged the Kantian view that the only specifically moral motivation is a sense of duty.[37] Such a motivation, so the criticism goes, excludes the loving concern that is due to our intimates. The critics suppose that it is the impartialist dimension of Kantianism which leads to the motivational emphasis on duty. If a sense of duty is troubling as a moral motive among loved ones, however, this problem is not limited to theories that ground relational duties on impartial considerations. The problem arises for any (deontological) view that holds there to be moral duties of partiality in close personal relationships,[38] whether these duties are accounted for in impartial or in partialist terms.

For certain particular relationships, and for many relationships on occasion, a sense of duty may be the only attitude available to motivate the required caretaking. A sense of duty may well be necessary in relationships based on some permanent tie, such as biological kinship, which endures independently of how the participants feel about each other. If one lacks affection for an elderly and infirm parent, then caring for her out of a sense of duty is surely preferable to neglecting her altogether. The lack of spontaneous compassion or concern does not diminish the caretaking responsibility and may engender additional responsibilities of self-control so that one's behavior does not reveal the lack of affection.[39]

Attitudes of loving concern, thus, are not necessarily owed to all our intimates at all times. A duty to be partial to family members and other intimates is a duty to treat them in certain ways, to favor them with care, protection, and so forth, over other persons whom one could also attend. Duties to favor certain particular persons in certain ways are, in the first instance, duties of behavior; they are

37. See the references in note 9 and the text at that point.
38. I am inclined to agree with Herman and Baron that the problems can be resolved; see the references in note 17.
39. For a similar point, see Baron, "The Alleged Moral Repugnance of Acting from Duty," pp. 204–5.

not necessarily duties to undertake the required behavior from certain motives. To be sure, (mutual) loving concern shared with those close to us is one of life's greatest joys, an ideal truly worth seeking to the extent that its realization lies within our power. In troubled relationships, however, this attitude may simply surpass our emotional capacities and lie beyond our abilities to control. It is not uncommon, in daily life, for people to care for those close to them primarily out of a sense of duty, given the vicissitudes of human affections.

Nonmarital family relationships, to return to the question of evaluating close relationships, persist independently of how we feel about the partner—indeed, they persist independently of whether or not the caretaking responsibilities are neglected. (Marital relationships can linger on in a similar manner.) My brother (supposing I had one) will remain my brother whether or not I am partial to him, emotionally or materially. As adults, he and I may choose to avoid each other's company, but our formal relationship continues. Being related in those ways is compatible with feelings of disrespect, spite, jealousy, contempt, hatred, or simple indifference. Partners in such relationships may loathe and mistreat each other, yet remain profoundly involved in each other's lives.

Perhaps it is because family relationships are so permanent that we place such a high premium on the emotional concern family members *could* provide for one another if such relationships functioned at their best. Our relationship conventions and practices, thus, include numerous rituals and occasions that serve, among other things, to promote affection and concern among loved ones: Mother's Day, Father's Day, celebrations of wedding anniversaries, family-oriented religious holiday traditions, and so on. A heavy suffusion of myths, clichés, and cultural idealizations permeate marriage and family relationship practices. In virtue of these myths and idealizations, our feelings about our own family relationships (like many aspects of our emotional lives) are subject to a good deal of social manipulation and dissemblance. Rituals, such as gift giving, may disguise the lack of affection among family members by simulating the manifestation of love. An accompanying set of clichés may blindly assert the existence of love regardless of the facts in a particular case. How often a young child, despondent over a parent's anger or neglect, is told, "of *course*, your father loves you; he simply doesn't know how to show it," by someone who, resorting to a stock cliché, has never even met the father in question.

These myths and idealizations can easily mystify our understandings of how it really is with us in our relationships, and, thereby, further complicate the already monumental task of assessing relationships. Philosophers, it seems, have a special responsibility to assist in the critical assessment of relationships by avoiding further mystification. One way to help penetrate through the mythic and idealized understanding of relationships is to resist arguments that sound like nothing more than appeals to unreflective opinions.[40]

Unreflective opinions about values and practices, however popular those opinions may be, are not decisively authoritative for critical moral reflection or moral theory. Such opinions are, to be sure, important starting points of such reflection. They certainly belong in the cultural dialogue about marital and family relationships, a type of dialogue which, as I urged in the previous chapter, should supplant an abstract, monological ideal of impartiality in the human quest for moral wisdom. Unreflective opinions, however (this is part of my own contribution to the dialogue), cannot constitute conclusive defenses of conventional practices because they simply exhibit (and confirm) the conventionality of those practices. The moral worth of particular relationship practices must be assessed, among other things, in terms of the daily reality of those relationships rather than in terms of the hopes or idealistic aspirations that mystify those practices. Real marriages, for example,

---

40. For an essay that violates this stricture, see Christina Hoff Sommers, "Philosophers against the Family," in George Graham and Hugh LaFollette, eds., *Person to Person* (Philadelphia: Temple University Press, 1989), pp. 82–105. My critical discussion of this and other essays by Sommers appears in my " 'They Lived Happily Ever After': Sommers on Women and Marriage," *Journal of Social Philosophy* 21 (Fall/Winter 1990): 57–65. A commentary by Sommers and my rejoinder to her commentary follow in the same journal issue, with a further response by Sommers in the following issue of the journal.

usually fall far short of their fairy-tale counterparts, which fade "happily ever after" into the sunset.

Even if unreflective opinions are not decisively authoritative for moral theory, it is nevertheless important to understand those opinions carefully. In this regard, the champions of traditional marriage and family who invoke popular support on behalf of these institutions usually make an additional mistake. A familiar adage tells us that actions speak louder than words. What people, in general, actually think about marriage is probably better revealed by the recent rise in the divorce rate than by idealistic popular pronouncements on the topic of marriage.

Some philosophers and social commentators, seeking a populist defense of traditional marriage and family, try to discount what the divorce rate reveals about popular views of marriage by finding culprits to blame for the "breakdown of the traditional family." Feminists, in particular, are frequent scapegoats for this alleged social disintegration.[41] Such an accusation misses an obvious point. Critics of the institution of marriage do not break into people's homes to serve them with mandatory divorce decrees. If feminism, for example, has anything to do with the rising divorce rate, it must be in virtue of the increasing plausibility, to more and more people, of feminist critiques of marriage.[42] Feminist criticisms of marriage are not the only analyses of marriage available for public consumption; there is no dearth of published apologetics on behalf of traditional marriage.[43] The inability of such marital defenses to stem

41. See Sommers, "Philosophers against the Family," pp. 82–83.

42. A growing divorce rate suggests that many people find their marriages to be unsatisfactory. By shifting responsibility for the rising divorce rate away from the divorcing parties and toward marriage critics, such as feminists (ibid., pp. 82–83, 99, and passim), Sommers, in effect, treats this widespread dissatisfaction as if it were merely the result of the manipulation of popular opinion by marriage critics. Such a low regard for popular opinion is curiously inconsistent with Sommers's insistence that philosophers heed the "opinions of the community" (p. 103). It appears that Sommers herself ignores popular opinion when it inconveniently does not support her views (in this case, about marriage).

43. George Gilder's defenses of traditional marriage and family were es-

the tide of divorces provides invaluable information about what people really think about the daily reality of their married lives.

The declining durability of marriages in general may be due to their frequent inability to provide, without undue personal costs, the protection and care needed by their participants. The context of changing economic circumstances is also significant. As Okin has well shown, when decent economic alternatives to marriage are available to a woman, her economic dependence on her husband diminishes, thus providing her with otherwise unavailable options to leave the relationship should it prove unsatisfactory.[44] Whether the current divorce trends, in themselves, reveal problems with marriage at the generic level, the formal conventional level, the informal conventional level, or merely in a substantially large number of instances is a matter for further investigation.

In the first part of this discussion, I suggested, following Robert Goodin, that duties of partiality in close relationships are based, in part, on the various vulnerabilities of persons in those relationships and, in part, on social conventions that assign responsibilities for the care of the vulnerable to others who stand in certain relationships to them. I cautioned, however, that the duties based on those conventions should be viewed as prima facie duties only, pending a deep evaluation of those conventional practices and the vulnerabilities to which they answer. I then outlined some difficulties in the crucial project of assessing those relationship practices.

In the next section, I turn to a different sort of problem with our practices of partiality in close relationships, namely, that many people lack sufficient resources for favoring their loved ones effectively.

2. PARTIALITY AND INADEQUATE RESOURCES

Derek Parfit poses an argument that challenges the simple notion that I should help my child rather than a stranger when they

pecially prominent during the Reagan presidency; See his *Sexual Suicide* (New York: Quadrangle, 1973).

44. Okin, *Justice, Gender, and the Family*, pp. 137–38, 167–68.

each face roughly equivalent dangers and when I cannot help both. Parfit asks and answers the following questions: "When I try to protect my child, what should my aim be? Should it simply be that he is not harmed? Or should it rather be that he is saved from harm *by me?* If you would have a better chance of saving him from harm, I would be wrong to insist that the attempt be made by me. This shows that my aim should take the simpler form."[45] Parfit later extends this point to cover any sort of benefiting of loved ones, not simply the saving of them from harm. Parfit subsequently qualifies his argument, as I note below. First, however, let us consider the position in its original form. Stated in this way, the argument is both right and wrong. Certainly, on a particular occasion when my child is threatened, I should want her to be saved from danger no matter who saves her.

Relationships, however, are long-term interpersonal involvements. Partialists do not generally defend partiality for its own sake. Their defenses always refer to some further value to be served by partiality, for example, the maintenance of close relationships (which might, in turn, derive their value from what they contribute to integrity or the good life). A relationship, as it endures, is at its best if its participants both feel that they derive something special from their partner and have something special to offer their partner.[46] This is part of the sense of uniqueness and irreplaceability that people feel about loved ones and about themselves in relation to their loved ones, when relationships are flourishing. This recognition of, and responsiveness to, uniqueness itself seems to require that people be able to do special things for each other, things which cannot be done by others or for others.[47]

Thus, wanting to have a close personal relationship with some-

45. Derek Parfit, *Reasons and Persons* (Oxford: Clarendon Press, 1984), p. 96.

46. This point is made by Williams, "Persons, Character and Morality," p. 15; and by John Hardwig, "In Search of an Ethics of Personal Relationships," in George Graham and Hugh LaFollette, eds., *Person to Person* (Philadelphia: Temple University Press, 1989), p. 67.

47. Blum extensively discusses this aspect of close relationships in *Friendship, Altruism, and Morality.*

one is more than simply wishing well for her; it also involves wanting to make a distinctive contribution to her well-being, wanting to be an irreplaceably valuable part of her life. Parfit does acknowledge this point. He subsequently amends his statement of the argument by noting that there may be some kinds of benefit "that my child should receive *from me.*"[48]

Parfit's initial argument, however, is not completely wrong. It remains true that in emergencies one should want loved ones to be saved, no matter by whom. This point can be extended as well to the whole of a relationship. Love for someone over the long haul should include not only a concern to be an irreplaceably valuable part of her life but also the simple concern for her well-being. Because I care for my loved ones, I should want them both to be cared for or benefited by me and to do well, to flourish. Both concerns blend in a loving relationship with someone.

Close personal relationships in any society, as noted earlier, are highly conventionalized by a variety of practices.[49] Those practices organize and normalize partiality, making it legitimate, even required, toward certain persons rather than others, and in certain forms. (If friends do not provide the special care, support, and assistance we think of as appropriate for friendship, then hardly anyone can be expected to do so. After all, what are friends for?) Substantial partiality is expected in close relationships and is normative for them.

The relationship practices by which I justify preferentially saving my child from a danger equally facing several other children (when I can only save one) are the same practices that justify another parent in abandoning my child and saving solely her own when she herself is able to save only one. That is, the practices in question may sometimes be detrimental to my own child, whose welfare is of overriding partial concern to me. Remember that love does (or should) involve not only wanting to benefit one's beloved

48. Parfit, *Reasons and Persons,* p. 96.

49. For Parfit's discussion of the role played by social convention in our relationship practices, see ibid., pp. 96–110.

oneself but also wanting to see the loved one do well. It should matter to the partialist whether or not actual practices of partiality, the conventions determining when and to what extent we should favor loved ones, really do promote overall the well-being of our loved ones. If particular conventions of partiality reduce the well-being of some of those we love, then they diminish the extent to which we together find fulfillment and integrity through close relationships.

A partialist might not be troubled by the fact that the same practices which lead me to favor my child will also lead others to disfavor my child. From the partialist's standpoint, some child or other is being favored on each occasion by someone who loves her. The result does not seem to involve a net loss of integrity or fulfillment and so should not worry the partialist. To ferret out the worrisome feature of unqualified partiality, we must think about conditions in the "real world" that are relevant to the partial ways in which we practice close personal relationships.

It is common among philosophers to think that extant relationship conventions are operative because people in general benefit from them.[50] Even if people in general do benefit from certain relationship conventions, this does not entail that each and every person benefits. Relationship norms do not take account of the varying social and economic conditions of people's lives. Whether someone benefits from certain conventions may have a lot to do with her "social location," her share in that all-important dispersion, the distribution of the benefits and burdens of social cooperation. Because of limited resources, some people, vulnerable children and elderly persons among them, do not derive from their close personal relationships the values we think those relationships ought to serve.

An indirect line of thought may best help us to approach this problem. Consider John Cottingham's 1983 attack on what he (in

---

50. R. M. Hare's view, for example, that strong maternal partiality promotes good care for children seems typical; see *Moral Thinking* (Oxford: Clarendon Press, 1981), p. 137.

that essay) presents as a close cousin of the impartiality requirement, the Christian maxim "love thy neighbor as thyself."[51] Passages in the Bible indicate that "neighbor" here refers to anyone
in need, not simply the person next door.[52] For the sake of argument, however, let us think about the meaning of this directive in
the narrower sense, an approach taken also by Cottingham in 1983.
Doing so will afford us a vehicle with which to explore some limits
to the partialist's perspective. Cottingham ridicules the maxim, in
its narrow sense, for demanding that one give the "same importance" to the interests of the person next door that one gives to
one's own interests. Cottingham's attack on the narrowly interpreted maxim has something to it, but his reasons miss a key point.

Whether my neighbor needs any special moral attention from
me depends, both literally and metaphorically, on where we live.
Until recently, I lived next door to a retired engineering professor
from Purdue. He spent every summer at his condominium in Colorado. For his months away, he hired a lawn service to maintain
the grounds around his home, including the dozen or so tomato
plants that he would install in his garden every spring. Each summer, before leaving for Colorado, he would invite me to help myself
to his homegrown, professionally watered tomatoes when they
started ripening in August, since he would not return from Colorado until September. My former neighbor deserves my deepest
gratitude, but he hardly needs my special moral concern.

The same cannot be said about those people across town who

51. Cottingham, *Partiality, Favoritism, and Morality*, p. 87.
52. According to the New Testament parable of the Good Samaritan (Luke
10:29–37), the "neighbor" is anyone in need. I am grateful to Cynthia Read
for bringing this passage to my (non-Christian) attention. Cottingham, as well,
has recently emphasized that the maxim to love thy neighbor as thyself applies
to any human being; see his "Ethics of Self-Concern," *Ethics* 101 (July 1991):
799, n. 5. Referring to an earlier draft of this chapter, Cottingham, in his
footnote, suggests that my discussion of the maxim is "off the mark" because
I interpret "neighbor" narrowly. Pace Cottingham, my narrow (mis)inter-
pretation is not a mistake; instead, it is designed to afford a useful vehicle for
making a point about resource differences between neighborhoods. Certainly,
Cottingham's own earlier, more literal reading of "neighbor" also served a
rhetorical purpose and was not a distortion of Christian doctrine.

have no condominiums in Colorado, no homes of their own any-
where, no lawn services, no tomato plants, and little else. It is not
really the neighbor as such who needs the special concern of others.
The one who really needs special attention is the person without
resources whose friends and family are equally lacking. She would
not be adequately cared for even if all her friends and family were
as partial toward her as they could be. There are radical disparities
among different "neighborhoods" in the distribution of the resources for caring and protecting others. Those of us who live in
comfortable middle-class neighborhoods (or better) need a metaphor other than "love thy neighbor" to express what impartiality
really calls for.

Interpreted narrowly, "love thy neighbor as thyself" is itself a
statement of one form of partiality: it is *thy* neighbor whom you
are exhorted to love, not neighbors in general or neighbors every-
where. Cottingham well knows that it is not the person next door
but all inhabitants of the planet who matter to the impartiality
thesis.[53] This means that Cottingham's (and my own) attack on the
narrow meaning of the injunction to love thy neighbor is actually
a criticism of a certain form of partiality and not an attack on the
impartiality thesis at all. It is no argument against impartiality that
I need not have paid any special moral regard to my engineer
neighbor, since he was doing splendidly without me.

Not so for the numerous others who live in dire need. Of
course, fulfilling relationships are logically—and empirically—possible under conditions of extreme material need, but they are certainly also severely threatened by such conditions. It is difficult to
find fulfillment or integrity, that is, wholeness, in life if those I love
are starving. If they continue to starve no matter how much favoritism I show them, because my resources are so meager, then
partiality, while it might be necessary for my integrity and fulfillment, is hardly sufficient. In many cases, this insufficiency is profound.

There are, to be sure, some reasons on behalf of favoring the
interests of neighbors and acquaintances, even those with re-

53. "Ethics and Impartiality," pp. 90–91.

sources, over the interests of unknown strangers. When one is acquainted with someone, then one knows something, however minimal, about her. One may be familiar with her needs, wants, situation, or the like. Knowing something about someone's particular circumstances makes it easier to help or care for her effectively than if one knows nothing in particular about her. In such cases of greater familiarity, the risk is lessened that the help or care one renders will be ineffective or, worse yet, detrimental to the recipient.

These considerations modify, but they do not override or even substantially diminish, the moral importance of social and economic conditions in determining how practices of partiality should be organized society-wide. Relationship norms, to reiterate, are silent about those conditions. It matters to the partialist's theoretical stance, however, that large numbers of people do not have adequate resources to favor their loved ones. (This is the point that I have approached indirectly.)[54] As a result, whether or not, and to what extent, someone benefits from certain partialist relationship conventions has a lot to do with her socioeconomic location. It hinges heavily on the sort of luck she had in being born to, adopted by, or linked by marriage to relations with adequate resources for her care, nurturance, and protection.

When many families are substantially impoverished, then practices of partiality further diminish the number of people who can achieve well-being, integrity, and fulfillment through close relationships. If we each tend to our own loved ones only, then some of those loved ones will flourish while others languish. Those who can care for their loved ones well, materially, emotionally, and so on, will enhance the well-being and life prospects of their loved ones and will thereby realize some measure of the sort of personal integrity and fulfillment that is attained through close relationships. Those who cannot take good care of their loved ones will not realize integrity or fulfillment through such relationships because they can do little to enhance the well-being of those they love. Partiality, if

54. For a related argument, see James Rachels, "Morality, Parents, and Children," in Graham and LaFollette, *Person to Person*, pp. 46–62.

practiced by all, untempered by any redistribution of wealth or resources, would appear to lead to the integrity and fulfillment of only some persons, but not all.

The implications of this line of thought are particularly relevant to the defenses of partiality that appeal to its role in furthering human integrity and fulfillment, an approach taken by Williams and Cottingham.[55] On such a view, partiality is not intrinsically valuable but derives its value largely from being a necessary ingredient in relationships that themselves realize integrity and fulfillment in someone's life because they are her relationships, connections through which she herself strives to promote the well-being of those she loves. As Cottingham puts it, "to be a person, to have a sense of identity and personal integrity, implies the possession of plans, projects and desires which have a *special status* in your scale of values precisely because they are yours."[56]

Recall the significance of Parfit's argument: in loving my loved ones, my aim is not simply that they be cared for by me, but that they be cared for *well*. If someone cannot care effectively for her loved ones, then her aims remain unrealized, putting her own integrity and fulfillment at risk along with the (to her) all-important well-being of her loved ones. Were the unqualified practice of partiality to lead to less integrity or fulfillment than is possible under other social arrangements, then, on this partialist account, there would be something wrong with the unqualified practice of partiality.

If the defense of partiality is predicated on the importance of human integrity and fulfillment in general, then the numbers must count theoretically.[57] It should matter to what I call the "fulfillment defense" of partiality that some people live in circumstances which

55. Other defenses of partiality, such as Fried's libertarian account, are not so clearly challenged by these considerations, although they might be if we could substitute freedom for integrity and fulfillment, mutatis mutandis.

56. Cottingham, "Ethics and Impartiality," p. 87.

57. A similar point is raised by David O. Brink against William's well-known hypothetical counterexample to utilitarianism involving the case of Jim and the nineteen villagers sentenced to death; "Utilitarianism and the Personal Point of View," *Journal of Philosophy* 83 (August 1986): 432.

critically compromise the care they can show to loved ones and which, accordingly, diminish their chances of achieving integrity and fulfillment through close personal relationships. If partiality is everyone's moral prerogative, and, more so, if it is everyone's responsibility, then, on certain partialist grounds alone, there ought to be a distribution of the resources for protecting, caring for, and otherwise favoring loved ones that permits as many of us as possible to do so in a fulfilling and integrity-conferring manner.

A defense of partiality toward loved ones is incomplete without a defense of the social conventions by which such partiality would be realized in practice and turned into a set of legitimated expectations for a society. Surely Bernard Williams is not merely trying to convince us that it is all right for him to favor members of the Williams clan, John Cottingham is not simply trying to justify his own partiality toward his loved ones, and so on. If partiality, as such, is to be justified, then the defense must be in general terms. If the very practices of partiality are not defensible, then particular instances of it lose one of their primary justifications.

The justification of practices, however, often takes a decidedly different form from the justification of actions that exemplify or fall under those practices.[58] If partiality is to be defended in virtue of the integrity and fulfillment it makes possible for *all* those who practice it, then we must consider the effects of practices of partiality on all who together engage in them, including those who lack the minimum resources for showing partiality effectively. The justification of practices requires us to consider people who are not our friends or relations, for whom we feel no particular affection, and whom we may not even know.

On a fulfillment defense of partiality, social institutions should be structured so that partiality, as practiced in close relationships, contributes to the well-being, integrity, and fulfillment of as many people as possible. I do not pretend to have a blueprint for thus restructuring our institutions. I have no formula for modifying our

---

58. This point has long been recognized. For what is, by now, a classic discussion and application of it, see John Rawls, "Two Concepts of Rules," *Philosophical Review* 64 (1955).

practices of partiality so as to alleviate the worldwide scarcity of caretaking resources while still preserving the values afforded by partiality itself.[59] The best solution, in my view, will arise out of the sort of public dialogue I urged in the previous chapter, a dialogue that its current participants should restructure so as to include in particular the voices of those who lack adequate means for favoring their loved ones effectively.

This conclusion, which appears to show consideration for all persons, is derived from certain partialist concerns. Thus, by viewing partiality as morally valuable because of what it ultimately contributes to human well-being, integrity, and fulfillment in life, and by considering the reality of inadequate resources for some, we are led to a notion that sounds suspiciously like my proposed method for promoting a modified, practicable moral impartiality.

In this chapter, I sketched the partiality debate and highlighted features of the practice of partiality that complicate its philosophical defense. First, I proposed that the moral value of partiality depends partly on the moral worth of the particular relationships in which it appears. Second, I suggested that practices of partiality must be tempered by the recognition that many persons lack adequate resources for favoring their loved ones effectively. In the next chapter, I contrast feminist and nonfeminist approaches to partiality and extend my feminist approach in certain new directions.

59. See Chapter 3, section 4, however, for my discussion of global moral concerns.

3

The Social Self
and the Partiality Debates

*I*n recent decades, the dissatisfaction with impartialist ethical traditions has grown widespread and diverse. Challenges to these traditions have arisen simultaneously from feminist moral philosophers and from some of their nonfeminist colleagues. In the previous chapter, I explored some nonfeminist arguments in defense of the moral importance of partiality and the claim that the moral value of partiality cannot be derived from an impartialist ethic. Some of the feminist critics of moral impartialism share these views with the nonfeminist critics.[1] In addition, nearly all the feminist critics and some of the nonfeminist critics contend that impartialist ethical theories do not take sufficient account of the inherently social nature of human persons.

This conceptual overlap between feminist and nonfeminist critiques of the tradition of moral impartialism might suggest that the underlying concerns of both groups coincide. That appearance, however, is largely an illusion. What seems on the surface to be a shared project of challenging moral impartialism in fact masks quite

1. Feminists who defend the moral importance of being especially attentive and responsive to loved ones and others to whom one has special relationships do not usually frame their arguments in terms of the notion of partiality. It is my own assessment that those feminist accounts can be grouped under this rubric.

different underlying presumptions and concerns. My aim, in this chapter, is to reveal some of those differences and to develop further the feminist alternative. In particular, I hope to clarify certain aspects of the social self by considering two important issues brought to light by nonfeminist critics of moral impartialism. For the most part, my discussion in this chapter will not take sides specifically on the challenge to moral impartiality or the defense of partiality.[2] The conception of the social self is the focal point for my discussion of what some moral philosophers have begun to call the "partiality-impartiality debates."

Here is my plan. I first review some of the arguments on behalf of partiality and introduce the conception of the social self. My sketch highlights some of the flavor of the partiality debates that I think will have special interest to feminists, for example, the variety of conceptions of the self that appear in these discussions and some hypothetical dilemmas used by the nonfeminist philosophers which rely on disturbing gender configurations.

In section 2, I turn to the first of two puzzles raised for a conception of the social self by nonfeminist defenses of partiality. Many nonfeminist critics of impartiality show a disturbingly conservative approach to our traditions for personal interrelationships. This conservatism prompts my first concern about the social self: a too-simplistic conception of the social self does not show us how persons critically reflect on social traditions or resist the hazardous features of those traditions—matters of deep importance to feminists. In this section, I sketch a way of understanding the social self that anchors the possibility of social critique and resistance.

In the third, and final, section, I consider a second puzzle for the conception of the social self. Many nonfeminist critics of impartiality defend partiality as the practice of "taking care of one's own." They explicitly deny that one should give the same moral consideration to distant and unknown people as one does to loved ones. They reject anything that hints at global moral concern. By contrast, feminist critics of impartiality, even while promoting the

---

2. See Chapter 1 for my challenge to moral impartialism and Chapter 2 for my critical discussion of partiality.

value of close personal relationships, continue to endorse global moral concern. The notion of global moral concern, however, does not fit well into the conception of the social self. This lack of fit seems to reveal one disquieting limitation to the social self, which I explore briefly.

1. THE PARTIALITY DEBATES (REVISITED) AND THE SOCIAL SELF

It has become a commonplace of contemporary mainstream ethics, as investigated in the preceding chapter, that we are each entitled to show favoritism, preferential treatment, partiality toward loved ones. Philosophers disagree, however, about whether partiality toward loved ones can adequately be justified by any of the dominant impartialist theories of modern moral philosophy. In the past two decades, both feminist and nonfeminist philosophers have challenged the requirement of moral impartiality and questioned its capacity to ground our responsibilities and prerogatives to favor those we love.

Moral impartiality, to reiterate, is variously characterized as an absence of bias and as equal consideration, in some important sense, for all persons. Moral philosophers have used a variety of fictional images to express what it would be for moral thinking to be genuinely impartial. One such image is that of the "ideal observer." According to Roderick Firth's classic 1952 depiction, the ideal observer is someone who is "omniscient with respect to nonethical facts," omnipercipient, disinterested, dispassionate, and consistent, but in all other respects, "normal."[3] A more recent image of impartial moral reasoning is R. M. Hare's "archangel," who can scan a novel situation and discern at a glance all its properties, including the future consequences of all alternative possible actions. Based on this superhuman knowledge, "he" frames a uni-

3. "Ethical Absolutism and the Ideal Observer," *Philosophy and Phenomenological Research* 12 (March 1952): 333. For an illuminating critique of the limitations of this and several other rhetorical fictions that are supposed to illustrate the moral point of view, see Margaret Walker, "Partial Consideration," *Ethics* 101 (July 1991): 758–74.

versal principle for behavior in that situation, a principle that would be acceptable to him from the standpoint of any role in that situation that he might have to occupy.[4] Thomas Nagel's image of impartial moral thinking (he calls it "objective" or "impersonal" thinking) is "the view from nowhere": to attain this view, one detaches oneself from one's own personal perspective, transcends "one's time and place," and "escapes the specific contingencies of one's creaturely point of view."[5]

From the impartial standpoint, one is to reason about moral matters detached from the influence of one's own specific contingencies, one's wants, needs, loyalties, and so on. The impartial attitude is supposed to overcome what is traditionally regarded as the pervasive human tendency toward self-serving partiality and egoism. From the impartialist point of view, one is permitted to take account of one's own particularities—but only as contextual details of the moral matter under consideration, a sort of "grist" for the "mill" (or "kant") of moral judgment. One is not to reason *from* those particularities, that is, from a perspective which, at the outset, prejudicially favors those interests.

Treating everyone impartially appears to mean treating each person, including oneself, with the same consideration—no more, no less—as anyone else. One gives equal consideration to "every person as a person," according to Paul Taylor, when one refrains from "counting the basic interests of one individual as having greater (or lesser) weight than the basic interests of another."[6]

This is hardly, however, the way to treat loved ones. Critics of moral impartialism charge that the array of attitudes called for by impartial theories is alienating in close personal relationships. It seems impossible to be especially loving when one is detached from one's personal concerns and loyalties, when one is disinterested, dispassionate, and attentive only to the generalized moral equality of all persons, thereby abstracting from individual partic-

---

4. *Moral Thinking* (Oxford: Clarendon Press, 1981), p. 44.

5. *The View from Nowhere* (New York: Oxford University Press, 1986), pp. 139, 9, and passim.

6. "On Taking the Moral Point of View," *Midwest Studies in Philosophy* 3 (1978): 37.

ularity and uniqueness. Close relationships call, instead, for personal concern, loyalty, interest, passion, and responsiveness to the uniqueness of loved ones, to their specific needs, interests, history, and so on.[7] In a word, personal relationships call for attitudes of partiality rather than impartiality.

Impartialist moral theories have also been criticized for failing to account adequately for the special values that personal relationships contribute to our lives. These include the intrinsic value that Lawrence Blum and Charles Fried find in benefiting one's own friends and loved ones.[8] In the opinion of Bernard Williams, devoting oneself preferentially to one's own ground projects, including personal relationships, is necessary in order to have character, integrity, motive force to face one's future, and reason for living.[9]

Those arguments are typical of critiques of impartiality that are not particularly feminist in orientation. My present concern is to highlight the feminist interests in these issues. Feminists, such as Sara Ruddick,[10] have generally endorsed partiality not merely for its own sake but rather as part of a larger project. This is the project of promoting esteem for, and an enriched understanding of, the caring and nurturing activities that women have traditionally undertaken in areas of life such as child care and health care. Those caring activities have essentially involved moral attention and responsiveness to the specific wants and needs of particular persons.

Also of concern to feminists, impartialist theorists have tended to emphasize moral matters, such as justice and rights, that pertain

7. John Kekes describes how the nature of intimacy renders impartiality inappropriate; see his "Morality and Impartiality," *American Philosophical Quarterly* 18 (October 1981): 299–302.

8. Lawrence Blum, *Friendship, Altruism, and Morality* (London: Routledge & Kegan Paul, 1980), chap. 3, "Friendship, Beneficence, and Impartiality"; and Charles Fried, *Right and Wrong* (Cambridge: Harvard University Press, 1978), p. 172.

9. Bernard Williams, "A Critique of Utilitarianism," in J. J. C. Smart and Bernard Williams, *Utilitarianism: For and Against* (Cambridge: Cambridge University Press, 1973), pp. 108–18; and Bernard Williams, "Persons, Character, and Morality," in *Moral Luck* (Cambridge: Cambridge University Press, 1981), pp. 1–19.

10. See Sara Ruddick, *Maternal Thinking* (Boston: Beacon Press, 1989).

to a public world in which people interact as equal but mutually disinterested persons.[11] Many feminists have contended, by contrast, that, in close personal relationships, the need for care overshadows the need for justice, perhaps rendering it altogether inappropriate.[12] Concepts of rights have been contested by feminists for relying on an atomistic or asocial conception of human individuals that is inimical to the interconnectedness of close personal relationships and damaging to the intimacy and mutual trust on which those relationships should be based.[13]

I have already noted that some critics of moral impartiality, nonfeminists such as Alasdair MacIntyre and Michael Sandel, and feminists such as Iris Young, have denied the very possibility of impartial reasoning.[14] This challenge is particularly germane to the present discussion, for it derives, in all those cases, from a certain metaphysical conception of the moral self. All three of these theorists argue that no self can reason as if dissociated from the contingencies which constitute her to be the self she is. There is no escape from the specifics of one's embodiment, historical situation, and relational connections to others. Impartial reasoning is impossible; the self is inherently partial.

Indeed, for MacIntyre, Sandel, and Young, the self is inher-

11. See John Rawls, *A Theory of Justice* (Cambridge: Harvard University Press, 1971), and the massive literature generated by Rawls's work.

12. See Carol Gilligan, *In a Different Voice* (Cambridge: Harvard University Press, 1982); and Nel Noddings, *Caring* (Berkeley: University of California Press, 1984). I discuss these views, especially those of Gilligan, in Chapters 4 through 6.

13. See Elizabeth Wolgast, *The Grammar of Justice* (Ithaca, N.Y.: Cornell University Press, 1987); and John Hardwig, "Should Women Think in Terms of Rights?" *Ethics* 94 (April 1984): 441–55. For an overview of feminist concerns about the legal applications of the concept of rights, see Carol Smart, *Feminism and the Power of Law* (London: Routledge, 1989), especially chap. 7, "The Problem of Rights."

14. See Alasdair MacIntyre, *After Virtue* (Notre Dame, Ind.: University of Notre Dame Press, 1981); Michael J. Sandel, *Liberalism and the Limits of Justice* (Cambridge: Cambridge University Press, 1982); and Iris Marion Young, "Impartiality and the Civic Public: Some Implications of Feminist Critiques of Moral and Political Theory," *Praxis International* 5 (January 1986): 381–401.

ently *social* to some degree or other. In its identity, character, interests, and preferences, it is constituted by, and in the course of, relationships to particular others, including the network of relationships that locate it as a member of certain communities or social groups. According to Sandel, we each have "constitutive attachments" of loyalty and allegiance which arise from our histories and have a moral force affecting our choices and behavior. Most important, these commitments partly define us and give us character. Living by these attachments "is inseparable from understanding ourselves as the particular persons we are."[15] For MacIntyre, as well: "We all approach our own circumstances as bearers of a particular social identity. I am someone's son or daughter, someone else's cousin or uncle; I am a citizen of this or that city, a member of this or that guild or profession; I belong to this clan, that tribe, this nation."[16] Relationships to others are intrinsic to identity, preferences, and so on, and the self can reason only as the social being she is.

The conception of the self as inherently social fits comfortably into the feminist project of incorporating women's moral perspectives into ethical theorizing. Caroline Whitbeck and Virginia Held argue that the conception of the social self, with its emphasis on the primacy of relationships, coincides with women's traditional experiences as mothers and care givers.[17] The concept of the social self also provides a theoretical underpinning for the feminist view that gender, in particular, is a socially constructed aspect of human identity, one that may, therefore, diverge from our present gender arrangements of pervasive male dominance.

If the self is inherently social, then a concern for other persons is fundamental to the self and is not reducible to a mere variety of self-concern. Indeed, the conception of the social self tends

15. Sandel, *Liberalism*, p. 179.
16. MacIntyre, *After Virtue*, pp. 204–5.
17. Caroline Whitbeck, "A Different Reality: Feminist Ontology," in Carol Gould, ed., *Beyond Domination* (Totowa, N.J.: Rowman & Allanheld, 1984), pp. 64–88; and Virginia Held, "Non-Contractual Society: A Feminist View," in Marsha Hanen and Kai Nielsen, eds., *Science, Morality, and Feminist Theory, Canadian Journal of Philosophy* suppl. vol. 13 (1987): 111–38.

somewhat to blur the distinction between self and other. If my relationship to someone or some group is internal to who I am, then she or they are somehow a part of me—admittedly, a metaphor that needs substantial clarification. In my partiality for those who are, in this way, near and dear to me, I show a moral attitude that is neither egoism nor self-denying altruism. The flourishing of loved ones promotes my own well-being, yet my motivation to care for them does not require me to compute how their well-being will further my own interests; I simply am interested in them. J. L. Mackie, following C. D. Broad, calls this attitude "self-referential altruism."[18] On this view, simple egoism is not the all-pervasive moral failing it has been theorized to be, and far too much ethical work has been expended in disputing it.

Despite these overlapping interests among feminist and nonfeminist partialists, there are other features of the arguments by nonfeminist partialists that deviate from, rather than coincide with, feminist concerns. To begin with, the social conception of the self is not shared by all critics of impartialism. Among nonfeminist partialists, conceptions of the self range from the individualistic atoms of libertarianism to the socially embedded subjects of communitarianism.

An example of an individualistic conception of selves is to be found in the works of Charles Fried, who has puzzled over the limits of moral impartiality at least since 1970. Fried presents a libertarian view: beyond the realm of justice, rights, and other duties to avoid injuring others, we are morally free to do what we want. On this view, morality has its limits, and beyond those limits, we may show partiality toward whomever we wish and ignore whomever we wish. Wants and wishes are left unexamined and the role of relationships in constituting wants and the wanting self is simply disregarded by Fried.[19] ·

18. J. L. Mackie, *Ethics* (Harmondsworth, England: Penguin Books, 1977), p. 132.

19. An *Anatomy of Values* (Cambridge: Harvard University Press, 1970), p. 227; and *Right and Wrong* (Cambridge: Harvard University Press, 1978), pp. 169–75.

Bernard Williams, a pioneering defender of partiality, relies on a conception of the self that is more social than that of Fried. Williams's conception of morality is richer, as well, and includes not only impartial moral demands but also matters of character and personal relations that, for him, are not to be understood in impartial terms. One important aspect of character is personal integrity. In Williams's view, the pursuit of integrity involves devoting considerable attention and energy to personal projects and commitments without which life would not be worth living. These projects, however, seem to Williams to compete with impartial moral concerns. A self who is too heavily encumbered with impartialist moral responsibilities to treat everyone with equal consideration will be alienated from close others and from her own self because she will not have time for her most fundamental, integrity-conferring relationships and projects.[20]

Williams's views[21] advance beyond Fried's in explicitly recognizing the importance of relationships to personal integrity and moral experience. But Williams's specific defense of his views is disturbing in virtue of the gender configurations that skew his examples. In an important essay on this topic, Williams contends that, in a hypothetical dilemma in which there is time to save only one person, one should save one's drowning "wife" rather than a drowning stranger.[22] One obvious problem with this sad example is its reliance on the unfortunate social stereotypes of active, heroic male and passive, helpless female.

A second, not-so-obvious gender configuration problem emerges when this example is compared to other examples deployed elsewhere in Williams's writings. In his famous essay on moral luck, Williams argues that a painter who abandons wife and

20. See Bernard Williams, *Moral Luck* (Cambridge: Cambridge University Press, 1981), especially "Persons, Character, and Morality," pp. 1–19.

21. For an excellent feminist critique of some of Williams's views, see Claudia Card, "Gender and Moral Luck," in Owen Flanagan and Amélie Oksenberg Rorty, eds., *Identity, Character, and Morality* (Cambridge, Mass.: MIT Press, 1990), pp. 199–218.

22. Williams, *Moral Luck*, pp. 17–18.

children altogether and heads off for Tahiti to develop his art will be retroactively justified if he thereby acquires the good fortune to paint great paintings.[23] Williams's larger body of writing, thus, gives the true measure of his nonimpartialist value hierarchy: wife trumps stranger, but great paintings trump wife.

Williams's writings aside, there are at least two more features of the nonfeminist partiality arguments that are noteworthy from a feminist perspective. First, in mainstream discussions of this topic, which I explored in the preceding chapter, partiality devolves into favoritism or preferential treatment. Mainstream discussions presuppose a context of competing interests. The emphasis is on what I do for my wife or child *at the expense of* someone else, including other wives, other children.

Hypothetical disasters abound as thought experiments in these discussions. The moral world of mainstream ethics is a nightmare of plane crashes, train wrecks, and sinking ships. Wives and children drown in this literature at an alarming rate. The nonfeminist impartiality critics never acknowledge how infrequent these emergencies are in daily moral life, or, therefore, how rare is the need to sacrifice someone else's wife in order to save one's own. And for those infrequent occasions, the nonfeminist impartiality critics never discuss the possibility of investing our moral energies in efforts to reduce beforehand those breathtaking contests for survival and love—for example, by better federal regulation of airline safety.

Second, although there is broad consensus about the legitimacy of partiality toward family members and friends, there is no consensus about other special relationships. Some theorists defend partiality toward the members of one's local and national communities, such as neighborhood, city, and nation. Communitarians

23. Ibid., in the essay "Moral Luck," pp. 20–39. Alison Jaggar is another feminist philosopher who expresses concern over Williams's use of this example: "Feminist Ethics: Some Issues for the Nineties," *Journal of Social Philosophy* 20 (Spring/Fall 1989): 97. In Chapter 6, I explore this example for what it reminds us about gender asymmetries in our practices of holding people accountable for caretaking.

especially, such as MacIntyre and Sandel, favor these examples.[24] It is remarkable, however, that nonfeminist participants in the partiality debates tend to neglect partialities of gender or race. Those few participants in this debate who deal with these relationships are usually defenders of moral impartialism who point out that some forms of partiality are unjustified, and who cite racism and sexism as examples.[25]

My point is that beyond the realm of close relationships, there is no consensus over the legitimacy of partiality. Note, however, that those who do defend partiality toward local or national communities ironically pay no attention to the historical specifics of interrelationships among communities and social groups—the hierarchies of group domination, the institutionalized oppressions, the imperialistic policies. Group loyalty is a form of partiality that covers a wide spectrum, for example, ethnic pride, group solidarity in the face of oppression, but also white supremacism, male chauvinism, and heterosexism. The moral worth of group loyalty varies with the relative needs, interests, powers, privileges, and history of the social group in question. At any rate, this issue has yet to find adequate treatment in the partiality debates.

2. On Being Social but Not Conventional

I now turn to the first of two problems faced by a social conception of the self, as suggested by the partiality debates.

In the preceding chapter, I observed that defenders of partiality tend to presume that close relationships are morally worthwhile without qualification. The nonfeminist defenses of partiality are

24. See MacIntyre, *After Virtue;* Sandel, *Liberalism;* and Oldenquist, "Loyalties," *Journal of Philosophy* 79 (April 1982): 173–93. I return to a discussion of communitarianism in Chapter 9.

25. See Alan Gewirth, "Ethical Universalism and Particularism," *Journal of Philosophy* 85 (June 1988): 298. John Cottingham is a singular example of a nonfeminist partialist who argues that not all partialities are justified and who worries about racism and sexism; see his "Partiality, Favouritism, and Morality," *Philosophical Quarterly* 36, no. 144 (1986): 357–73.

particularly susceptible to this criticism. Many nonfeminist impartiality critics invoke certain conventionally defined roles and relationships as if these relationships as such legitimate the partiality shown within them. If my child or friend is in danger, then I may—or, rather, I should—help her first before I help others who are in lesser or equivalent or, even, slightly greater danger. According to most nonfeminist impartiality critics, that someone is related to me in certain ways *of itself* warrants partiality toward that person. On this view, certain conventional social relationships are intrinsically legitimate reference points for partiality.

The explicit appeals to social convention are expressed by communitarian critics of impartiality.[26] In their view, social traditions, practices, and roles determine the particulars of individual moral lives. I am someone's daughter, someone's friend, someone's mother, and I, therefore, have certain filial, friendship, and parental responsibilities toward certain other particular persons, responsibilities that I do not have to persons to whom I am not thus related. The basis for these responsibilities is at least partly a matter of tradition, a matter of the way caretaking work is socially allocated. Impartiality calls for the humanly impossible detachment from those particulars about oneself that make certain social conventions relevant. Thus, on the communitarian view, partiality in special relationships simply fulfills socially assigned responsibilities in the context of traditional relationship practices that define the "starting points" of individual moral identity.

In the nonfeminist literature on this topic, the general consensus is that one should show special favoritism to people in the following relationships to oneself: spouse, child, parent, and friend. These are by far the most commonly invoked nonfeminist examples. Even nonfeminist theorists who disagree on how to *justify* partiality in these relationships nevertheless agree that partiality is legitimate in these relationships. Nonfeminist impartiality critics, thus, treat these traditionally sanctioned relationships as paradigms of partiality, betraying an uncritical attitude toward our traditions of intimate relationships.

26. MacIntyre, *After Virtue*; and Sandel, *Liberalism*.

Our traditions for interrelating closely with people, the traditions that make partiality legitimate for each of us toward certain others, for example, traditions of marriage and family, are problematic in a variety of ways. The preceding chapter dealt extensively with two of these problems and noted a third one in passing.[27] First, those traditions are sometimes unfairly exclusionary. In such cases, only certain particular types of people can be related to each other in the specified ways. By legal and religious tradition, for example, no women are qualified to be my spouse. Because of those restrictive traditions, lesbian and gay relationships are widely scorned and otherwise socially obstructed. To the extent that relationship traditions provide genuine value for the participants, the unfairly exclusionary nature of some of those practices is a moral wrong.

Second, even the permitted forms of traditional relationships can be morally treacherous. Shielded from public scrutiny by a veil of "privacy," conventional intimate relationships have permitted abuses as well as favoritism.[28] Many of the socially sanctioned relationships for partiality and favoritism have been sites of privatized power imbalances. The same social traditions that confer prerogatives of favoring loved ones have permitted, to those with

27. It should be obvious that to emphasize, as I do, the problems with certain traditions is not to deny the possibility that the traditional practices in question also provide valued (or valuable) goods to their practitioners. Even if the traditions do provide such goods, however, the problems should not, for that reason, be casually dismissed.

28. Among nonfeminist theorists in the partiality debate, as far as I have been able to determine, this point is brought out only by Robert E. Goodin, in "What Is So Special about Our Fellow Countrymen?" *Ethics* 98 (July 1988): 663–86. Goodin's work is also noteworthy for not invoking conventional relationships uncritically; instead, he justifies partiality by reference to the underlying values that are supposed to be served by special relationships; see *Protecting the Vulnerable: A Reanalysis of Our Social Responsibilities* (Chicago: University of Chicago Press, 1985); and Chapter 2, above, for my discussion of some of Goodin's arguments. Among feminist theorists, there is an extensive literature on the problems in traditional close relationships; see, for example, Irene Diamond, ed., *Families, Politics, and Public Policy* (New York: Longman, 1983).

greater power, privileges of hurting those same loved ones. Historically, men have been able to assault, batter, and rape the women to whom they were married and parents can assault, batter, and impound their children. Traditional forms of partiality, or "preferential treatment," have often come at a price. The "favoritism" shown by husbands toward wives has not always been so favorable. However, most nonfeminist impartiality critics provide no critical evaluation of the social roles they take to warrant partiality. They disregard the costs of that partiality for those "favored" by it—not to mention the costs of that partiality to those disfavored by it or excluded from it.[29]

Third, as I argued in the preceding chapter, we live in a world in which many people do not have adequate resources for caring for their loved ones effectively. Under these circumstances, the social practices by which we each favor only our respective "own," if untempered by any methods for redistributing caretaking resources, would result in gravely inadequate care for many of the world's people.

To summarize: the nonfeminist defenses of partiality generally show a complacency about our social traditions for close personal relationships. But these traditions, despite the genuine values they afford their participants, are morally problematic in at least two different ways. First, relationship traditions are sometimes exclusionary, and, often in such cases, they stigmatize any similar kind of relationship that falls outside conventional bounds. Second, relationship traditions harbor the potential for abuse and exploitation, problems that are disregarded by nonfeminist partialists in their haste to endorse the partiality featured in those relationships. Third, relationship traditions ignore the inadequacy of the resources of many people for favoring their loved ones effectively. The nonfeminist partialists, thus, inadvertently remind us of the need for a socially critical perspective on relationship traditions, a perspective that I began to outline in the previous chapter.

This need for a critical attitude toward relationships bears on

29. Cottingham, to reiterate, is an exception; see his "Partiality, Favouritism, and Morality."

the conception of the social self in an important way. The social self identifies herself, at least in part, by her relationships to others, including the social groups of which she is a part. She is, for example, someone's daughter, someone's sister, someone's aunt, she is black, she is heterosexual, she is middle class, she's a Hoosier. Doubtless, she understands those relationships in terms of whatever, if any, social norms and conventions govern them. But if she has a socially critical perspective, then she does not necessarily act in accordance with those relational norms or with the conventions for her group. Instead, she may resist and subvert them.

This conception seems, on the face of it, mysterious. How can someone both identify in terms of certain relationships and, at the same time, cast doubt on those relationships by questioning the underlying social norms on which they are based? How can someone resist constituents of her very self? How can such independent attitudes be possible? Would they not also be socially constituted? If so, would that not negate the possible social independence of attitudes?

We know, however, that attitudes and behavior sometimes *are* independent. We know that there are social critics and social deviants. From that assumption, it is plausible to modify the conception of the social self so as to account for the existence of social criticism and resistance. The beginnings of such an account lie in some commonplace observations we may make about the development of selves and the social conditions under which they develop.

The potential for deviating from relationship norms must lie predominantly, it seems to me, in the complexity of selves and the diversity of ways in which we are constituted by our social contexts. A complex self can depart from this or that particular social influence, even those which (partially) constitute her identity, because of the combined effect of her various and varied identity constituents. Selves do not simply replicate a small cohesive set of social norms.

What are some of those varied identity constituents? First, as social beings, we reflect a variety of relationships. Few people show the influence of only one single formative affiliation. Where there is variety, however, there is likely to be divergence and inconsistency. From political activist friends, many years ago, I learned to distrust the patriotism I was taught in school. From love relationships, I learned to resist the sexual norms of femininity that gripped my teenage consciousness. We can move back and forth among a plurality of partial identities, now interrogating this or that relational norm from the standpoint of other commitments.[30]

Second, this movement between aspects of identity is assisted, in our culture, by capacities for distrusting, doubting, interrogating, criticizing, and resisting that are socially learned to varying degrees. When someone finds out that she can "just say no" to drug dealers, she is also learning how to say no to other demands. These techniques generalize and can be deployed against the conventional as well as the unconventional, both to scrutinize others and in self-scrutiny.

Third, there are aspects of the social that are not normative, conventional, or rule-governed. Only some of what we derive from social origins is the orderly implementation of rules applied consistently across all social contexts. Our society is heterogeneous, complex, confused, contradictory, and, sometimes, incoherent. Some of what we derive from our social relationships is unregulated, disorderly, chaotic.

This social irregularity, in turn, has at least two dimensions. First, relational norms themselves are usually general and do not dictate the specific ways they are to be realized in any particular case; this must inevitably depend on the specifics of the persons and circumstances involved. For example, we are taught to care for our parents when they are old and infirm, but there are no

---

30. The importance of plurality among partial identities is also emphasized by Elizabeth Young-Bruehl in "The Education of Women as Philosophers," *Signs* 12 (Winter 1987): 207–21. This part of my discussion reveals one of many remaining areas of obscurity in the conception of the social self. If we conceive of the self as being *wholly* constituted by its complex of socially derived identity constituents, then it is not clear who or what it is that moves "back and forth" among the "plurality of partial identities." I do not address this metaphysical conundrum in this book.

specific guidelines about exactly how to do this. The best affordable medical care might be available only in a nursing home, but your mother might rather be dead than enter one. Filial and other social norms are often general, and we are left to work out the specific applications for ourselves.

A second dimension of the unregulated nature of the social is the chaos of socially unsanctioned abuses. The sexual molestation of children is not explicitly condoned by our dominant cultural ideology or by our conventional norms of relationship to children. It is, however, encouraged by suggestive advertising and inadequately punished by law. As we are socially constituted, we are affected by these lawless social elements along with what is rule-bound, norm-governed.

And let us not forget the chaos of being constituted a woman, female, the "other"—lacking a sense of justice, lacking the authority of reason, lacking a you-know-what, fleshy, mysterious, and insatiable, the human source of original sin. Some theorists now construe female embodiment itself as a social construct.[31] Certainly it is the source of much disconcerting "female trouble."

To summarize: Selves are complex. Even though they are socially constituted, they can adopt points of view independent of this or that norm-governed relationship which constitutes their very identities. This complexity of selves includes: (1) the variety exhibited by the personal relationships that contribute to any one person's identity and that afford her differing and sometimes contradictory points of view; (2) learned techniques of doubt, critical reflection, resistance, and insubordination; and (3) elements of social life that exceed the limits of social regulation, elements of disorder within the heart of society and culture, including female nature and, to the extent that it is also a social construct, female embodiment as well. It is because of the complexity of the social that even socially constituted selves can evade thorough social regulation.[32]

31. See Judith Butler, *Gender Trouble* (New York: Routledge, 1990).
32. If Diana T. Meyers is right, men are more capable of such evasions than women. See her illuminating and disturbing study of the ways in which

If this survey of social influences on self-identity is correct, then the conception of the self as inherently social allows for the possibility that a self might criticize or resist this or that relationship convention which is, nevertheless, constitutive of her very identity.

3. On Being Partial But Not Parochial: Global Moral Concern

In this final section, I turn to a different issue. I mentioned earlier that moral impartiality is currently understood in terms of giving equal consideration to all persons. As interpreted by many nonfeminist critics of impartiality, this requirement calls for the moral agent to devote literally equal amounts of time, energy, and resources to all persons, that is, to all persons in the world.[33] I should not be buying my own child such luxuries as toys when there are children (and adults) across the oceans, or across town, who don't even have food to eat. An equality of global moral concern, then, is an important part of what impartiality represents or entails for many nonfeminist impartiality critics and is a primary target for them.

Such a moral requirement would, of course, be impossibly demanding. It would call for us to consider the interests of all strangers and unloved acquaintances equally with the interests of loved ones. It would call for humanly impossible knowledge about the particular situations facing each of the world's inhabitants. It would call, in addition, for the humanly impossible division of

---

feminine socialization fails overall to develop as much of what Meyers calls "autonomy competency" as does masculine socialization: *Self, Society, and Personal Choice* (New York: Columbia University Press, 1989). Some traditions of thought, psychoanalytic theories among them, posit natural, or presocial, drives and impulses to help explain the "discontents" of civilization. I do not deny the possibility of presocial drives or impulses which might manifest themselves in contrasocial forms of behavior. The concept of the "natural," however, is profoundly complicated by social myths and mystifications; see ibid. I bypass this thorny issue in the present discussion.

33. See Cottingham, "Ethics and Impartiality," *Philosophical Studies* 43 (1983): 90–91.

one's time, energy, and resources into microscopic shares to be distributed to each of those inhabitants. Given this interpretation, it is no wonder that nonfeminist partialists balk at the requirement of moral impartiality.

Nonfeminist partialists also frequently attack a less ludicrous, but still extreme, version of the requirement of impartiality. This is the view that I should give equal consideration and moral attention to all persons directly involved in whatever situation is at hand. The situation may be very intimate and may encompass only a few persons besides myself. On this less extravagant version, if my "wife" and someone else are drowning, for example, I should weight their interests equally and decide whom to save by, perhaps, flipping a coin.[34]

Neither of these interpretations of what moral impartiality requires is typical or representative of what moral impartialists themselves say about their own theories. Only a few moral impartialists have explicitly articulated the requirement of impartiality in either of these uncompromising sets of terms. William Godwin and Peter Singer are convenient targets for the partialists because they have each advocated an uncompromisingly extreme impartiality.[35] Peter Singer's early writings called for each of us to show concern for all the starving millions in the global village. Proximity and close relationship, Singer contended at that time, carry no moral weight.[36]

William Godwin (ironically, the husband of the late-eighteenth-century English feminist Mary Wollstonecraft), writing early in the nineteenth century, was the one who invited us to consider this now philosophically infamous dilemma: Should I rescue my beloved but socially worthless mother (or father, depending on which edition one consults), a mere chambermaid (or valet, respectively), or should I rescue, instead, François de Salignac de la Mothe Fenelon, the archbishop of Cambray, in a disaster that prevents me

34. See Fried, *An Anatomy of Values,* p. 227.

35. William Godwin, *Enquiry Concerning Political Justice,* ed. K. Codell Carter (Oxford: Clarendon House, 1971); and Peter Singer, *Practical Ethics* (Cambridge: Cambridge University Press, 1979), pp. 10–11.

36. Peter Singer, *Practical Ethics,* pp. 10–11; and "Famine, Affluence, and Morality," *Philosophy and Public Affairs* 1 (Spring 1972).

from rescuing both? Godwin advocates choosing the archbishop. "What magic is there in the pronoun 'my'," he asks, "that should justify us in overturning the decision of impartial truth?"[37] That someone is "my" mother or father has no moral significance, on Godwin's view, and impartiality, he thinks, calls for a decision based instead on social worth.

That there are remarkably few such extreme statements of the impartiality requirement in philosophical literature suggests that, on the question of equal concern for others, moral impartiality means something else to most impartialists—what it means will be reiterated shortly—and that nonfeminist partialists often attack a straw person.

And attack it they do, supplanting it with the moral ideal of partiality. With the fervor of political activists defending a social cause, partialists advance the case for "taking care of one's own." Nonfeminist partialists seem especially troubled by moral demands that they attend to people with whom they have no particular relationship and for whom they feel no special concern. On the nonfeminist partialist view, overriding priority goes to what we should or can do for loved ones and others to whom we are close. At best, some of these partialists do acknowledge some moral responsibilities to distant others and strangers,[38] sometimes linking these responsibilities to the duties that define certain positions of public office.[39] At worst, nonfeminist partialists simply neglect to mention any such responsibilities, concentrating their attention entirely on what should or can be done for those who are close.

Cottingham is one partialist who has no quarrel with, for example, giving money to Oxfam. What Cottingham challenges is the idea that morality requires giving the sum total of one's money

---

37. *Enquiry Concerning Political Justice*, p. 71. Carter notes that Godwin's first edition used the terms "mother," "sister," and "chambermaid," while the later edition substitutes "father," "brother," and "valet" (see Carter's editorial note 2 on p. 71).

38. See Kekes, "Morality and Impartiality," p. 299.

39. See Blum, *Friendship, Altruism, and Morality*, p. 47. I do not mean to imply that Blum is not feminist. The point is, rather, that his book on friendship is not obviously so and has been widely cited by nonfeminist partialists.

to Oxfam, to the point at which one has no more money than any of the starving recipients of Oxfam relief.[40] Aside from Godwin and the early Singer, however, few defenders of moral impartiality actually recommend that we divest ourselves of our resources to so radical an extent.

Contemporary impartialists make it clear that impartial moral theories do not require each of us to devote the entirety of our resources to helping the world's needy. Global moral concern, as a duty or responsibility of daily moral life, differs from impartiality as a criterion of adequate moral justification. To thus clarify moral impartiality is not, of course, to defend moral impartiality as conventionally defined. I argued in Chapter 1 that the typical abstract notion of impartiality is not something we could knowingly realize in practice. Nevertheless, it is important to clear away the misinterpretations of what moral impartiality actually requires.

As construed by its current defenders, impartiality is a requirement only of the principles, practices, or institutions that justify specific actions.[41] Conceptualized in this way, impartiality does not a priori require each of us to devote substantial moral attention to those we do not love or for whom we feel no special attachment. It does not require us to be indifferent between the sufferings of loved ones and strangers. The specific duties that are required of us, on this view, need merely exemplify principles, practices, or institutions which themselves best promote, overall, the interests of all persons. It is those principles, practices, or institutions that must be impartially morally justified. If the interests of all persons, for example, were best served by the social practice of each parent devoting herself exclusively to her own children, then, on impartialist grounds, child-care duties for each person would require only the care of her own children.

Thus, impartialists do not necessarily differ from partialists when it comes to matters of practice, including global affairs.[42] The

40. Cottingham, "Ethics and Impartiality," p. 91.
41. See Chapter 2, especially at notes 14–17, for a survey of some examples of this strategy.
42. For a detailed discussion of other theoretical and practical differences

real practical difference in global matters lies between partialists, on the one hand, and, on the other hand, those extreme impartialists who are also globalists, that is, who specifically advocate that duties of concern for those in need around the world override duties to loved ones. The partialist either denies that there are specific duties of global moral concern or denies that they ever override competing duties to family members and others who are close. It is this approach to global moral matters in particular that contrasts, in practice, with the extreme impartialist (i.e., globalist) view.

The point that I wish to emphasize here is that feminists who dispute the requirement of moral impartiality tend to differ from their nonfeminist counterparts in respect to the issue of global moral concern.[43] Global concerns and international connections among feminists have nourished our wider movement.[44] Most feminists would insist on the importance of a cross-cultural variety of women's issues and of forging cross-cultural connections and solidarity among women.[45] The responsibility to be concerned about distant peoples, particularly for those with relatively greater social and economic privileges, is, thus, one implication of moral impartiality that I think most feminists would wish to retain. It is not in this particular respect that the notion of moral impartiality has worried feminists.

It is important to beware of possible equivocation over the notion of global moral concern. The difference between nonfem-

---

between partiality and impartiality, see Marcia Baron, "Impartiality and Friendship," *Ethics* 101 (July 1991): 836–57.

43. But see the skepticism expressed over the notion of universal moral concern in Nel Noddings, *Caring: A Feminine Approach to Ethics and Moral Education* (Berkeley: University of California Press, 1984), pp. 91–94. It is noteworthy that Noddings uses the word "feminine" rather than "feminist" in her subtitle.

44. See Charlotte Bunch, *Bringing the Global Home* (Denver: Antelope, 1985); and Chandra Talpade Mohanty, Ann Russo, and Lourdes Torres, eds., *Third World Women and the Politics of Feminism* (Bloomington: Indiana University Press, 1991).

45. Gloria I. Joseph and Jill Lewis, *Common Differences: Conflicts in Black and White Feminist Perspectives* (Boston: South End Press, 1981).

inist and feminist impartiality critics on this point is subtle. Even feminists with money to burn and whose histories of charitability are second to none are not usually relinquishing all their resources to social movements or political reforms. So what exactly is the point at issue? The dispute, in my estimation, concerns a matter of degree and a matter of moral paradigm. It has to do with what is honored and who the heroes are.

First, the matter of degree. Between, at one extreme, distributing all one's resources evenly among all the starving members of the global village and, at the other extreme, hoarding all one's resources for loved ones alone, there are countless intermediate positions. There are an indeterminate number of proportions in which to combine concern for the world's needy with devotion to "one's own." Although feminist partialists, who are concerned to establish the moral value of close personal relationships, do not tend to be so extreme in their globalism as Godwin or Singer, nevertheless, they tend to give more philosophical weight or emphasis to global moral concerns than do nonfeminist partialists.

Few globalists, whether impartialist or feminist partialist, utterly abandon their loved ones, in practice, for the sake of serving the world's needy. And, as noted earlier, at least some nonfeminist partialists acknowledge that some concern for the world's needy may fit comfortably into a life devoted largely to friends and loved ones. Some partialists, however, concede merely that charity toward distant peoples is acceptable, all the while counting partiality, by contrast, as intrinsically necessary for such preeminent moral ends as intimacy, integrity, fulfillment, and flourishing in life. The result is to cast partiality in the mold of the morally exemplary and to diminish the moral importance of any wider circle of concern. Nonfeminist partialists seem to be more ready than impartial globalists or feminist partialists to count global moral concerns as supererogatory rather than a matter of strict duty or stringent responsibility.

This de-emphasis on global concerns is not unrelated to the other aspect of divergence that I note between nonfeminist partialists, on the one hand, and feminist partialists and other globalists on the other. Moral paradigms constitute that other important point of divergence, paradigms exemplified by the specific sorts of actions either lauded or despised, and by the sorts of persons honored as heroes or condemned as villains or fools. We may learn quite a bit about the orientation of a moral perspective by noting whom it counts as a paragon of virtue and whom it counts as a rogue.

For the nonfeminist partialist, favoring "one's own" becomes paradigmatic of moral virtue and of responsible moral practice. Christina Hoff Sommers, for example, contrasts the notion of a family member dutifully caring for her elderly parents with "Mrs. Jellyby," a fictional Charles Dickens mother who neglects her family in order to save the world's poor, evidently none "nearer than Africa," in Dickens's words.[46] (Those with ancestral ties to Africa or who feel a sense of connection to African people might resent the use of this example to illustrate what Sommers describes as "someone whose moral priorities are ludicrously disordered.")[47] In any case, Sommer's contrast elevates the dutiful family member to the status of moral paradigm and disparages globally oriented social activism by associating it with neglect of family, as if this were one of its necessary consequences. This differential emphasis, in addition, casts partiality in the mold of the morally exemplary and disparages any wider circle of concern. The moral exemplars are parents, children, spouses, and friends insofar as they favor their "own."

If this is the practical orientation arising from a nonfeminist approach (and I reiterate that not all nonfeminist partialists agree in attributing so little value to global concerns), then it has sad, potentially tragic, implications. Some very familiar notions of moral virtue and heroism are undermined by this approach. Efforts by European Gentiles to save Jews from death camps in Nazi Ger-

46. Christina Hoff Sommers, "Filial Morality," *Journal of Philosophy* 83 (1986): 442–43. (Mrs. Jellyby is a character in Charles Dickens's *Bleak House*.) Although Sommers, in later writings, declares herself to be a feminist, her account in the above-cited paper shows no explicitly feminist concerns; hence, as with Lawrence Blum's *Friendship, Altruism, and Morality*, I group it with the nonfeminist partialists.

47. Sommers, "Filial Morality."

many,[48] famine relief efforts for distant peoples, civil rights activism on behalf of social groups other than one's own, feminist changes initiated by men—these efforts receive no special endorsements from a nonfeminist partialist perspective. At best, such concerns would be required only for those whose "ground projects" (à la Williams) encompassed those particular ends. Even then, they would be derivative moral requirements, necessary only in case they contributed to a particular person's integrity. If we formed our ground projects carefully enough, we could avoid such burdensome obligations. Do we really want a moral theory that honors us for no greater efforts than taking care of "our own," a moral theory that demands no greater heroism than that?[49]

Feminist partialists, by contrast, devote much more theoretical attention to developing concern for those who are not "one's own." This is the significance of all the work that feminists put into theorizing "difference"[50] and into trying to incorporate a diversity of racial and class consciousness into feminist theory. Cross-cultural connections, theoretical and practical, are highly revered feminist achievements. Thus, for feminists, "global moral concern" does

48. Although Lawrence Blum's book on friendship is generally grouped with writings by the nonfeminist partialists, some of his other writings show both feminist concerns and, indeed, global interests that range more widely than is typical of the nonfeminist partialists. See his illuminating comparative study of heroic efforts by several European Gentiles to save Jews during the Nazi regime: "Moral Exemplars: Reflections on Schindler, the Trocmes, and Others," *Midwest Studies in Philosophy* 13 (1988): 196–221. For an example of Blum's feminist writings, see his "Gilligan and Kohlberg: Implications for Moral Theory," *Ethics* 98 (April 1988): 472–91.

49. James Fishkin, in commenting on an earlier version of this discussion when it was presented at a conference on "Impartiality and Ethical Theory" (Hollins College, Hollins College, Virginia, June 1990), drew attention to the difficulties of theorizing an appropriate balance between heroic responses to distant others and moral obligations to loved ones. I do not pretend to solve that problem. My aim in the present discussion is far more modest, namely, to illuminate the practical differences between, on the one hand, nonfeminist partialists and, on the other hand, the impartialists and feminist partialists who have more wide-ranging global moral concerns.

50. See Hester Eisenstein and Alice Jardine, eds., *The Future of Difference* (New Brunswick: Rutgers University Press, 1980).

not call for exactly equal consideration for the interests of all persons, but it does call for substantially more concern for distant or different people than is recommended by nonfeminist partialists.

Global moral concerns, however, raise a unique problem for the conception of the social self. A self whose identity is defined in terms of relationships to certain others is capable of having immediate and direct moral concern for those others. Her moral concern for them does not need to be mediated by calculations of how their well-being might serve her own interests. The question raised by the issue of global moral concern is whether concern for distant and unknown people is an immediate moral motivation of the social self.

The likeliest source of such a motivation is group identity and consciousness.[51] We are familiar with the sort of group consciousness that attaches to racial, ethnic, and national communities. What about consciousness of membership in the human community? Unfortunately, it is not clear just what role it plays in self-identity. Philosophy has been of no help on this question. Philosophical works that have inquired into what it means for us to be "men" and not brutes aim to clarify how we are different from (nonhuman) animals, but not to foster among all human beings a sense of globally shared mutual interest. Human group consciousness is an aspect of the conception of the social self that awaits further clarification.

Virginia Held suggests that we acquire concern for, say, starving children elsewhere by learning to empathize with them.[52] One learns what it is like for children close to home to starve, and one recognizes that distant children are like those close to home. One's empathetic capacities, developed in relationships with persons known closely, are engaged by more distant people through the recognition of their similarity to those we know. This approach,

---

51. On the moral nature and importance of group identity, see Larry May, *The Morality of Groups* (Notre Dame, Ind.: University of Notre Dame Press, 1987).

52. Virginia Held, "Feminism and Moral Theory," in Eva Feder Kittay and Diana T. Meyers, eds., *Women and Moral Theory* (Totowa, N.J.: Rowman & Littlefield, 1987), p. 118.

however, does not spring solely from motives that are rooted in self-identity. It requires, in addition, reasoning and analogical insight.

Interpreted in this way, global moral concern is a rational achievement but not an immediate motivation. It is, furthermore, an achievement only for some selves. It is a result of moral thinking that has no necessary motivational source in the self, so not everyone will find it convincing. (Think about those who *fail to see* the similarity between "them" and "us.") Since so many persons appear to lack global moral concern, Held's view is quite plausible—regrettably so.

This result does not threaten the conception of the social self. However, it brings us face to face with what seems to be one important limit of that concept: its inability to ground the widest sort of concern for others in unmediated constituents of the self. We, thus, confront the apparent fragility of the human motivation of global concern, even in socially constituted selves.

In this chapter, I reviewed the partiality-impartiality debates and sketched the conception of the social self. I then focused on two problems faced by a conception of the social self: first, the need to account for the possibility of fundamental social criticism by selves, and, second, the need to grapple with the notion of global moral concern. I argued that the first problem is easily solved by recognizing that the self is social in complex ways. The second problem remains vexing. While it does not undermine the conception of the social self, nevertheless, it exposes some moral limits of a social self.

PART II

Care and Justice

4

Care and Context
in Moral Reasoning

Carol Gilligan heard a "distinct moral language" in the voices of women who were subjects in her studies of moral reasoning. Though herself a developmental psychologist, Gilligan has put her mark on contemporary feminist moral philosophy by daring to claim the competence of this voice and the worth of its message. In her book *In a Different Voice,*[1] which one theorist has aptly described as a best-seller,[2] and in a number of subsequent writings,[3] Gilligan has explored the concern with care and contextual detail that she discerned in the moral reasoning of women and has con-

1. *In a Different Voice* (Cambridge: Harvard University Press, 1982).
2. Frigga Haug, "Morals Also Have Two Genders," trans. Rodney Livingstone, *New Left Review* 143 (1984): 55.
3. "Do the Social Sciences Have an Adequate Theory of Moral Development?" in Norma Haan, Robert N. Bellah, Paul Rabinow, and William M. Sullivan, eds., *Social Science as Moral Inquiry* (New York: Columbia University Press 1983), pp. 33–51; "Reply," *Signs* 11 (1986): 324–33; "Moral Orientation and Moral Development," in Eva Feder Kittay and Diana T. Meyers, eds., *Women and Moral Theory* (Totowa, N.J.: Rowman & Littlefield, 1987), pp. 19–33; and "Remapping the Moral Domain: New Images of the Self in Relationship," in Thomas C. Heller, Morton Sosna, and David E. Wellbery, eds., *Reconstructing Individualism* (Stanford: Stanford University Press, 1986), pp. 237–52; reprinted in Carol Gilligan, Janie Victoria Ward, Jill McLean Taylor, with Betty Bardige, eds., *Mapping the Moral Domain* (Cambridge: Harvard Center for the Study of Gender, Education, and Human Development, 1988), pp. 3–20.

trasted it with the orientation toward justice and abstract principles that she found to typify the moral reasoning of men.

The story is, by now, very familiar. According to Gilligan, the standard, more typically "male," moral voice articulated in moral psychology derives moral judgments about particular cases from abstract, universalized moral rules and principles that are substantively concerned with justice and rights. For justice reasoners, the major moral imperative enjoins respect for the rights of others; the concept of duty is limited to reciprocal noninterference; the motivating vision is one of the equal worth of self and other; and one important underlying presupposition is a highly individuated conception of persons.[4]

By contrast, the different, more characteristically "female," moral voice that Gilligan heard in her studies eschews abstract rules and principles. This moral voice derives moral judgments from the contextual detail of situations grasped as specific and unique. The substantive concern for this moral voice is care and responsibility, particularly as these arise in the context of interpersonal relationships. Moral judgments, for care reasoners, are tied to feelings of empathy and compassion; the major moral imperatives center around caring, not hurting others, and avoiding selfishness; and the motivating vision of this ethics is "that everyone will be responded to and included, that no one will be left alone or hurt."[5]

When gender differences first appeared in the studies of moral reasoning that were based on Lawrence Kohlberg's research[6] into cognitive moral development, it seemed that women, on average, did not attain as high a level of moral reasoning as men, on average. In other words, it seemed that women's moral reasoning was typically more immature than that of men. According to Gilligan, however, women's moral reasoning is not an immature form of the cognitive moral development that men attain, despite those early research findings. Rather, women's moral reasoning char-

4. *In a Different Voice*, pp. 63, 100, 147.
5. Ibid., pp. 19, 63, 69, 90, 100.
6. Lawrence Kohlberg, *The Philosophy of Moral Development* (San Francisco: Harper & Row, 1981).

acteristically incorporates a different moral perspective altogether—
a morality of care and responsibility that is particularly attentive
to personal relationships. This alternative framework, this "different voice" for dealing with moral dilemmas, contrasts with Kohlberg's framework, which centers around the notions of justice and
rights. If Gilligan is right, Kohlberg's framework expresses the
moral concerns that typify the male moral voice.

In addition to the predominance of relationships as the central
substantive moral concern of Gilligan's different voice, that voice
also exhibits what Gilligan calls "contextual relativism."[7] In Gilligan's usage, "contextual relativism" actually encompasses two distinct features: first, a great sensitivity to the details of situations;
and second, a reluctance to make moral judgments. My discussion
will concentrate on the first of these two features.

Gilligan suggests that women, more often than men, respond
to hypothetical dilemmas (such as the famous Heinz dilemma used
in Kohlbergian tests of moral reasoning, a dilemma I will explore
shortly) by evading a forced choice between two proffered alternatives and seeking more details before reaching a conclusion.
Women, more than men, are likely to seek the detail that makes
the suffering clear and that engages compassion and caring. In
Gilligan's view, such responses have often been misunderstood by
the interviewers who administered the tests in their studies of
moral reasoning. Interviewers tended to regard such responses as
revealing a research subject's failure to comprehend the dilemmas
or the problems to be solved. On the contrary, Gilligan argues,
these responses challenge the way the problem is posed; in particular, they question its capacity to allow any real or meaningful
choice.

Gilligan's insights, while often unsophisticated about the tech-
nicalities of philosophical theories of justice or rights, have nevertheless inspired needed rethinking of major ethical themes and
presuppositions.[8] In this and the next two chapters, I use Gilligan's

7. *In a Different Voice*, p. 22.
8. The literature on these themes has mushroomed rapidly in recent years.
The following are important collections of papers that, in whole or in part,

work as a springboard for extending certain of those themes in new directions. The importance of both care and context in moral reasoning is the topic of this chapter. In section 1, I deploy a sequence of hypothetical narratives to ferret out a few of the ways considerations of care and relationships may sometimes override considerations of justice and rights in overall moral reasoning. In the second section I explore the role of contextual detail in moral reasoning, the philosophically important core of the "contextual relativism" that has caught Gilligan's attention.

I postpone until the next chapter a discussion of whether it can be empirically confirmed that the moral reasoning of women in general shows greater concern with care and contextual detail than that of men. I also postpone until the next two chapters my discussion of the limitations of care as a moral orientation.

1. CARE

Gilligan's views about the differences between men's and women's moral judgments have become highly controversial. Most of the controversy has centered around two claims: first, the claim that women tend to score lower then men when measured according to Kohlberg's moral reasoning framework; and second, her contention that Kohlberg's framework is male-biased and fails to take account of the "different" moral perspective oriented toward care that is more distinctively the perspective of women.

If women did not score significantly differently from men on Kohlberg's scale when matched against men of similar educational and occupational background, then there would be little evidence of a gender difference in moral reasoning. There would also be a good deal less evidence for the second controversial claim, namely,

---

deal with care ethics: *Social Research* 50 (Fall 1983); Kittay and Meyers, eds., *Women and Moral Theory;* Marsha Hanen and Kai Nielsen, eds., *Science, Morality, and Feminist Theory, Canadian Journal of Philosophy* suppl. vol. 13 (1987); Claudia Card, ed., *Feminist Ethics* (Lawrenceville: University Press of Kansas, 1991); and Eve Browning Cole and Susan Coultrap-McQuin, eds., *Explorations in Feminist Ethics* (Bloomington: Indiana University Press, 1992).

that Kohlberg's framework is male-biased for ignoring the distinctly different moral orientation of women. Even if Kohlberg's framework were not biased toward a moral perspective typical of males, however, that would not entail the absence of all bias. If nothing else, Gilligan's research has uncovered a substantial bias toward certain particular moral considerations that comprise only a part of the whole range of our moral concerns.

Kohlberg himself acknowledges[9] that Gilligan's research prompted him to take account of the importance to overall moral development of notions of care, relationships, and responsibility and to consider how these moral concerns augment his own prior emphasis on reasoning having to do with justice and rights.[10] He suggests that his previous concern had been with "justice reasoning" only, and that it was unfortunate that it had been called simply "moral reasoning," a label that implied that it represented the whole breadth and substance of the cognitive moral domain. In Kohlberg's later view, care and justice both appear as cognitive moral concerns, but their appearance is not linked specifically to gender. Instead, the type of orientation used in moral reasoning (by either males or females) depends on "the type of moral problem defined" and the environment in which the problem is located.[11] Moral dilemmas located, for example, in a family context are more likely to invoke caring considerations (from both sexes), whereas dilemmas located in a secondary institution of society, such as government, are more likely to invoke justice considerations (from both sexes).

This concession, in Kohlberg's later writings, that care and relationships are indeed morally important, is noteworthy. Yet Kohlberg does not as readily accept Gilligan's view that care and justice define mutually distinct moral perspectives. Kohlberg contends that justice and caring are not "two different tracks of moral development which are either independent or in polar opposition

---

9. In Lawrence Kohlberg, Charles Levine, and Alexandra Hewer, *Moral Stages: A Current Reformulation and Response to Critics* (Basel: S. Karger, 1983).
10. Ibid., pp. 20, 122–23.
11. Ibid., p. 132.

to one another,"[12] that "many moral situations or dilemmas do not pose a choice between one or the other orientation, but rather call out a response which integrates both orientations," and that considerations of caring need not conflict with those of justice "but may be integrated into a response consistent with justice, especially at the postconventional level."[13] Several decades ago, we learned that "separate" was inherently unequal;[14] we cannot, however, assume that integration is inherently equal. In Kohlberg's most recent formulation, although he claims that care can be integrated with justice, nevertheless, considerations of justice remain "primary in defining the moral domain."[15]

For Kohlberg, a morality of care pertains to special relationships among particular persons which contrast with the universalistic relationships handled by justice reasoning. Kohlberg suggests that "central to the ethic of particularistic relationships are affectively-tinged ideas and attitudes of *caring, love, loyalty, and responsibility.*"[16] In Kohlberg's estimation, special relationships should be regarded as supplementing and deepening the sense of generalized obligations of justice. For example, in the famous Heinz dilemma,[17] Heinz's care for his wife would be regarded as supplementing the obligation that he has to respect her right to life. But an ethic of care cannot, in Kohlberg's view, supplant a morality of justice, for "an ethic of care is, in and of itself, not well adapted to resolve justice problems; problems which require principles to resolve conflicting claims among persons, all of whom in some sense should be cared about."[18] Furthermore, "morally valid forms of caring and

12. Ibid., p. 137.
13. Ibid., p. 134.
14. *Brown v. Board of Education of Topeka, Kansas,* 347 U.S. 483, 1954.
15. Kohlberg et al., *Moral Stages,* p. 91.
16. Ibid., pp. 20–21.
17. The Heinz dilemma is the most famous moral dilemma used by researchers in the Kohlberg tradition to test the cognitive moral development of research subjects. Subjects are asked to solve the dilemma, and to defend their solutions with reasons; the reasons are then scored. I present and explore the Heinz dilemma later in this section of the present chapter.
18. Kohlberg et al., *Moral Stages,* pp. 21–22.

community presuppose prior conditions and judgments of jus-tice."[19]

Kohlberg admits that the primacy of justice was not "proven" by his previous research and that, instead, it had been a guiding assumption of the research, based on certain methodological and metaethical considerations.[20] The primacy of justice is, first of all, based on a "prescriptivist conception of moral judgment"; that is, moral judgment is treated not as the interpretation of situational fact but rather as the expression of universalizable "ought" claims. Second, it derives from a search for moral universality, that is, for "minimal value conceptions on which all persons could agree." Third, the primacy of justice stems from Kohlberg's cognitive, or rational, approach to morality. In Kohlberg's words, "justice asks for 'objective' or rational reasons and justifications for choice rather than being satisfied with subjective, 'decisionistic', personal com-mitments to aims and to other persons."[21] Finally, the most im-portant reason for the primacy of justice, in Kohlberg's view, is that it is "the most structural feature of moral judgment." As Kohl-berg puts it, "With the moral domain defined in terms of justice, we have been successful in . . . elaborating stages which are struc-tural systems in the Piagetian tradition."[22] Care reasoning, accord-ing to Kohlberg, may not be capable of being represented in terms of the criteria that he takes to define Piagetian cognitive stages.

Kohlberg's arguments for according primacy to justice reason-ing are unsatisfactory, for several reasons. First, the methodological considerations to which he appeals entitle us to infer only that justice is primary in that domain of morality which can be repre-sented in terms of Piagetian hard stages but not to infer that justice is primary to morality as such. Second, his appeal to certain meta-ethical considerations is controversial at best, question begging at worst. Whether moral judgments express universalizable prescrip-

19. Ibid., p. 92.
20. Ibid., pp. 93–95.
21. Ibid., p. 93.
22. Ibid., p. 92.

tions rather than interpretations of situational facts, whether there are "minimal value conceptions on which all persons could agree," whether "personal commitments to aims and to other persons" are excluded as rational justifications of choice, as Kohlberg seems to suggest, are all issues that cannot be resolved simply by presuming the primacy of a type of reasoning that has these features. Each of these assumptions is controversial and calls for defense in its own right.

Kohlberg's definition of the moral domain in terms of the primacy of justice is troubling for a third reason. Kohlberg claims that higher scores on his scale of moral development are correlated with participation in the secondary institutions of society, such as government and the workplace outside the home. By contrast, care reasoning is supposed to be relevant only to special relationships among "family, friends, and group members."[23] These two sorts of moral reasoning exemplify, respectively, the "public," or "political," realm and the "private," or "personal," realm. Kohlberg's primacy of justice reasoning coincides with a long-standing presumption of Western thought that the world of personal relationships, of the family and of family ties and loyalties, that is, the traditional world of women, is a world of lesser moral interest and importance than the public world of government and the marketplace, that is, the male-dominated world outside the home.

For Kohlberg, considerations of justice and rights have to do with abstract persons bound together by a social contract to act in ways that show mutual respect for rights which they possess equally. Considerations of justice do not require that persons know each other personally. Relatives, friends, or perfect strangers all deserve the same fair treatment and respect. In Kohlberg's view, considerations of special relationship and of caring seem merely to

---

23. Ibid., pp. 129–31. Kohlberg relied heavily for this assessment on Lawrence J. Walker's meta-analysis of research into cognitive moral development: "Sex Differences in the Development of Moral Reasoning," *Child Development* 55, no. 3 (1984): 677–91. This meta-analysis has more recently been challenged: see Diana Baumrind, "Sex Differences in Moral Reasoning: Response to Walker's (1984) Conclusion That There Are None," *Child Development* 57 (1986): 511–21.

enrich with compassion the judgments that are based on prior considerations of justice. In no way would considerations of special relationship, for Kohlberg, override those of justice and rights. Unless caring and community presupposed prior judgments of justice, they would seem, in Kohlberg's terms, not to be "morally valid."[24]

For those interpersonal relationships which lack mutual concern, or even personal acquaintance, considerations of justice may have to suffice morally. But this does not entail that those considerations are of overriding moral importance for those relationships which involve mutual interest and personal concern. To explore what it might mean for caring and the closeness of relationships to override the moral significance of justice and rights, I shall tell (and retell) some tales. My stories will not, of course, show that the duties of special relationships override, in all cases, considerations of justice; indeed, I do not believe that to be the case. My aim is, rather, to investigate some of the possible interconnections between considerations of justice and considerations of special relationship that could yield the priority of the latter.

First recall the biblical story in which God asks Abraham for the sacrifice of Abraham's only child, his son Isaac. In this familiar tale, Abraham shows himself willing to carry out the command. Only at the last moment does God intervene to provide a sacrificial ram and permission for Abraham to substitute it for Isaac. Abraham's faith in God has been tested and has proved unshakeable.

Both Carol Gilligan[25] and Owen Flanagan[26] refer to this story when discussing the controversy about sex differences in moral reasoning. They each use it as an illustration of what can go wrong with Kohlberg's highest or principled stage of moral reasoning, a stage, as Flanagan puts it, "where 'principle' always wins out in conflicts with even the strongest affiliative instincts and familial obligations."[27] Kohlberg, on the other hand, disagrees with the

24. Kohlberg et al., *Moral Stages*, p. 92.

25. Gilligan, *In a Different Voice*, p. 104.

26. "Virtue, Sex, and Gender: Some Philosophical Reflections on the Moral Psychology Debate," *Ethics* 92 (April 1982): 501.

27. Ibid.

Gilligan-Flanagan interpretation of the Abraham story, offering an alternative construal that, when measured according to Kohlberg's own framework of moral development, demotes the cognitive status of Abraham's reasoning to the preprincipled level:

> By no stretch of the imagination could Abraham's willingness to sacrifice Isaac be interpreted by Gilligan or myself as an example or outcome of principled moral reasoning. It is, rather, an example of an action based on reasoning that the morally right is defined by authority (in this case God's authority) as opposed to universalizable moral principles. For both Gilligan and myself such judgment based on authority would represent conventional (stage 4) moral judgment, not postconventional (principled) moral judgment.[28]

Contra Gilligan, Flanagan, as well as Kohlberg, however, I suggest yet a third interpretation of the Abraham story, one that draws upon the writings of Søren Kierkegaard and one that I believe to be the most plausible and insightful of the three. On this third interpretation, Abraham's choice to sacrifice Isaac derives from the considerations of a (uniquely) special relationship that Abraham takes to override, in its importance, the duties derived from justice.

In *Fear and Trembling*, Kierkegaard reminds us that Abraham's faith in and love for God were being tested by God's command that Abraham sacrifice his only son. In Kierkegaard's view, "to the son the father has the highest and most sacred obligation."[29] Abraham's test of faith was to be asked by God precisely to violate a most sacred obligation. Remember that Abraham is a good man. On this Kierkegaardian construction, Abraham's act cannot derive from what Kohlberg considers to be the stage 4 reasoning that whatever God says is right since, in that case, it would lose its significance as a test of religious faith. The supreme test of the faith of a moral person would be to ask that person to commit what she

28. "A Reply to Owen Flanagan and Some Comments on the Puka-Goodpaster Exchange," *Ethics* 92 (April 1982): 520.

29. Translated by Walter Lowrie (Princeton, N.J.: Princeton University Press, 1941), p. 39.

continues to regard as a grave sin, even as she acts. Thus, what Abraham is commanded to do remains morally *wrong* throughout. This sort of action would constitute the greatest sacrifice that a supremely virtuous person could make. If the command of God made the sacrifice of Isaac morally permissible, then it would not be the most supreme sacrifice that a moral person such as Abraham could make, and hence, would be no test of the faith of such a person.

Viewed in this way, the story of Abraham represents the moral dilemma of someone having either to choose to uphold the right to life, thereby sacrificing relationship with a Supreme Being, or, rather, to choose relationship with a Supreme Being, thereby sacrificing all considerations of rights. Abraham's story thus, surprisingly, becomes more accountable from a care perspective than from a justice perspective: relational considerations (of a uniquely theistic sort) are taken to override all (other) moral requirements. Those relational considerations do not render morally right what was morally wrong; they require, however, that wrong be done in order to risk achieving a greater relational good.

My second retold tale involves Euthyphro's story from the Platonic dialogue. Socrates, the reader will recall, encounters Euthyphro just after the latter has arranged to prosecute his father for murder. The victim, a slave in Euthyphro's home, had killed another domestic servant in a drunken fit. Socrates is astonished that Euthyphro would prosecute his own father for bringing about such a death. Socrates' reaction is complicated by certain troubling suggestions: an emphasis on the servant status of the man killed by Euthyphro's father and an emphasis on the father's status as "master," as if this role conferred privileges of life and death over servants. Let us ignore these disturbing suggestions; they would take us too far afield of our main concern.

Socrates is concerned about the charge of murder being brought against a father by his own son. Euthyphro tries to defend his action by appealing to piety, a virtue that both Socrates and Euthyphro agree is a part of justice. At a famous stage in the argument, Euthryphro defines piety as "acting in a way the gods approve (or that the gods command)." Kohlberg cites this literary example in order to showcase Socrates's rational approach to morality. Kohlberg construes Euthyphro's view as an example of a prerational, logically confused, divine command theory that commits the "naturalistic fallacy" by deriving "X ought to be done" from "X is a command of God."[30] On this construction, Euthyphro simply defers uncritically to a supposed moral authority while Socrates rises to a rational, postconventional perspective that recognizes morality's autonomy with respect to religion.

Another strand of thought, however, pervades the discussion between Socrates and Euthyphro, one that Kohlberg either disregards or fails to notice. In addition to deferring to divine moral commands, Euthyphro also articulates a conception of piety in terms of a universal rule. The rule in question calls for "prosecuting anyone who is guilty of murder, sacrilege, or of any similar crime—whether he be your father or mother, or whoever he may be—that makes no difference."[31] Socrates, as we know, challenges this universalized, impartial injunction even before he questions Euthyphro's deference to the gods; it is this view of Euthyphro's which first irks Socrates and prompts his cross-examination of Euthyphro's position. In this earlier part of the discussion, most importantly, Socrates intimates that the responsibilities deriving from family relationships might outweigh even considerations of piety, which constitutes a part of justice.

Socrates has been singled out by Kohlberg as one of the few human beings ever to have reached what Kohlberg then regarded as the highest stage of moral reasoning, the sixth stage.[32] It is, therefore, a noteworthy irony for the figure of Socrates, in this early Platonic dialogue, to suggest that impartial and universalizable considerations of justice may be overridden by personal responsibilities arising out of particularized familial relationships.

Perhaps the responsibilities deriving from particular relation-

30. Kohlberg, *Philosophy of Moral Development*, pp. 314–15.

31. Translated by Benjamin Jowett. In Irwin Edman, ed., *The Works of Plato* (New York: Modern Library, 1928), pp. 39–40.

32. Kohlberg, *The Philosophy of Moral Development*, pp. 85, 139, 401, and chap. 2, passim.

ships are indeed universalizable; some have argued as much.[33] For example, if it is true that certain behavior is owed to someone simply because that person is my father, then such behavior is owed prima facie by anyone to whoever happens to be that person's father. While this response is very plausible, it will not resolve all the problems raised by the story of the *Euthyphro* for a Kohlbergian justice perspective. First, and especially relevant to Kohlberg's conception of justice at the highest stages, many of the personal relationships that matter to us do not originate in mutual consent or with anything that can suitably be represented by the metaphor of a social contract, most kinship ties in particular.[34] Yet, as one moves up Kohlberg's scale of moral, that is, justice, reasoning, social contract becomes increasingly important as the justification of universalizability in moral reasoning. Rather than derive the responsibilities arising out of personal relationships from Kohlbergian justice principles, it seems more plausible to seek a direct grounding of those responsibilities in the nature of personal relationships themselves and the moral values they promote.[35]

Second, a moral consideration might be universalizable without being a matter of justice in any substantive sense. Thus, in contrast to Gilligan's understanding of the care perspective as nonprincipled and therefore nonuniversalizable, I do not exclude universalizability from care ethics. In addition, a maxim requiring that one's kin be treated as exempt from the principles of justice that are to apply to all (other) persons hardly seems itself to be a principle of justice. It seems, rather, to be a side constraint that delimits the scope of application of principles of justice. Thus, even if (some) responsibilities to one's kin could be subsumed under universalizable requirements of justice, they could hardly include the Socratic recommendation to Euthyphro that considerations of justice be overridden for the sake of one's kin.

33. See John Cottingham, "Partiality, Favouritism, and Morality," *Philosophical Quarterly* 36, no. 144 (1986): 359.

34. The full significance of this point for moral theory is well developed in Virginia Held, "Non-Contractual Society," in Hanen and Nielsen, *Science, Morality, and Feminist Theory*, pp. 111–38.

35. This is the approach I recommend in Chapter 2.

Thus far my stories have all been about men. Yet Gilligan's importance to moral investigation stems at least in part from her work on the moral development of women. My remaining stories will remedy the imbalance by featuring women as protagonists. I shall take the liberty of performing a sex-change operation on the Heinz dilemma, the most famous of the dilemmas used by Kohlberg to measure the level of moral reasoning of his research subjects. The original dilemma is as follows:

> In Europe, a woman was near death from cancer. One drug might save her, a form of radium that a druggist in the same town had recently discovered. The druggist was charging $2000, ten times what the drug cost him to make. The sick woman's husband, Heinz, went to everyone he knew to borrow the money, but he could only get together about half of what it cost. He told the druggist that his wife was dying and asked him to sell it cheaper or let him pay later. But the druggist said, "No." The husband got desperate and broke into the man's store to steal the drug for his wife. Should the husband have done that? Why?[36]

Of course, there is already a woman in the Heinz dilemma, namely, Heinz's wife. She is easy to forget since, unlike Heinz, she has no name, and unlike both Heinz and the also unnamed druggist, she is the only person in the story who does not act. Instead she is simply the passive patient who is there to be saved, the one whose presence provides both Heinz and the druggist with their moral opportunities for heroism and villainy. Let us remove her from this oblivion. First, she needs a name: I will call her Heidi. Next, let us change her role from that of patient to that of agent. Finally, let us suppose that the druggist, another unnamed character in the original dilemma, is also a woman; I will call her Hilda. Now we are ready for our new story: the "Heidi dilemma":

> In Europe, a *man* was near death from cancer. One drug might save him, a form of radium that a druggist in the same town, a

36. Lawrence Kohlberg, "Stage and Sequence: The Cognitive-Developmental Approach to Socialization," in D. A. Goslin, ed., *Handbook of Socialization Theory and Research* (Chicago: Rand McNally, 1969), p. 379.

woman named Hilda, had recently discovered. The druggist was charging $2000, ten times what the drug cost her to make. The sick man's *wife*, Heidi, went to everyone she knew to borrow the money, but she could only get together about half of what it cost. She told Hilda, the druggist, that her husband was dying and asked Hilda to sell the drug cheaper or let her, Heidi, pay later. But Hilda said no. *Heidi* got desperate and broke into the woman's store to steal the drug for her husband. Should the *wife* have done that? Why?

It would be interesting to speculate on whether any of our responses to the dilemma have changed as a result of the sex-change operation and the emergence of women as protagonists. For surely there are new questions to ask: What risks does theft pose for a woman that are not posed for a man? What unique indignities are inflicted on a woman who is arrested for a street crime? Gilligan's portrait of women's care orientation finds an interesting test case in this hypothetical example. Would a female druggist not care about the dying patients who cannot afford her medication? Would she not spare some of the drug if only she could afford to do so? Would she not spare some of the drug even if she could not afford to do so? Is a woman's intransigence in the face of someone's likely death as believable as that of a man?[37]

With women as the protagonists, the very plausibility of the Heinz dilemma as an exercise in forced choice seems to diminish dramatically. This change, however, is not my real concern. An even more modified version of the original dilemma brings me closer to my main point; version number 1 was just a transitional stage. Consider Heidi dilemma number 2:

37. In Chapter 5, I go on to suggest that gender stereotypes may lie behind any tendency we have to think that women are care, but not justice, oriented and that men are justice, but not care, oriented. This possible stereotypic bias does not, however, undermine the point toward which the present discussion is tending. My point here is that our judgments about the right thing to do under the circumstances of the Heinz dilemma, even those judgments that invoke the moral authority of justice itself, are strongly affected by who the players are and how they are interrelated. If our judgments also exhibit gender biases regarding the identities of the players, then this reinforces my point.

In Europe, a man was near death from cancer. One drug might save him, a form of radium that a druggist in the same town, a woman named Hilda, had recently discovered. The druggist was charging $2000, ten times what the drug cost her to make. A *perfect stranger*, a woman named Heidi, chanced to read about the sick man's plight in the local newspaper. She was moved to act. She went to everyone she knew to borrow the money for the drug, but she could get together only about half of what it cost. She asked the druggist to sell the drug more cheaply or to let her, Heidi, pay for it later. But Hilda, the druggist, said no. Heidi broke into the woman's store to steal the drug *for a man she did not know.* Should Heidi have done that? Why?

If Kohlberg's dilemma can indeed be resolved through impartial considerations of justice and rights, then the solution to the dilemma should not depend upon the existence of any special relationship between the person who is dying of cancer and the person who might steal the drug. I suggest, however, that the conviction many of us have, that Heinz should steal the drug for his nameless wife in the original dilemma, rests at least in part on our notion of responsibilities arising out of the sort of special relationship that marriage is supposed to be. Without this relationship, our conviction that theft ought to be committed might well, on grounds provided simply by the story, be much weaker than it is. If the patient and the prospective thief were absolute strangers, I suspect that we would be far less likely to say that a serious personal risk should be undertaken to steal the drug, break the law, and harm the druggist—even to save a life.

In *Moral Stages,* Kohlberg considers the question of whether the solution to the original dilemma depends only upon considerations of justice or rather upon considerations of special relationship as well. To illustrate what he regards as cognitive improvement in answering this question, Kohlberg cites an interview with an eleven-year-old boy with whom he discussed the Heinz dilemma. The boy was asked whether a "man" should steal a drug to save the life of a stranger, "if there was no other way to save his life." The boy's first response was that it does not seem that one should steal for someone about whom one does not care.

Subsequently, the boy revised his judgment: "But somehow it doesn't seem fair to say that. The stranger has his life and wants to live just as much as your wife; it isn't fair to say you should steal it for your wife but not for the stranger."[38] For Kohlberg, as illustrated by his young respondent, a concern for universalizing a moral judgment leads to a preference for justice reasoning and away from reasoning in terms of care and special relationship.

What are we to make of such an example? First, the boy's reasoning is quite perceptive: it is *not* fair to steal the drug for one's spouse but not for a stranger. Considerations of fairness would not lead to this distinction among needy persons. If there is a moral distinction of this sort between what is owed to one's kin and what is owed to strangers, the distinction would derive from some other moral consideration, most probably the special nature of the relationship to one's kin. If my duty to steal in order to save a life is owed to my kin in virtue of my kinship relationship to them, then the fact that it is not fair that I do not have this duty toward strangers does not entail that, all things considered, I therefore have the same duty toward strangers that I have toward my kin. We cannot presuppose in advance that considerations of justice have moral primacy, never to be outweighed by considerations of special relationship. Considerations of justice and rights do not necessarily lead to the conclusion that, all things considered, we owe to all persons the special treatment that is due to our families and friends. It may indeed not be fair, but fairness is not our only moral concern.

This is, of course, not to deny altogether the moral importance of justice. In the next chapter, I argue for the need to integrate considerations of justice with those of care. In Chapter 2, I explored an issue of distributive justice: the inadequate resources of many people for favoring their loved ones effectively. Because of those inadequacies, I urged that practices of partiality be tempered with social mechanisms for redistributing such resources. I sought to show that such redistributions were called for by the very values that made partiality itself a matter of moral concern. Practices of

38. Kohlberg et al., *Moral Stages*, p. 92.

partiality in caretaking and protecting others should take into account the interests of distributive justice and should, in turn, transform those interests.

My approach is, thus, integrationist through and through. Neither justice nor care is necessarily overriding under any and all circumstances. The specific features of each particular case are critical in determining which moral concerns take priority in that case. In the original Heinz dilemma in particular, the marital relationship between Heinz and the sick woman, and not considerations of justice alone, seems to be what finally tips the balance of *competing* moral concerns toward the conclusion that Heinz should steal the drug to save the woman's life.

The second problem with Kohlberg's eleven-year-old respondent who thought that Heinz should steal the drug to save the life of any impoverished, dying stranger is that it is (forgivably) naive about moral practice. Kohlberg's justice framework, we should recall, is designed to measure only abstract moral reasoning, reasoning detached from any necessary connection to moral practices. Kohlberg's framework neither measures nor evaluates the sorts of moral commitments that motivate behavior. Few persons, even at the higher stage of justice reasoning, would judge, in a manner that would impel the corresponding behavior, that anyone ought to steal to save the life of a stranger. If you are not persuaded that this is so, then please consider one final modified form of the Heinz dilemma: the *you* dilemma:

> *You* are the perfect stranger who has just read in your morning paper about a person dying of cancer and about the only drug that can save her, but which she cannot afford. *You* are the stranger who fails to convince the druggist to sell the drug more cheaply. Will you (really) take the risk of stealing the drug to save the life of someone you do not know? What moral judgment (and practical resolution) will you (really) reach in this dilemma?

How many of those who endorse the judgment that you should steal to save the life of a stranger actually act on it? Yet this failure to act does not stem from a lack of impoverished, critically ill persons in our society or from a lack of knowledge by most people about the tragic existence of such cases. (The AIDS epidemic has ensured widespread knowledge about the crisis in health care delivery.) The *you* dilemma confronts us with the gap between moral reasoning and moral behavior. It discloses the limited bearing on true moral maturity of those moral judgments upon which we do not act.

In addition, the *you* dilemma alerts us to another factor that may differentiate a justice orientation from a care orientation. With our verbalized moral judgments, we lay claim to our moral identities, to the sorts of persons we, morally, aspire to be—and wish others to think we are. We express the purported sweep of our moral visions and our moral aspirations. A justice orientation, with its strict impartiality and grandiose universality, lends itself to a more "heroic"[39] form of moral expression than does a care orientation. Judgments based upon considerations of justice and rights seem permeated with an impersonal nobility of moral concern, unlike considerations of "my husband," "my sister," or "my body."

Nobility of moral concern is especially easy to affect when one is merely responding to a test interviewer or when real commitment, for some other reason, is not measured and deeds need not follow upon words. Of course, some individuals in our world really do steal or undertake other grave risks to save the lives of strangers.[40] Moral thinking would be sorely impoverished without such heroic exemplars.[41]

Many people, however, who judge that "one" should steal to save a dying stranger are not manifesting a genuine readiness to act. Most such judgments are cut off from any link with practice. Such judgments might be naively sincere and betoken understandable moral inexperience (as with Kohlberg's eleven-year-old boy)

39. Eva Kittay suggested the relevance of heroism to this part of my discussion.

40. See Philip Hallie, *Lest Innocent Blood Be Shed* (New York: Harper & Row, 1979); and Lawrence Blum, "Moral Exemplars: Reflections on Schindler, the Trocmes, and Others," *Midwest Studies in Philosophy* 13 (1988): 196–221.

41. See my brief discussion in Chapter 2 of the way the orientation of a moral theory is revealed in part by its particular choice of heroic exemplars.

or forgivable moral weakness; or they might, instead, be insincere and exhibit moral hypocrisy. Of greatest relevance to the present discussion, perhaps, such judgments are seldom acted upon because the complexities of our lives interweave the universalizing demands of justice with other competing and equally imperative moral concerns.

2. CONTEXT

In addition to a substantive orientation to care and relationships, the "different voice" of Gilligan's studies shows certain distinctive formal features as well. Gilligan suggests that women, more than men, respond inadequately to such dilemmas as the Heinz dilemma because of their hypothetical nature. In Gilligan's view, the dilemmas are too abstract and, as she puts it, they separate "the moral problem from the social contingencies of its possible occurrence."[42]

Gilligan's insight can be strengthened by a change in focus. Of greater importance than whether the dilemmas are real or hypothetical, I believe, is the extent of the contextual detail in which they are described. A work of literature or a film can portray a moral crisis with enough detail to make the responses and behavior of the protagonist plausible, even compelling, to readers or viewers. The hypothetical nature of the moral dilemmas facing numerous protagonists of fiction does not at all preclude thoughtful moral consideration or profound moral insight about those fictional cases.

Perhaps Gilligan has been distracted by the fact that when we learn of real-world moral dilemmas, we typically know the people and a good bit about their lives and their current situations. We rely upon this tacit but crucial background information to help generate alternative possible solutions for those problems. Hypothetical dilemmas have no social or historical context outside their own specifications; lacking any background information, we require longer stories in order to feel that we know most of the

42. *In a Different Voice*, p. 100.

pertinent information that can be expected in cases of this sort. What matters, I contend, is having sufficient detail for understanding the story at hand, whether the story is of a real moral dilemma or a hypothetical one.

Gilligan shows convincingly how the hypothetical Heinz dilemma would be significantly altered were it to be enriched by some very plausible details. Commenting on the response to the Heinz dilemma given by one subject, Gilligan says:

> Heinz's decision to steal is considered not in terms of the logical priority of life over property, which justifies its rightness, but rather in terms of the actual consequences that stealing would have for a man of limited means and little social power.
>
> Considered in the light of its probable outcomes—his wife dead, or Heinz in jail, brutalized by the violence of that experience and his life compromised by a record of felony—the dilemma itself changes. Its resolution has less to do with the relative weights of life and property in an abstract moral conception than with the collision between two lives, formerly conjoined but now in opposition, where the continuation of one life can occur only at the expense of the other.[43]

In order to emphasize the importance of contextual detail, let us elaborate the Heinz-Heidi dilemma even further.

The woman who is dying of cancer is weary and depressed from the losing battle she has been fighting for several years. It all began with cancer of the colon, and her doctors convinced her to resort to a colostomy. Now, several years later, it is clear that the malignancy was not stopped by this drastic measure. Experiencing her own present embodiment as unacceptably disfigured, weakened, and in pain from the cancer that continues to poison her system, bedridden and dependent on others for her daily functioning, she has lost hope and grown despondent about a fate that, to her, is worse than death. How does this woman really measure the value of her own life?

And perhaps there is more to the druggist's story as well. Her husband deserted her and her three children years ago and has

43. Ibid., p. 101.

paid not a penny of his court-ordered child-support money. So the druggist struggles mightily day after day to keep her family together and tends a small pharmacy that barely meets the material needs of her children, let alone her own. Moreover, she lives in a society that jealousy guards the private ownership of its property. Were she and her children to fall into poverty, that society would throw her a few crumbs of welfare support, but only after she had exhausted all other resources and at the cost of her dignity and the invasion of her privacy.

In this society, the tiny share of goods on which she can labor and whose fruits she can sell are the slender means of livelihood for her and her family. The notion of property does not mean the same thing to a single mother with dependent children, living at the margins under the constraints of a "free enterprise" economy, as it does to the affluent shareholders of General Dynamics. The druggist, too, is a person of flesh and blood with a story of her own to tell.

There are other contingencies that could be imaginatively explored. I have already referred to one of Gilligan's interviews in which the subject ponders the risks and uncertainties of theft for a person who lacks the skill or experience to bring the job off successfully—burglary is no mean accomplishment. Then there are the possible deleterious side effects of drugs that are proclaimed as cancer cures in all the glittering hyperbole of the mass media before they have been adequately tested. When the story is filled out with such additional considerations, it is no longer possible to resolve the dilemma with a simple principle asserting the primacy of life over property. Economic constraints can turn property into a family's only means to life and can force a competition of life *against* life in a desperate struggle not all can win.

Indeed, the most pervasive and universalizable problems of justice in the Heinz dilemma lie entirely outside the scope of its narrowly chosen details. The significance of the larger justice problem in the Heinz dilemma is neglected in Kohlberg's discussions. His construction of the dilemma as one individual's own moral problem forces a choice between two alternatives that actually are identical in at least one important respect: neither threatens the institutional context that partly structures Heinz's (and his wife's) problem.

The significance of this more fundamental justice problem has also not been commented on by Gilligan, although she perceptively sees the importance of grasping the situation in terms of rich contextual detail. Gilligan seems to think that contextual detail is a concern only of people whose moral reasoning centers on care and relationships. She does not appear to realize that in reasoning about justice and rights, it is equally inappropriate to draw conclusions from highly abbreviated descriptions of situations. Gilligan's position would be strengthened, I believe, by incorporating this insight.

In Heinz's hypothetical situation, in addition to the justice dilemma of life vs. property, there are also broad issues of social justice at stake regarding the delivery of health care. These issues cannot be resolved or even properly understood from the scanty detail that is provided in any of Kohlberg's formulations of the dilemma. We must have background knowledge about the inadequacy of health care provided for people without financial resources in a society that allows most health care resources to be privately owned, privately sold for profit in the marketplace, and privately withheld from people who cannot afford the market price or the insurance rates. And before we can resolve the problem, we must know what the alternatives are and must assess them for the degree to which they approximate an ideal of fair and just health care available to all and the degree to which they achieve, or fall short of, other relevant moral ideals.

Should we, for example, allow health care resources to remain privately owned while we simply implement a Medicaid-like program of government transfer payments to subsidize the cost of health care to the needy? Or should the government provide mandatory health insurance for everyone, with premiums taken from those who can pay, as a kind of health care tax, and premiums waived for those who cannot pay, as an in-kind welfare benefit? Or should we instead abolish private ownership of health care resources altogether, and, if so, should our alternative be grassroots-organized health care cooperatives or state-run socialized medicine? Selecting an answer to these questions and resolving the larger justice dilemma that the Heidi-Heinz situation merely intimates requires an inordinate amount of detail as well as a complex theoretical perspective on matters of economics, politics, and social and domestic life. Thus, contextual detail is of overriding importance to matters of justice as well as to matters of care and relationships.

Despite my general agreement with Gilligan's emphasis on contextual detail in moral reasoning, there is a second feature of her approach that I question. Gilligan believes that a concern for contextual detail moves a moral reasoner away from principled moral reasoning in the direction of "contextual relativism." She suggests that persons who exemplify this form of moral reasoning have "difficulty in arriving at definitive answers to moral questions" and show a "reluctance to judge" others.[44] Obviously, many people experience this reluctance at some time or other, and some people experience it all the time. But we misunderstand moral reasoning if we regard this as a necessary or inevitable outcome of being concerned with contextual detail.

Kohlberg's response to Gilligan on this point, however, is oversimple. In Kohlberg's view, the notion of a principle is the notion of that which guides moral judgment in a way that allows for exceptions. On this construal, a responsiveness to contextual details and a willingness to alter moral judgments depending upon the context do not, therefore, imply an abandonment of moral principles or a genuine moral relativism.[45] For Kohlberg, an increasing awareness of context need only indicate an increasing awareness of the difficulties of applying one's principles to specific cases. There is something to this: sensitivity to contextual detail need not carry with it the relativistic view that there simply are no moral rights or wrongs, or the slightly weaker view that there is merely no way to decide such matters. Contextual sensitivity need only reflect uncertainties about just which principles to apply to a

44. Ibid., pp. 101–2.
45. Kohlberg et al., *Moral Stages*, pp. 145–48.

particular case, or a concern that one does not yet have sufficient knowledge to apply one's principles—or a worry that one's principles are themselves too general and abstract to deal with the endless moral variety of human life.

This last alternative merits special emphasis. Kohlberg seems unconcerned about the excess generality and abstractness of most moral rules and principles. Yet, when we heed attentively the variety and complexity of contextual detail in real everyday situations, we see how limited is the help afforded by abstract moral principles in reaching conclusive moral judgments. A principle that asserts the primacy of life over property is obviously not wrong; in the abstract, few of us would challenge the point. Its relevance to a particular situation, however, depends on countless details about the quality of the particular lives at stake, the meaning of that particular property, the identities of those involved, the range of available options, the potential benefits and harms of each, the institutional setting that structures the situation and the lives of its participants, and the crucial possibility (or its absence) of changing that institutional context.

These details are ordinarily very complex; some sway us in one direction, some in another. In no time at all, we need principles for the *ordering* of our principles. Kohlberg's suggestion that contextual detail helps one to figure out which principle to apply simply does not get us very far in understanding how we finally decide what ought to be done in the complex, institutionally structured situations of our everyday lives. And this is true whether the reasoning is about care and relationships or about matters of social justice.

Kohlberg acknowledges that his scale of moral development does not measure the whole of moral reasoning; it is limited to what he calls structural stages in the development of reasoning about justice and rights. Drawing upon Gilligan's gender-based critique of Kohlberg, I have discussed two other limitations: first, the absence of any genuine integration of moral considerations having to do with care and relationships; and second, the absence of an adequate account of how people reason about complex and richly specified situations in terms of general and abstract moral rules and principles. In the next two chapters, I turn to care ethics and explore some of its complexities.

5

Gendered Morality

Care, personal relationships, and attentiveness to contextual detail are crucial matters of ordinary moral reasoning which have yet to be well represented in academic moral theorizing. Carol Gilligan's psychological research into the moral perspectives of women has provided one crucial stimulant for the sort of reconstruction of ethics which would incorporate these matters adequately.[1]

Gilligan, to reiterate, identifies two coherent and distinct moral orientations in the reasonings of her research subjects. These orientations are differentiated by certain features of content and form and by gender association. Coincident with the major traditions of moral theorizing is the typical moral perspective of men, oriented toward matters of justice and rights and dominated by abstract principles. Divergent from those traditional theories is a moral perspective found most frequently among women; it is oriented

---

1. *In a Different Voice* (Cambridge: Harvard University Press, 1982); "Do the Social Sciences Have an Adequate Theory of Moral Development?" in Norma Haan, Robert N. Bellah, Paul Rabinow, and William M. Sullivan, eds., *Social Science as Moral Inquiry* (New York: Columbia University Press, 1983), pp. 33–51; "Reply," *Signs* 11 (1986): 324–33; and "Remapping the Moral Domain: New Images of the Self in Relationship," in Thomas C. Heller, Morton Sosna, and David E. Wellbery, eds., *Reconstructing Individualism* (Stanford: Stanford University Press, 1986), pp. 237–52, reprinted in Carol Gilligan, Janie Victoria Ward, Jill McLean Taylor, with Betty Bardige, eds., *Mapping the Moral Domain* (Cambridge: Harvard Center for the Study of Gender, Education, and Human Development, 1988), pp. 3–20. All page references inserted in the text are to *In a Different Voice*.

toward matters of care and relationships and permeated with a sensitivity to contextual detail.

The divergent women's moral perspective challenges moral philosophy in several ways. First, care ethics calls upon philosophy to upgrade its estimate of the theoretical importance of caring and personal relationships, matters too long neglected in modern ethical traditions. In addition, care ethics challenges philosophy to develop a better understanding of the role of situational detail in moral reasoning. Finally, the possible link between moral outlook and gender appears to belie the universalist claims of much moral theorizing and suggests the possible distortion of moral philosophy due to a deeply rooted bias toward male moral methods and concerns.

Despite the obvious moral significance of care, however, I doubt its capacity to generate a comprehensive moral outlook. In addition, I question the view that care and justice so distinctively divide the genders as some of the Gilligan-inspired research might suggest. In the first section of this chapter, I review the supposed gender difference in moral reasoning. I propose that even if actual statistical differences in the moral reasoning of women and men cannot be confirmed, there is nevertheless a real difference in the moral norms and values culturally associated with each gender. The genders are "moralized" in distinctive ways. Moral norms about appropriate conduct, characteristic virtues, and typical vices are incorporated into our conceptions of femininity and masculinity, female and male. The result is a dichotomy that exemplifies what can be called a "division of moral labor"[2] between the genders.

In the second section, I consider a different (admittedly incomplete) explanation of why actual women and men may not show a divergence of reasoning along the care-justice dichotomy,

2. This term is used by Virginia Held to refer, in general, to the division of moral labor among the multitude of professions, activities, and practices in culture and society, though not specifically gender roles. See *Rights and Goods* (New York: Free Press, 1984), chap. 3. Held acknowledges in her book that gender roles are part of the division of moral labor but she mentions this topic only in passing (p. 29).

namely, that the notions of care and justice overlap more than Gilligan, among others, has realized. Morally adequate care involves considerations of justice. Thus, the concerns captured by these two moral categories do not define necessarily distinct moral perspectives in practice.

In section 3 I propose that, even if care and justice do not define distinct moral perspectives, nevertheless, these concepts do illuminate other important differences in moral orientation. The difference I explore here concerns relationships to other persons, the corresponding forms of moral commitment that underlie those relationships, and the nature of the resulting moral thought. To anticipate: an orientation toward matters of care emphasizes responsiveness to particular persons in their uniqueness and commitment to them as such. By contrast, an orientation toward matters of justice focuses on abstract moral rules, values, and principles and undergirds the treatment of individuals in terms of the abstract and general normative categories they instantiate.

Let us turn first to the issue of gender difference.

1. THE GENDER DIFFERENCE CONTROVERSY

Gilligan advances at least two different positions about the care and justice perspectives. One is that the care perspective is distinct from the moral perspective centered on justice and rights. I call this the "different voice" hypothesis about moral reasoning.[3] Gilligan's other hypothesis is that the care perspective is most commonly the moral voice of women, while the justice perspective is typically, or characteristically, the moral voice of men. Let us call this the "gender difference" hypothesis about moral reasoning.

The truth of Gilligan's gender difference hypothesis has been a matter of controversy. Some empirical studies do show gender differences in moral reasoning between female and male research subjects at one or more age levels.[4] Other studies, by contrast,

3. Gilligan, "Reply," p. 326.
4. These studies include Norma Haan, M. Brewster-Smith, and Jeanne

show no gender differences in moral reasoning for those same age levels.[5] In some of her studies, psychologist Norma Haan discerned two distinct moral voices among her research subjects but found them to be used to approximately the same extent by both females and males.[6]

In a meta-analysis of all the cognitive moral development research to that time, Lawrence Walker concluded in 1984 that the apparent gender difference in moral orientation was better ana-

---

Block, "Moral Reasoning of Young Adults: Political-Social Behavior, Family Background, and Personality Correlates," *Journal of Personality and Social Psychology* 10 (1968): 183–201; James Fishkin, Kenneth Keniston, and Catharine MacKinnon, "Moral Reasoning and Political Ideology," *Journal of Personality and Social Psychology* 27 (1973): 109–19; Constance Holstein, "Irreversible Stepwise Sequence in the Development of Moral Judgment: A Longitudinal Study of Males and Females," *Child Development* 47 (1976): 51–61 (showing gender differences in middle adulthood but not for other age categories); Sharry Langdale, "Moral Orientations and Moral Development: The Analysis of Care and Justice Reasoning across Different Dilemmas in Females and Males from Childhood through Adulthood" (Ed. D. diss., Harvard Graduate School of Education, 1983), cited by Gilligan, in "Reply," p. 330; D. Kay Johnston, "Adolescents' Solutions to Dilemmas in Fables: Two Moral Orientations—Two Problem-Solving Strategies," in *Mapping the Moral Domain*, pp. 49–72.

5. These studies include E. Turiel, "A Comparative Analysis of Moral Knowledge and Moral Judgment in Males and Females," *Journal of Personality* 44 (1976): 195–208; C. B. Holstein, "Irreversible Stepwise Sequence in the Development of Moral Judgment: A Longitudinal Study of Males and Females" (showing gender differentiation in middle adulthood but no differences in childhood or adolescence); Norma Haan et al., "Family Moral Patterns," *Child Development* 47 (1976): 1204–6; M. Berkowitz et al., "The Relation of Moral Judgment Stage Disparity to Developmental Effects of Peer Dialogues," *Merrill-Palmer Quarterly* 26 (1980): 341–57; and Mary Brabeck, "Moral Judgment: Theory and Research on Differences between Males and Females," *Developmental Review* 3 (1983): 274–91.

6. Norma Haan, "Two Moralities in Action Contexts," *Journal of Personality and Social Psychology* 36 (1978): 286–305. Also see Norma Haan, "Hypothetical and Actual Moral Reasoning in a Situation of Civil Disobedience," *Journal of Personality and Social Psychology* 32 (1975): 255–70; and Gertrude Nunner-Winkler, "Two Moralities? A Critical Discussion of an Ethic of Care and Responsibility versus an Ethic of Rights and Justice," in William M. Kurtines and Jacob L. Gewirtz, eds., *Morality, Moral Behavior, and Moral Development* (New York: John Wiley & Sons, 1984), pp. 348–61.

[120]

lyzed in terms of differences in occupation and education.[7] Since occupational and educational differences have long been integral to the social construction of gender, Walker's conclusion does not genuinely eliminate gender as a source of differing moral perspective, but merely decomposes it into two of its most salient constituents. On the other hand, those studies which show no *apparent* gender difference in moral reasoning have been harder to explain away.

In an attempt to dismiss the research-based objections to her gender difference hypothesis, Gilligan now asserts that her aim was not to disclose a statistical gender difference in moral reasoning but rather simply to disclose and interpret the differences in the two perspectives.[8] Psychologist John Broughton claims that if the gender difference is not maintained, then Gilligan's whole explanatory framework is undermined.[9] Broughton, however, is wrong about this. The different voice hypothesis has a significance for moral psychology and moral philosophy that would survive the demise of the gender difference hypothesis. At least part of its significance lies in revealing some of the obsessions that have distorted theories of morality in both disciplines until recently. Theoretical attention to universal and impartial conceptions of justice and rights eclipsed the moral importance of particular, interpersonal relationships based on partiality and affective ties. In part because of Gilligan's work and related studies in feminist ethics, this lopsidedness is diminishing.

Furthermore, researchers who otherwise believe that the over-

7. Lawrence J. Walker, "Sex Differences in the Development of Moral Reasoning," *Child Development* 55 (1984): 677–91. This "meta-analysis" was later disputed: see Norma Haan, "With Regard to Walker (1984) on Sex 'Differences' in Moral Reasoning" (University of California, Berkeley, Institute of Human Development mimeograph, 1985); this source is cited by Gilligan in "Reply," p. 330; see also Diana Baumrind, "Sex Differences in Moral Reasoning: Response to Walker's (1984) Conclusion That There Are None," *Child Development* 57 (1986): 511–21.

8. Gilligan, "Reply," p. 326.

9. John M. Broughton, "Women's Rationality and Men's Virtues: A Critique of Gender Dualism in Gilligan's Theory of Moral Development," *Social Research* 50 (Fall 1983): 636.

all evidence disconfirms any claims of female-male differences in moral reasoning nevertheless acknowledge that many female readers of Gilligan's book find its postulated gender difference to "resonate . . . thoroughly with their own experience."[10] Gilligan notes that it was precisely one of her purposes to expose the gap between women's experience and the findings of psychological research,[11] and, we may suppose, to critique the latter in light of the former.

The unsystematic, personal observations that females and males do differ in ways examined by Gilligan's research should lead us either (1) to question and examine carefully the methods of the empirical research that does not reveal such differences; or (2) to suspect that a gender difference exists but in some form that is not, strictly speaking, a matter of statistical differences in the moral reasoning of women and men. Gilligan has herself expressed the first of these alternatives. I would like to explore the second possibility.

Suppose that there were a gender difference of a sort, but one that was not a simple matter of differences among the form or substance of women's and men's moral reasonings. A plausible account might take this form. Among the white middle classes of such Western industrial societies as Canada and the United States, women and men are associated with different moral norms and values at the level of the stereotypes, symbols, and myths that contribute to the social construction of gender. One could say that morality is "gendered" and that the genders are "moralized." Our very conceptions of femininity and masculinity, female and male, incorporate norms about appropriate behavior, characteristic virtues, and typical vices.

Much of conventional morality exhibits a division of labor along gender lines, a division rooted in historical developments pertaining to family, state, and economy. The tasks of governing, regulating social order, and managing other public institutions have been monopolized by men as their privileged domain, and the tasks

10. Catherine G. Greeno and Eleanor E. Maccoby, "How Different Is the 'Different Voice'?" *Signs* 11 (1986): 314–15.

11. Gilligan, "Reply," p. 325.

of sustaining privatized personal relationships have been undertaken by or imposed on women.[12] The genders have thus been conceived in terms of special and distinctive moral projects. Justice and rights have structured male moral norms, values, and virtues, while care and responsiveness have defined female moral norms, values, and virtues. The division of moral labor has served both to prepare us for our respective socially defined domains and to promote our incompetence to manage the affairs of the realm from which we have been excluded. That justice is symbolized in our culture by the figure of a woman[13] is a remarkable irony; her blindfold hides more than the scales she holds.

To say that the genders are moralized is to say that specific moral ideals, values, virtues, and practices are culturally conceived as the special projects or domains of specific genders. These conceptions determine which commitments and behaviors are to be considered normal, appropriate, and expected of each gender, which commitments and behaviors are to be considered remarkable or heroic, and which commitments and behaviors are to be considered deviant, improper, outrageous, and intolerable. Men who fail to respond to the cry of a baby, fail to express tender emotions, or fail to show compassion in the face of the grief and sorrow of others are likely to be tolerated, perhaps even benignly, while women who act similarly can expect to be reproached for their coldness and hard-heartedness. Women, however, are seldom required to devote themselves to service to their countries or to international struggles, such as struggles for human rights or against colonialism. Women are seldom expected to display any of the special virtues associated with political life. At the same time, women still carry the burden of an excessively restrictive and oppressive sexual ethic; sexual aggressiveness and promiscuity are vices for which women in most social groups are roundly con-

12. For a discussion of this historical development, see Linda Nicholson, "Women, Morality, and History," *Social Research* 50 (1983): 514–36; and her *Gender and History* (New York: Columbia University Press, 1986) especially chaps. 3 and 4.

13. On the metaphoric uses of "woman," see Eva Feder Kittay, "Woman as Metaphor," *Hypatia* 3 (September 1988): 63–86.

demned, even while many of their male counterparts win tributes for their "virility."

Social science provides ample literature to show that moral gender differences are alive and well at the level of popular perception. Both men and women, on average, still conceive women and men in a moralized fashion. For example, expectations and perceptions of women's greater empathy and altruism are expressed by both women and men.[14] The gender stereotypes of women center around qualities that some authors call "communal." These include a concern for the welfare of others; the predominance of caring and nurturant traits; and, to a lesser extent, interpersonal sensitivity, emotional expressiveness, and a gentle personal style.[15]

By contrast, men are stereotyped according to what are referred to as "agentic" norms.[16] These norms center primarily around assertive and controlling tendencies. The paradigmatic behaviors are self-assertion, including forceful dominance, and independence from other people. Also encompassed by these norms are patterns of self-confidence, personal efficacy, and a direct, adventurous personal style.

If reality failed to accord with myth and symbol, if actual women and men did not fit the traits and dispositions expected of them, this might not necessarily undermine the myths and symbols, since perception could be selective and disconfirming experiences could be reduced to the status of "occasional exceptions"

14. See Nancy Eisenberg and Roger Lennon, "Sex Differences in Empathy and Related Capacities," *Psychological Bulletin* 94 (1983): 100–131.

15. See Alice H. Eagly, "Sex Differences and Social Roles" (Paper presented at Experimental Social Psychology, Tempe, Ariz., October 1986), esp. p. 7. This paper summarizes material that is presented in greatly expanded form in Alice Eagly, *Sex Differences in Social Behavior: A Social Role Interpretation* (Hillsdale, N.J.: Erlbaum, 1987). Also see Alice H. Eagly and Valerie J. Steffen, "Gender Stereotypes Stem from the Distribution of Women and Men into Social Roles," *Journal of Personality and Social Psychology* 46 (1984): 735–54.

16. The stereotypes of men are not obviously connected with justice and rights, but they are connected with the excessive individualism that Gilligan takes to underlie the justice orientation. See Eagly, "Sex Differences and Social Roles," p. 8.

and "abnormal, deviant cases." "Reality" would be misperceived in the image of cultural myth, as reinforced by the homogenizing tendencies of mass media and mass culture, and the popular imagination would provide little foothold for the recognition that women and men were not as they were mythically conceived to be.

If I am right, then Gilligan has discerned the symbolically female moral voice and has disentangled it from the symbolically male moral voice. The moralization of gender is more a matter of how we think we reason than of how we actually reason, more a matter of the moral concerns we attribute to women and men than of true statistical differences between women's and men's moral reasonings. Gilligan's findings resonate with the experiences of many people because those experiences are shaped, in part, by the cultural myths and stereotypes of gender that even feminist theorizing may not dispel. Thus, both women and men in our culture expect women and men to exhibit this moral dichotomy, and, on my hypothesis, it is this expectation that has shaped both Gilligan's observations and the plausibility we attribute to them. Or, to put it somewhat differently, whatever moral matters men concern themselves with are categorized, estimably, as matters of "justice and rights," whereas the moral concerns of women are assigned to the devalued categories of "care and personal relationships."

It is important to ask why, if these stereotypic beliefs are so pervasive, they might, nevertheless, still not produce a reality in conformity with them.[17] How could those critics who challenge Gilligan's gender hypothesis be right to suggest that women and men show no significant differences in moral reasoning, if indeed women and men are culturally educated, trained, pressured, expected, and perceived to be so radically different?[18]

17. Eagly argues both that people do show a tendency to conform to the expectations of others about their behavior and that a division of labor that leads people to develop different skills also contributes to differential development: ibid. It follows from Eagly's view that if the genders are stereotypically "moralized," they are likely to develop so as to conform to the different expectations.

18. Eagly and Steffen find that stereotypic beliefs that women are more communal and less agentic than men and that men are more agentic and less

Philosophy is not, by itself, capable of answering this question adequately. My admittedly incomplete answer to it depends upon showing that the care-justice dichotomy is rationally implausible and that the two concepts are conceptually compatible. This conceptual compatibility creates the empirical possibility that the two moral concerns are intermingled in practice. That they are actually intermingled in the moral reasonings of real women and men is, of course, not determined simply by their conceptual compatibility but requires as well the wisdom and insight of those women and men who comprehend the relevance of both concerns to their experiences.[19] Philosophy does not account for the actual emergence of wisdom. That the genders do not, in reality, divide along those moral lines is made possible, though not inevitable, by the conceptual limitations of both a concept of care dissociated from considerations of justice and a concept of justice dissociated from considerations of care. Support for this partial explanation requires a reconceptualization of care and justice—the topic of the next section.

2. Surpassing the Care-Justice Dichotomy

I have suggested that if women and men do not show statistical differences in moral reasoning along the lines of a care-

---

communal than women are based more deeply on occupational role stereotypes than on gender stereotypes: "Gender Stereotypes Stem from the Distribution of Women and Men into Social Roles." In this respect, Eagly and Steffen force us to question whether the gender categorization that pervades Gilligan's analysis really captures the fundamental differences among persons. I do not address this question in the present work.

19. In correspondence, Marcia Baron has suggested that one factor accounting for the actual emergence of "mixed" perspectives in women and men may have to do with the instability of the distinction between public and private realms to which the justice-care dichotomy corresponds. Many men have roles to play in family life and, in practice, many women have participated, out of choice or necessity, in such segments of the public world as that of paid labor. The result is a blurring of the experiential segregation that otherwise might have served to reinforce distinct moral orientations.

justice dichotomy, this should not be thought surprising since the concepts of care and justice are mutually compatible. People who treat each other justly are in an important albeit limited sense engaged in providing a kind of care for each other. (To care for someone, that is, to take care of her, does not necessitate any fond feelings or feelings of concern about her.) Conversely, personal relationships are arenas in which people have rights to certain forms of treatment and in which fairness itself can be reflected in ongoing interpersonal mutuality. It is this latter insight—the relevance of justice to close personal relationships—that I emphasize here.

Justice, at the most general level, is a matter of giving people their due, of treating them appropriately. Justice is relevant to personal relationships and to care precisely to the extent that considerations of justice determine appropriate ways to treat friends or intimates. Justice as it bears on relationships among friends or family or on other close personal ties might not involve duties that are universal, in the sense of being owed to all persons simply in virtue of shared moral personhood. But this does not entail the irrelevance of justice among friends or intimates.

Moral thinking has not always dissociated the domain of justice from that of close personal relationships. The earliest Greek code of justice placed friendship at the forefront of conditions for the realization of justice and construed the rules of justice as being coextensive with the limits of friendship. The reader will recall that one of the first definitions of justice which Plato sought to contest, in the *Republic*, is that of "helping one's friends and harming one's enemies."[20] Although the ancient Greek model of justice among friends reserved that moral privilege for free-born Greek males, the conception is, nevertheless, instructive for its readiness to link the notion of justice to relationships based on affection and loyalty. This provides an important contrast to modern notions of justice which are often deliberately constructed so as to avoid presump-

---

20. Book 1, pp. 322–35. A thorough discussion of the Greek conception of justice in the context of friendship can be found in Horst Hutter, *Politics as Friendship* (Waterloo, Ont.: Wilfrid Laurier University Press, 1978).

tions of mutual concern for those to whom the conception is to apply.

Consider John Rawls's well-known requirement that principles of justice be decided, metaphorically speaking, by taking up the "original position" behind the "veil of ignorance," a reflective mode of thought which is supposed to exclude mutual interest among the contracting parties. Each party is assumed to be concerned, first and foremost, for the advancement of her own interests and to care about the interests of others only to the extent that her own interests require it. This postulate of mutual disinterestedness is intended by Rawls to ensure that the principles of justice do not depend on such "strong assumptions" as that of "extensive ties of natural sentiment."[21] Rawls is seeking principles of justice that apply to all people in all their social interrelationships, whether or not those relationships are characterized by affection and a concern for one another's well-being. While such an account promises to disclose duties of justice owed to all other parties to the social contract, friend or foe, lover or stranger, it may fail to uncover special duties of justice that arise in close personal relationships whose foundation is affection or kinship rather than contract. The methodological device of assuming mutual disinterest might blind us to the role of justice among mutually interested or intimate parties.

Gilligan herself suggests that mature reasoning about care incorporates considerations of justice and rights. But Gilligan's conception of what this means is highly limited. It appears to involve simply the recognition "that self and other are equal," a notion that serves to override the problematic tendency of the ethic of care to become *self-sacrificing* care in women's practices.[22] However important it may be, this notion hardly does justice to justice.

There are several ways in which justice pertains to close personal relationships. The first two ways I will mention are appropriate only among friends, relatives, or intimates who are mature

21. John Rawls, *A Theory of Justice* (Cambridge: Harvard University Press, 1971), pp. 13 and 129.
22. *In a Different Voice*, p. 149.

moral persons or, at least, morally competent adults. The third sort of relevance of justice to close relationships, which I will discuss shortly, pertains to family relationships, a context in which adults often interrelate with children and which provides a more challenging domain for the application of justice. But first the easier task.

One sort of role for justice in close relationships among competent moral persons emerges clearly when we consider that a personal relationship is a miniature social system, which provides valued mutual intimacy, support, and concern for those involved. The maintenance of a relationship requires effort by the participants. One intimate may bear a much greater burden for sustaining a relationship than the other participant(s) and may derive for her efforts less support, concern, and so forth than she deserves. Justice sets a constraint on such relationships by calling for an appropriate sharing, among the participants, of the benefits and burdens that constitute their relationship.

Marilyn Frye, among many other theorists, has explored what amounts to a pattern of violation of this requirement of justice in heterosexual relationships. She argues that women of all races, social classes, and societies can be defined as a coherent group in terms of a distinctive function that is culturally assigned to them. This function is, in Frye's words, "the service of men and men's interests as men define them."[23] This service work includes personal service (satisfaction of routine bodily needs, such as hunger, and other mundane tasks), sexual and reproductive service, and ego service. Says Frye, "at every race/class level and even across race/class lines men do not serve women as women serve men."[24] Frye is, of course, generalizing over societies and cultures, and the sweep of her generalization encompasses both ongoing close personal relationships and other relationships that are not close or are not continued beyond specific transactions, for example, that of prostitute to client. By excluding the latter cases for the time being and applying Frye's analysis to familial and other close ties between

23. *The Politics of Reality* (Trumansburg, N.Y.: Crossing Press, 1983), p. 9.
24. Ibid., p. 10.

women and men, we may discern the sort of one-sided relational exploitation, often masquerading in the guise of love or care, that constitutes this first sort of injustice.

Justice is relevant to close personal relationships among competent moral persons in a second way as well. The trust and intimacy that characterize special relationships create special vulnerabilities to harm. Commonly recognized harms, such as physical injury and sexual assault, become more feasible, and special relationships, in corrupt, abusive, or degenerate forms, make possible certain uncommon emotional harms not even possible in impersonal relationships. When someone is harmed in a personal relationship, she is owed a rectification of some sort, a righting of the wrong that was done her. The notion of justice emerges, once again, as a relevant moral notion.

Thus, in a close relationship between competent moral persons, care may degenerate into the injustices of exploitation or oppression. Woman battering, acquaintance rape, and sexual harassment are but a few of the many recently publicized injustices of so-called personal life. The notion of distributive or corrective injustice seems almost to understate these indignities, involving, as they do, violations of bodily integrity and an assumption of the right to assault and injure. To call these harms injustices, however, is certainly not to rule out other terms of moral condemnation.

The two requirements of justice I have just discussed exemplify the standard distinction between distributive and corrective justice. They illustrate the role of justice in personal relationships regarded in abstraction from a social context. Personal relationships may also be considered in the context of their various institutional settings, such as marriage and family. Here justice emerges again as a relevant ideal, its role being to define appropriate institutions to structure interactions among family members, other household cohabitants, and intimates in general. The family, for example,[25] is a miniature society, exhibiting all the major facets of large-scale

25. For an important discussion of the relevance of justice to the family, see Susan Moller Okin, *Justice, Gender, and the Family* (New York: Basic Books, 1989).

social life: decision making affecting the whole unit; executive action; judgments of guilt and innocence; reward and punishment; allocation of responsibilities and privileges, of burdens and benefits; and monumental influences on the life chances of both its maturing and its mature members. Any of these features by itself would invoke the relevance of justice; together, they make the case overwhelming.

Women's historically paradigmatic role of mothering provides a multitude of insights that can be reconstructed as insights about the importance of justice in family relationships, especially those relationships involving remarkable disparities in maturity, capability, and power.[26] In these familial relationships, one party grows into moral personhood over time, gradually acquiring the capacity to be a responsible moral agent. Considerations of justice pertain to the mothering of children in numerous ways. For one thing, there may be siblings to deal with, whose demands and conflicts create the context for parental arbitration and the need for a fair allotment of responsibilities and privileges. Then there are decisions to be made involving the well-being of all persons in the family unit, whose immature members become increasingly capable over time of participating in such administrative affairs. Of special importance in the practice of raising children are the duties of child rearers to nurture and foster the development of their charges, toward the end of enhancing the life prospects of those children. These duties have public counterparts of a sort in the welfare rights viewed by many as a matter of social justice.[27] Motherhood continually presents its practitioners with moral problems best seen in terms of a complex framework that integrates justice with care, even though the politico-legal discourse of justice has not shaped its domestic expression.[28]

26. For insightful discussions of the distinctive modes of thought to which mothering gives rise, see Virginia Held, "The Obligations of Mothers and Fathers," in Joyce Trebilcot, ed., *Mothering: Essays in Feminist Theory* (Totowa, N.J.: Rowman & Allanheld, 1983), pp. 7–20; and Sara Ruddick, *Maternal Thinking* (New York: Ballantine Books, 1989).

27. This point was suggested to me by L. W. Sumner.

28. John Broughton also discusses the concern for justice and rights that

I have been discussing the relevance of justice to close personal relationships. A few words about my companion thesis, the relevance of care to the public domain of justice, is also in order.[29] In its more noble manifestations, care in the public realm would show itself, perhaps, in foreign aid, welfare programs, famine or disaster relief, or other social programs designed to relieve suffering and attend to human needs. If untempered by justice in the public domain, care degenerates precipitously. The infamous "boss" of Chicago's old-time Democratic machine, the late mayor Richard J. Daley, was legendary for his nepotism and political partisanship; he cared extravagantly for his relatives, friends, and political cronies.[30]

In recounting the moral reasoning of one of her research subjects, Gilligan once wrote that the justice perspective fails "to take into account the reality of relationships."[31] Gilligan evidently presumes that a justice perspective emphasizes only a self's various rights to noninterference by others. If this is all that a concern for justice involves, then such a perspective would indeed disregard the moral value of positive interaction, connection, and commitment among persons.

However, Gilligan's interpretation of justice is far too limited. For one thing, it fails to recognize positive rights, such as welfare

---

appears in women's moral reasoning as well as the concern for care and relationships featured in men's moral reasoning: "Women's Rationality and Men's Virtues," esp. pp. 603–22. For a historical discussion of male theorists who have failed to hear the concern for justice in women's voices, see Carole Pateman, " 'The Disorder of Women': Women, Love, and the Sense of Justice," *Ethics* 91 (1980): 20–34.

29. Francesca M. Cancian warns that we should not narrow our conception of love to the recognized ways women love, which researchers find to center around the expression of intimate feelings and verbal self-disclosure. Such a conception ignores forms of love that are stereotyped as characteristically male, including instrumental help and the sharing of activities. See "The Feminization of Love," *Signs* 11 (1986): 692–709. I discuss Cancian's essay in greater detail in Chapter 6.

30. See Mike Royko, *Boss: Richard J. Daley of Chicago* (New York: New American Library, 1971).

31. *In a Different Voice*, p. 147.

rights, which may be endorsed from a justice perspective. In addition, and more important, Gilligan fails to acknowledge the potential for violence and harm in human interrelationships and human community.[32] The concept of justice, in general, arises out of relational conditions in which most human beings have the opportunity, the capacity, and, for too many, the inclination to treat each other badly.[33]

Thus, notions of distributive justice are fostered by the realization that people who together comprise a social system may not share fairly in the benefits and burdens of their social cooperation. Conceptions of rectificatory, or corrective, justice are founded on the concern that when harms are done, action should be taken either to restore those harmed as fully as possible to their previous state or to prevent further similar harm or both. Furthermore, the specific rights that people are variously thought to have are just so many manifestations of our interest in identifying ways in which people deserve protection against harm by others. The complex reality of social life encompasses the human potential for helping, caring for, and nurturing others as well as the potential for harming, exploiting, and oppressing others. Thus, Gilligan is wrong to think that the justice perspective neglects "the reality of relationships." Rather, it arises from a more subtle and multivalent assessment of the complexities of human relationships.

In light of these reflections, it seems wise both to reconsider the seeming dichotomy of care and justice and to question the moral adequacy of either orientation dissociated from the other. Our aim would be to advance "beyond caring," that is, beyond

32. Claudia Card has criticized Gilligan's work for ignoring the harms to which women have historically been subjected in heterosexual relationships such as (but not only) marriage; see her "Gender and Moral Luck," in Owen Flanagan and Amélie Oksenberg Rorty, eds., *Identity, Character, and Morality* (Cambridge, Mass.: MIT Press, 1990), pp. 199–218. A related discussion, based on an earlier, unpublished version of Card's paper, is Barbara Houston's "Rescuing Womanly Virtues: Some Dangers of Moral Reclamation," in Marsha Hanen and Kai Neilsen, eds., *Science, Morality, and Feminist Theory, Canadian Journal of Philosophy* suppl. vol. 13 (1987): 237–62.

33. In Chapters 2 and 3, I discuss the problems of abuses and harms in personal relationships.

mere caring dissociated from a concern for justice. In addition, we would do well to progress beyond gender stereotypes that assign distinct and different moral roles to women and men. Our ultimate goal should be a nongendered, nondichotomized moral framework in which all moral concerns could be expressed.

3. COMMITMENTS TO PARTICULAR PERSONS

Although care and justice do not define mutually exclusive moral frameworks, it is still too early to dispose of the "different voice" hypothesis. It is worth considering whether there are indeed different moral orientations, even if the concepts of care and justice do not capture the principal differences and even if the differences do not correlate statistically—or symbolically—with gender differences.

An interesting distinction can be drawn between different sorts of primary moral commitments. Let us begin with the observation that, from the so-called care standpoint, responsiveness to other persons in their wholeness and their particularity is of singular importance. This idea, in turn, points toward a notion of moral commitment that takes particular persons as its primary focus.[34] In contrast to this person-based sort of commitment, other moral commitments may be defined by reference to general and abstract rules, values, or principles. It is no mere coincidence that Gilligan found the so-called justice perspective to feature an emphasis on rules.[35]

In the preceding section, I contended that the concepts of jus-

---

34. My discussion in this section draws upon Claudia Card's "Gender and Moral Luck"; and Seyla Benhabib, "The Generalized and the Concrete Other: The Kohlberg-Gilligan Controversy and Moral Theory," in Eva Feder Kittay and Diana T. Meyers, eds., *Women and Moral Theory* (Totowa, N.J.: Rowman & Littlefield, 1987), pp. 154–77. Note that Card, in her paper, explores a dichotomy she finds undergirds that between justice and care; this is the difference between moral thinking that is focused on formal and impersonal relationships and moral thinking that is focused on informal and personal relationships; see esp. pp. 208–14.

35. *In a Different Voice*, e.g., p. 73.

tice and care are mutually compatible and, more than that, both necessary for a morally adequate perspective on personal interrelationships. The same might well be true for those personal relationships that are the farthest removed from close intimacy, relationships with complete strangers to whom we are connected only as conationals or comembers of the global community. If so, then the justice perspective could be said to rest, at bottom, on the insight that the best way to care for persons in general is to respect their rights and to accord them their due, both in distribution of the burdens and benefits of social cooperation and in the rectification of wrongs done. To uphold these justice principles, however, it is not necessary to respond with emotion, feeling, passion, or compassion to other persons. A commitment to justice does not require the full range of human responsiveness toward every person.

By contrast, the explicit ethic of care stresses an ongoing responsiveness. This ethic is, after all, the stereotypic moral norm for women in the domestic role of sustaining a family in the face of the harsh realities of a competitive marketplace and an indifferent polis. The domestic realm has been idealized as the realm in which people, as specific individuals, are to be nurtured, cherished, and succored. The care perspective discussed by Gilligan is a limited one; it is not really about care in all its complexity, since Gilligan excludes the just treatment that I maintain is necessary to morally adequate caring, and she neglects the sense in which justice, even toward strangers, can itself be construed as a kind of care. Gilligan's care perspective does seem, however, to capture some important dimensions of what it means to relate to particular persons as such. These dimensions center around attentiveness and responsiveness to another person's emotional states, individuating differences, specific uniqueness, and whole particularity. Gilligan's care orientation focuses on whole persons and deemphasizes adherence to moral rules.

Thus, the important conception that I am extracting from Gilligan's care perspective is that of commitment to particular persons and commitment to them *in their particularity*. What is the nature of this form of moral commitment? Commitment to a specific person, such as a lover, child, or friend, takes as its primary focus the needs, wants, attitudes, judgments, behavior, and overall way of being of that particular person. It is specific to that individual and is not generalizable to others. Attending to someone's needs, enjoying her successes, deferring to her judgments, and finding inspiration in her values and goals simply because they are hers are all ways of being committed to someone primarily as the unique person she is. If it is precisely and exactly who she is, and not her actions or traits subsumed under general rules, that matters as one's motivating guide, then one's responsiveness to her reflects an exclusively person-oriented, and not a rule-based, moral commitment.

Thus, both the care and the justice perspectives take account of human relationships in some way; both may legitimately incorporate a concern for justice as well as care (although in a different order of priority or focal concern) and both aim to avoid harm to others and (at the highest stages) to the self. Nevertheless, the two perspectives seem to exhibit substantive differences in the nature of their primary moral commitments. From the standpoint of care, self and other are conceptualized in their particularity rather than as instances for the application of generalized moral notions, as they would be according to the justice perspective.

This analysis requires a subtle expansion. Like care and justice, commitments to particular persons and commitments to values, rules, and principles are not mutually exclusive within the entire panorama of one person's moral concerns. Doubtless, they are intermingled in most people's moral outlooks. Pat likes and admires Mary because of Mary's resilience in the face of tragedy, her intelligent courage, and her good-humored audacity. Pat thereby shows a generalized commitment to resilience, courage, and good-humored audacity as traits of human personality.

In Mary, however, these traits coalesce in a unique manner: perhaps no one will stand by a friend in deep trouble quite so steadfastly as Mary; perhaps no one can fight an impersonal bureaucracy as effectively as Mary. The traits that Pat likes, in general, converge to make Mary, in Pat's eyes, an especially admirable human individual, a sort of moral exemplar. In virtue of Pat's loyalty to her, Mary may come to play a role in Pat's life that exceeds, in its weightiness, the sum total of the values that Pat sees in Mary's virtues taken individually and in abstraction from any particular human personality.

Pat is someone with commitments both to moral abstractions and to particular persons. Pat is, in short, like most of us. When we reason morally, we can take up a stance that makes either of these forms of commitment the focal point of our attention. The choice of which stance to adopt at a given time is probably, like other moral alternatives, most poignant and difficult in situations of moral ambiguity or uncertainty when we do not know how to proceed. In such situations, one can turn either to the guidance of abstract conceptions of value, right conduct, or human virtue, or one can turn to the guidance that inheres in the example set by a trusted friend or associate—the example of how she, in particular, interprets those same moral ambiguities or how she resolves those same moral uncertainties.

Commitments to a particular person, obviously, are evident in more situations than simply those of moral irresolution. The experience of moral irresolution, however, may clarify the different sorts of moral commitments that structure our thinking. Following cherished values will lead one out of one's moral uncertainties in a very different way from following someone else's example. I return to this point below.

The insight that each person needs some others in her life who recognize, respect, and cherish her particularity in its richness and wholeness is one distinctive motivating vision of Gilligan's care perspective.[36] The sort of respect for persons that grows out of this vision is not the abstract respect that is owed to all persons in virtue of their common humanity but, rather, a respect for individual worth, merit, need, or even idiosyncrasy. It is a form of respect that involves admiration and cherishing, when the distinctive qualities are valued intrinsically, and that, at the least, involves toleration when the distinctive qualities are not valued intrinsically.[37]

36. For this part of my discussion I am indebted to Claudia Card.

37. For a discussion of the sort of respect generated by care, see Robin Dillon, "Care and Respect," in Eve Browning-Cole and Susan Coultrap-

There is, indeed, an apparent irony in the notion of personhood that underlies some philosophers' conceptions of the universalized moral duties owed to all persons. The rational nature that, in Kant's view, for example, gives each person dignity and makes each of absolute value and, therefore, irreplaceable,[38] is no more than an abstract rational nature in virtue of which we are all alike. But if we are all alike in this respect, it is hard to understand why we would be irreplaceable. Our common rational nature would seem to make us indistinguishable and, therefore, mutually interchangeable. Specific identity would be a matter of indifference, so far as our absolute value is concerned. It seems that only in virtue of our distinctive particularity could we each be truly irreplaceable.

Of course, particularity does not exclude the possibility of a common nature, conceptualized at a level of suitable generality. We still deserve equal respect in virtue of our common humanity. We are also, however, more than abstractly and equivalently human. It is this "more" to which we commit ourselves when we care for others in their particularity.

Can a primary commitment to abstract principles and values be integrated with a primary commitment to particular persons or are we necessarily doomed to a forced choice between them? On this issue, as on the question of whether care and justice are necessarily distinct, my approach is integrationist. One possible sort of integration between person-based and abstract moral commitments is to seek intimate, responsive, and committed relationships with people we know well enough to be reliably familiar with their needs, desires, beliefs, and so on and to settle for abstract, rule-based, equal respect toward that vast number of others we cannot know in any particularity.

Another possible sort of integration is to try to forge and sustain a dynamic, although uneasy, balance between abstract commitments to important values and principles (including equal respect

---

McQuin, eds., *Explorations in Feminist Ethics* (Bloomington: Indiana University Press, 1992), pp. 69–81.

38. See Immanuel Kant, *Groundwork of the Metaphysics of Morals*, trans. Lewis White Beck (Indianapolis: Bobbs-Merrill, 1959), pp. 46–47, 53–54.

for common moral personhood), on one hand, and particularized commitments to the people we care about, on the other. I can, for example, stand loyally and supportively by a friend who has done something wrong, yet at the same time, if she is open to my counsel, try privately to guide her toward change. I combine my commitment to her and all the loyalty, care, and protectiveness that requires with my commitments to abstract moral values and principles, threading my way through a complex web of responses that uphold the importance of both sorts of commitments, sacrificing neither. I show respect for my friend and for my abstract commitments simultaneously. I respect my friend both by supporting her at a time of trouble in her life and by appealing to her as an autonomous being, one capable of reflectively considering the moral standards I now champion to her. I respect my own deeply held values and principles by defending them to my friend.

In a situation in which my friend has done something only moderately wrong and in which the values at stake are of only moderate importance to me, the balance I strive to sustain between my two sorts of commitment, though it takes some thoughtful effort, does not seriously challenge me. At other times, however, the tension between such commitments poses challenges of a more troubling sort. Our friends might turn out to be not merely petty thieves or inconsiderate oafs, but genuine villains, vicious and monstrous. They might outreach our capacities for moral persuasion, being firmly entrenched in practices from which no amount of pleading can dissuade them. What should become of our moral priorities then? What should happen to the uneasy balance between abstract justice and caring loyalty?

In practice, we sometimes do, but sometimes do not, abandon our loved ones even when they violate those values or principles to which we adhere most strongly. Is it blind loyalty to stay thus committed to a loved one, a cherished friend, when she has committed the seemingly unthinkable, the apparently outrageous? In Chapter 7, I defend a complicated answer to this question. Sometimes when we allow such abiding commitments to trusted friends to override our abstract commitments to values and principles, we open ourselves to the possible transformation and enrichment of

[139]

our moral perspectives. Our friends may inspire us to discern that something happens to be extremely wrong with the very moral norms and conventions against which they have "sinned." Personal loyalties, in other words, may help us to ascend to a level where we put our own values and principles into question; the result may be to reach a new plateau in our critical moral understanding and insight.

The contrary risk is, of course, that we may follow fools and charlatans as well as genuine moral revolutionaries. In my view, there is no principled way to discern, in advance of the particulars of each case, which possibility we are confronting at any one time. Actual cases might not be clear-cut; perhaps my friend really did some wrong, but perhaps the standards by which she is being judged are not entirely well grounded, or perhaps the wrong she did is genuine enough but counterbalanced by as yet unrecognized benefits.

This much may be said. To suppose that the abstract commitments to values and principles that we happen to hold at a particular time should always prevail in any conflict with our commitments to loved ones would be to cut ourselves off from an invaluable source of inspiration for critical moral rethinking. In addition, to thus subject our loved ones perpetually to scrutiny according to abstract standards is, at a deep level, to make one's intimacies and loving connections always conditional on whether the loved one adheres to the particular, fallible, humanly limited standards that we happen to have at any contingent time in our lives.

It is sadly true that some intimate relationships are oppressive; sometimes, those who love us endanger our integrity and well-being at the deepest levels. For one's own sake, commitments to such persons should be conditional; some loved ones need continual scrutiny in light of one's best-considered standards. One does not owe to someone who is not helplessly in need of care the sort of unqualified personal commitment that would violate one's most cherished values or compromise one's fundamental well-being. A life, however, in which one must always love others conditionally, cautiously, and suspiciously, because of their oppressiveness or one's own excessive vulnerability, is a life deprived of a potential source of human joy. To the extent that social conditions and arrangements support such oppressiveness and vulnerability, social conditions themselves undermine the possibilities for wholehearted, unconditional love and interpersonal commitment.

Thus, Gilligan's investigation of the care and justice frameworks reveals other facets of moral thinking that also admit of important contrasts. The contrast I have explored pertains to certain sorts of moral commitments that structure moral thought and to the resulting nature of the responses to other persons. A justice orientation treats people as instances of abstract, generalized moral categories and disregards their unique particularity. A care orientation, by contrast, makes recognition of, and commitment to, persons in their particularity one of its overriding moral concerns.[39] Such alternative forms of moral commitment, however, do not define two competing, or even alternative, moral frameworks. They simply represent another facet of the variety in moral thinking, one that seems to overlie the difference between care and justice and one that is equally mutually compatible.

To tie together the varied threads of this discussion, we may conclude that nothing intrinsic to gender demands a division of moral norms that assigns particularized, personalized commitments to women and universalized, rule-based commitments to men. With luck, we may yet abolish the stereotypic gendered division of moral labor, advance beyond the dissociation of justice from care, and learn how to forge a vital and flexible integration of our personal and abstract moral commitments. Let us hope for no less than the symbolic (and genuine) access of each gender to all available conceptual and social resources for the sustenance and enrichment of our collective moral life.

39. For a helpful discussion on this topic, see Margaret Walker, "Moral Particularism," *Metaphilosophy* 18 (1987): 171–85.

6

Liberating Care

Critical thinking about care and caring relationships is a burgeoning area of moral theory. The widespread attention shown by most of the theorists in this area to women's experiences and perspectives is utterly unique in the history of philosophical ethics and a momentous, if sadly belated, achievement. This is not to suggest, however, that all theorists of care ethics share similar approaches or concerns. In the growing and lively field of care ethics, there is a great deal of diversity and debate. The previous chapter touched on one major area of controversy: the relationship between considerations of care and considerations of justice. This chapter addresses the adequacy—or inadequacy—of an ethic of care to illuminate women's cultural subordination.

A brief review of Gilligan's approach to the interconnections between care and justice will soon bring issues of women's subordination into view. In the previous chapter, I argued that morally adequate care incorporates considerations of justice. Gilligan herself, at times, proposes this integration by suggesting that the highest level of moral reasoning, the postconventional level, combines considerations of care with those of justice.[1] In Gilligan's view, the important assumption that a justice and rights perspective adds to a care perspective is that "self and other are equal." The concept of rights also carries with it the notion that "the interests of the

1. Carol Gilligan, *In a Different Voice* (Cambridge: Harvard University Press, 1982), e.g., p. 174.

self can be considered legitimate." On the basis of this insight, women, as care givers, are enabled "to consider it moral to care not only for others but for themselves."[2] Beyond this point, psychologist Gilligan understandably does not develop in detail the philosophical possibilities of her own proposed integration.

Feminists diverge over the relevance of justice to care. Some agree with Gilligan that the integrative route is very promising and have further developed the philosophical details of this approach.[3] Others eschew the integrative approach altogether. Nel Noddings, for example, regards the ethic of universal justice as a masculine illusion.[4]

It is noteworthy that Gilligan's later writings do not claim that care and justice are the *only* two moral perspectives available. These are the only two perspectives she investigates, however, and she regards them as the two most widely preferred orientations.[5] On

2. Ibid., p. 149.

3. These works include Annette Baier, "The Need for More than Justice," in Marsha Hanen and Kai Nielsen, eds., *Science, Morality, and Feminist Theory, Canadian Journal of Philosophy* suppl. vol. 13 (1987): 41–56; Owen Flanagan and Kathryn Jackson, "Justice, Care, and Gender: The Kohlberg-Gilligan Debate Revisited," *Ethics* 97 (April 1987): 622–37; Susan Moller Okin, "Reason and Feeling in Thinking about Justice," *Ethics* 99 (January 1989): 229–49; Susan Moller Okin, *Justice, Gender, and the Family* (New York: Basic Books, 1989); and Claudia Card, "Gender and Moral Luck," in Owen Flanagan and Amélie Oksenberg Rorty, eds., *Identity, Character, and Morality* (Cambridge, Mass.: MIT Press, 1990), pp. 199–218. In the previous chapter, after suggesting that the equality of self and other is not all there is to the full-blown notion of justice, I went on to outline other considerations of justice that integrate in a relevant way with considerations of care in intimate relationships.

4. Nel Noddings, *Caring: A Feminine Approach to Ethics and Moral Education* (Berkeley: University of California Press, 1984), p. 90. More recently, in response to debate over this point, Noddings has postponed her final verdict on the relevance of justice to care; see her "A Response," *Hypatia* 5 (Spring 1990): 120.

5. Gilligan writes, "The tendency for people to organize experiences of conflict and choice largely in terms of justice or of care has been a consistent finding of research on moral orientation": "Prologue: Adolescent Development Reconsidered," in Carol Gilligan, Janie Victoria Ward, Jill McLean Taylor, with Betty Bardige, eds., *Mapping the Moral Domain* (Cambridge: Harvard Center for the Study of Gender, Education, and Human Development, 1988), p. xviii.

Gilligan's view, "people tend to focus their attention either on problems of unfairness or on problems of disconnection."[6]

Many feminists criticize care ethics for its relative silence about oppressive social practices and the cultural subordination of women. Gilligan seems to regard a concern for "problems of oppression" and "problems stemming from inequality" as reflecting the justice perspective.[7] Although many feminist concerns about oppression and subordination do reflect an orientation to matters of justice and injustice,[8] not all of them have this foundation. Not all problems of oppression are problems of unfairness or the violation of rights.

Some features of women's subordination pertain to the varied forms of care, the nature of traditional caretaking practices in our culture, and the complications of moral personality and moral identity that emerge with deep, long-term involvement in care giving. Care ethics has neglected the way caring practices themselves have been bound up with women's subordination. As a result of this neglect, care ethics as currently formulated seems incapable of sufficiently grounding the efforts to overcome the diverse forms of subordination affecting women. This is the issue to which we now turn.

I begin in section 1 by surveying some feminist criticisms of care ethics that point to its failure to illuminate women's cultural subordination or the means necessary to overcome it. This survey is followed, in section 2, by an exploration of the importance of care for female care givers themselves and some of the varied forms that care should take. Bernard Williams's quasi-hypothetical example of a painter seeking moral luck, who abandons his family to pursue his art, sets the stage for my query, in section 3, about the heavier caretaking responsibilities that befall women as compared to men. My discussion concludes in section 4 with a comparative exploration of the different sorts of care that women and

6. Ibid., p. xix.
7. Ibid., pp. xvii–xviii.
8. See Susan Moller Okin, *Justice, Gender, and the Family* (New York: Basic Books, 1989).

men provide each other in the context of heterosexual relationships and the way this difference contributes to women's subordination.

1. A Critical Feminist Overview of Care Ethics

Care ethics offers at least one very alluring feature: high moral esteem for the traditional caring work done by women. Yet, because of certain problems in care ethics, feminists wonder whether, on balance, this ethic hinders more than it helps women seeking to overcome their cultural subordination. Claudia Card and Joan Tronto, for example, observe that merely presenting care ethics as a distinctively female ethic is not enough to establish its moral adequacy or its moral superiority to other ethical perspectives.[9] Barbara Houston worries that to celebrate feminine virtues and perspectives is to risk glorifying the oppressive conditions under which they arose.[10]

Card and Tronto point out that relationships differ in their worth, that not every relationship is valuable, and that care ethics provides no basis for critical reflection on relationships.[11] Card suggests that, having developed under conditions of oppression, the

9. Card, "Gender and Moral Luck," p. 201; Joan Tronto, "Beyond Gender Difference to a Theory of Care," *Signs* 12, no. 4 (1987): 646.

10. Barbara Houston, "Rescuing Womanly Virtues: Some Dangers of Moral Reclamation," in Hanen and Nielsen, *Science, Morality, and Feminist Theory*, p. 247. On this point, Houston draws extensively upon Joan Ringelheim, "Women and the Holocaust: A Reconsideration of Research," *Signs* 10, no. 4 (1985): 759–60. In that essay, Ringelheim offers a newly cautious rereading of some of her own previous research findings which had adopted a "cultural feminist" approach. Cultural feminism, in general, honors the behavior, values, and perspectives of women more highly than those of men, even when the former have arisen under conventional conditions. Ringelheim's later skepticism about a cultural feminist approach directly responds to the temptation that a feminist might feel to regard care ethics as a sign of women's moral superiority.

11. Card, "Gender and Moral Luck," p. 215; Tronto, "Beyond Gender Difference to a Theory of Care," p. 660.

care perspective has been needed for adaptation to those oppressive conditions and may not embody genuine virtue.[12] In the views of both Card and Houston, care ethics ignores the possibility that a history of oppression has inflicted moral damage on women. Of special concern to feminists is the moral damage that further entrenches women's subordination,[13] for example, the morally hazardous forms of deference that are a frequent risk when women care for men.[14]

Card and Sarah Hoagland, in addition, both point out that care ethics lacks a political or institutional focus. It ignores the institutionally structured differentials of power and authority among different persons, especially those that constitute the gender hierarchy. It is thereby incapable of conceptualizing the oppressive, institutionally patriarchal context in which care takes place and that may compromise the otherwise high moral value of care.[15] In Jeffner Allen's view, the nonviolence of care is a liability to women under oppressive circumstances, for it disables women from resisting whatever abuse they experience in heterosexual relationships.[16]

Hoagland and Tronto, furthermore, recognized that care ethics ignores moral responsibilities to distant strangers and those for whom we do not feel particularly caring; care ethics thereby threat-

12. Card, "Gender and Moral Luck," pp. 204–5, 215–16.

13. Ibid., p. 216; Houston, "Rescuing Womanly Virtues," p. 253.

14. See Sandra Bartky, *Femininity and Domination* (New York: Routledge, 1990), especially chap. 7, "Feeding Egos and Tending Wounds: Deference and Disaffection in Women's Emotional Labor"; also see my "Moral Integrity and the Deferential Wife," *Philosophical Studies* 47 (January 1985): 141–50.

15. Card, "Gender and Moral Luck," p. 205; Sarah Hoagland, "Some Thoughts about 'Caring,' " in Claudia Card, ed., *Feminist Ethics* (Lawrence: University Press of Kansas, 1991), pp. 253, 260. For a good, early discussion of how care may be compromised by an institutionally oppressive context, see Larry Blum, Marcia Homiak, Judy Housman, and Naomi Scheman, "Altruism and Women's Oppression," in Sharon Bishop and Marjorie Weinzweig, eds., *Philosophy and Women* (Belmont, Calif.: Wadsworth, 1979), pp. 190–200; reprinted from *Philosophical Forum* 5 (1975).

16. Jeffner Allen, *Lesbian Philosophy* (Palo Alto, Calif.: Institute for Lesbian Studies, 1986), p. 35.

ens to devolve into a mere defense of conventional relationships.[17] Care ethics also fails to represent diversity among women. Either it suffers from positive biases of race, class, ethnicity, and national culture, as Michele Moody-Adams charges,[18] or, at the very least, it suffers by its simple failure to represent specific differences among women, such as the racial diversity discussed by Carol Stack.[19]

Despite such limitations, care ethics, in my view, makes a profound contribution to contemporary moral theory. This contribution is qualified but not fundamentally undermined even by the limitations mentioned above.[20] Care ethics raises caring, nurturing, and the maintenance of interpersonal relationships to the status of foundational moral importance. It directs our attention to the realms of human life in which these activities have been the primary focus, especially family life, friendship, and sexual and other close personal relationships. These realms of life have, until the last two decades or so, been neglected or relegated to a derivative and

17. Hoagland, "Some Thoughts about Caring," pp. 260–61; Tronto, "Beyond Gender Differences to a Theory of Care," ibid., pp. 659–60.

18. Michele Moody-Adams, "Gender and the Complexity of Moral Voices," in Card, *Feminist Ethics*, pp. 198–200.

19. Carol Stack, "The Culture of Gender: Women and Men of Color," *Signs* 11 (Winter 1986): 321–24. Gilligan does occasionally note, of her various findings, that they are based on "a small and highly educated sample.": *In a Different Voice*, p. 156. However, the language in which she reports those findings fails to repeat this limitation. Thus, she introduces certain of her findings in this way: "I want to restore in part the missing text of *women's development*, as *they* describe their conceptions of self and morality in the early adult years. In focusing primarily on the differences between the accounts of *women and men*, my aim is to enlarge developmental understanding by including *the perspectives* of both the sexes. While the judgments considered come from a small and highly educated sample, they elucidate a contrast and make it possible to recognize not only what is missing in *women's* development but also what is there" (p. 156).

20. Houston also applauds current work on care ethics even while worrying about the limitations of that work. The risk in abandoning care ethics altogether is that, to borrow Houston's terms, "a very large part of women's moral experience will again become invisible or will suffer a devaluation": "Rescuing Womanly Virtues," p. 260.

secondary theoretical status by most (although not all) of the major theorists of modern moral philosophy, both those who founded and those who further developed Kantian moral philosophy and utilitarianism.[21]

Care ethics, furthermore, makes an important contribution to contemporary moral theory by raising esteem for women in virtue of their primary identification with the caring and nurturing realms of social life. Cheshire Calhoun sees this development as a crucial step in overcoming ethical theory's own tendency to reinforce the pervasive societal bias toward the masculine.[22] This tendency is manifested both in an explicit devaluing of (traditionally female) moral experiences in the domestic and familial realm, and in selective attention only to (traditionally male) realms of moral experience in the public world. For advocates of care ethics to have turned women's traditional moral concerns into a fundamental focus of attention for moral theory was a ground-breaking endeavor. The importance of such an advance in moral philosophy and, in particular, its importance for feminism, should not be underestimated.

Care ethics is inspired and engaged by a respect for women's traditional domestic and familial care-giving labor. Any system of thought that shows such esteem combats the aspect of women's

21. Annette Baier finds much in the writings of David Hume that bears on contemporary feminist ethics; see "Hume, The Women's Moral Theorist?" in Eva Feder Kittay and Diana T. Meyers, eds., *Women and Moral Theory* (Totowa, N.J.: Rowman & Littlefield, 1987), pp. 37–55. John Stuart Mill, in collaboration with Harriet Taylor, is noteworthy for his extensive writings on the subordination of women; see their *Essays on Sex Equality*, ed. Alice S. Rossi (Chicago: University of Chicago Press, 1970). These investigations, however, do not appear in his major work of moral theory, *Utilitarianism*, and the subsequent tradition in moral philosophy has not canonized his writings on women. The major metaethical developments that dominated the early- to mid-twentieth century in moral philosophy, e.g., intuitionism, emotivism, and linguistic analysis, also ignored the realm of caring. This observation is scarcely noteworthy, however, since those trends tended to neglect important matters of moral substance in *most* realms of human activity.

22. Cheshire Calhoun, "Justice, Care, Gender Bias," *Journal of Philosophy* 85 (1988): 451–63.

oppression that has to do with the cultural devaluation of women's work. Feminist critics of care ethics, however, worry that, on balance, more harm than good may arise from promoting care ethics as a distinctively *female* ethical perspective. The subordination of women has included many more dimensions than simply the devaluation of women's traditional forms of labor, and it is not clear what contribution is made by care ethics toward alleviating these other problems. Women's subordination has included the denial to women of opportunities for full participation in public life and the concomitant confinement of women to traditionally female forms of labor, whether as unpaid or (under)paid workers. It has included whatever constriction of moral competency follows upon the loss of opportunity to cope with the circumstances, persons, and relationships of the public sphere. These concerns are ignored by care ethics.

Care ethics also neglects the historical male control of women's sexual and reproductive capacities and activities, whether by obstetric practitioners and other scientific experts,[23] by governments,[24] or by husbands and male lovers, as made possible by the practice of obligatory heterosexuality and prohibitions against lesbianism.[25] Care ethics tends to ignore the distinctive forms of violence and violation to which women, far more than men, have been subjected. The lamentably familiar examples include incest, rape, sexual harassment, and domestic battering.[26] Although a care ethic certainly condemns any form of violence and brutality, it is by no means clear what response it will advise for a woman or girl who has been the victim of, say, rape or battering by someone close to her.

23. Barbara Ehrenreich and Deirdre English, *For Her Own Good: 150 Years of the Experts' Advice to Women* (Garden City, N.Y.: Anchor Books, 1978).

24. For a discussion of the legal aspects of governmental control of reproductive and family policy, see Deborah L. Rhode, *Justice and Gender* (Cambridge: Harvard University Press, 1989), esp. chaps. 6, 7, and 9.

25. See Adrienne Rich, "Compulsory Heterosexuality and Lesbian Existence," *Signs* 5 (Summer 1980): 631–60.

26. For a recent discussion of the legal aspects of these social problems, see Rhode, *Justice and Gender*, chap. 10, "Sex and Violence."

Traditional moral theories and traditional concepts of justice and rights may fare better than care ethics in handling problems of violence. Traditional moral theories offer grounds for judging that one has been harmed or wronged in certain important ways, and they also articulate rationales for the criminal punishment of wrongdoers.[27] Theorists of care ethics have been notably silent about these matters.[28]

Gilligan touches on the issue of violence in intimate relationships when she discusses some empirical data that summarize the reactions of female and male research subjects to certain suggestive visual images. In one study, women and men had to tell a story about two trapeze artists who were pictured performing a dangerous aerial act. Women, more often than men, added safety nets in their stories. Partly on the basis of such data, Gilligan concludes that, unlike men, women do not generally regard personal relationships as dangerous: "the women saw the scene on the trapeze as safe because, by providing nets, they had made it safe."[29] Perhaps, on the contrary, women added nets as external safety devices precisely because they perceived the relationships as being, in themselves, *unsafe*.

It would be a mistake to think that a care perspective need not countenance the possibilities of harm in close personal relation-

27. Feminists debate the legal and moral adequacy of traditional conceptions of rights for dealing with such problems as that of violence against women; see Carol Smart, *Feminism and the Power of Law* (London: Routledge, 1989), esp. chap. 7, "The Problem of Rights." I do not assume that traditional conceptions have been rendered fully adequate to the problem. However, as stated in the text, they "may fare better" than care ethics. In addition, we should not underestimate the dynamic power of such systems of thought to grow and change in light of feminist concerns; see Carl Wellman, "Doing Justice to Rights," *Hypatia* 3 (Winter 1989): 153–58.

28. Moody-Adams argues persuasively that moral perspectives quite different from that of care might have emerged in Gilligan's studies had the underlying research been based on interviews with women who were coping with the experience of rape or domestic battering rather than (as was the case) on interviews with women who were struggling with abortion decisions: "Gender and the Complexity of Moral Voices," pp. 202–3.

29. *In a Different Voice*, p. 43; the entire discussion appears on pp. 39–45.

ships, and that such concerns are imported into morality only by way of a concern with justice. Sara Ruddick, for example, systematically confronts issues concerning violence as an inherent part of her care-based maternal ethic.[30] Ruddick examines "maternal practice through the lens of nonviolence" and asks "if there are principles in the practices of mothering that coincide" with ideals of nonviolence.[31] However, the mothering relationship, which is the focus of Ruddick's investigation, has limited usefulness as a source of insight about everyday adult interrelationships. Morally competent adults, in relationships with each other, do not usually have motherlike responsibilities for each other's preservation, growth, or social acceptability.[32] In addition, the domain to which Ruddick primarily applies, and in which she expands, the nonviolent insights of mothering is that of military politics, not the domain of domestic or sexual violence.

To sum up: resisting the varied forms of female subordination calls for more than simply elevating esteem for women's traditionally sanctioned forms of labor and attendant modes of consciousness. To elevate social esteem for care ethics is to combat women's subordination to the extent of resisting only one of its many manifestations. This approach, by itself, does not (yet) constitute a sufficiently rich or fully liberatory *feminist* ethic. Worse yet, care ethics appears to bolster some of the practices and conceptions that subordinate women.

To portray care ethics as a distinctively female ethic reinforces the stereotypic gender assumptions that women are especially suited for the domestic, nurturing realm, that men are unsuited for this realm, and that women are particularly unsuited for the traditionally masculine worlds of public work and activity. The apparent incapacity of care ethics to deal with the moral relationships of public life, relationships among strangers, or among persons who share no affective ties, contributes greatly to this

30. Sara Ruddick, *Maternal Thinking: Towards a Politics of Peace* (New York: Ballantine Books, 1989).

31. Ibid., p. 161.

32. These are the three demands that, in Ruddick's view, are imposed by maternal work and that "constitute" such work: ibid., p. 17.

impression. If care ethics is supposed to represent the preferred perspective of substantial numbers of women, and if its mutual integration with justice considerations is not widely convincing, then the promotion of care ethics as a female ethic cannot help but reinvigorate stereotypes of women's incapacity to handle the moral challenges of public life.

Furthermore, care ethics might also undermine women's resolve to resist, say, violence or reproductive control by others, by appearing to endorse the *overridingness* of the moral duties to care, nurture, and maintain relationship with anyone with whom one comes into intimate contact, regardless of the moral quality of the relationship. Gilligan's focus on what she sees as the inclusiveness of the caring attitude suggests this unqualified orientation simply to maintaining connections with others.[33] A care ethic, in this respect, is vulnerable to Hoagland's objection that it morally nullifies some of the most effective strategies available to women for resistance to abuse, exploitation, and coercion, strategies such as withdrawal altogether from relationship.[34]

It is noteworthy that Gilligan's writings are not univocal on this point. In one passage, for example, she writes approvingly of a decision by "Sarah," a research subject, to end a heterosexual relationship that seemed to Sarah to reduce her to a "nonentity." Sarah resolves to leave the relationship in a way that does not compromise her own needs. For Gilligan, this example illustrates mature, postconventional care reasoning. Gilligan emphasizes, however, that Sarah strives to end the relationship "in a responsible way," still attentive to the needs of her soon-to-be former partner and seeking to minimize his hurt.[35] Sarah exhibits supposed mature care reasoning by departing caringly from the very partner in af-

33. For example, *In a Different Voice*, p. 160.
34. Hoagland, "Some Thoughts about 'Caring,' " p. 256. Nel Noddings explicitly rejects the appropriateness of withdrawal from a relationship as a response to someone else's wrongdoing; see "A Response," *Hypatia* 5 (Spring 1990): 124.
35. Gilligan, *In a Different Voice*, p. 95. I am grateful to Diana Meyers for bringing this passage to my attention.

filiation with whom she felt effaced.[36] Thus, although Gilligan's care perspective does permit withdrawal as one resolution for relationships that oppress women, the moral option of withdrawal as such is deemphasized and attention is refocused elsewhere. This brief reference by Gilligan to withdrawal from relationship, furthermore, contrasts with her characteristic formulation of a mature care ethic in terms of a recognition of *everyone's* need for care and a sense of personal responsibility for answering to that omnipresent need.[37]

Another way that care ethics fails to challenge the subordination of women is through its neglect of the wider sense of female community or collectivity that has been so crucial for feminist activism. The formulations of care ethics by Gilligan and Noddings tend to focus on dyadic relationships, relationships between two persons considered in isolation from any larger relational network. With the exception of Ruddick's work, care ethics usually fails to attend to the larger social context in which such relationships are embedded, the wider social networks or the communities at large.

Even those women who are comfortable with traditional heterosexual lives usually depend heavily, if not exclusively, on female relatives and friends for the practical advice and help, companionship, and emotional support that they need to cope with the minor and major relational challenges of daily life. Financial need and outright poverty, social marginalization, child rearing, domestic labor, the stresses and strains of marital and other sexually intimate relationships, illness, injury, bereavement, and the rest are borne more easily with support. Women have long been one anothers' primary supporters in such matters.[38] Female relational networks, so crucial for women, are radically underrepresented and underappreciated in our culture, a culture which, like most others, never-

36. "Reduced to a nonentity," are Sarah's own words, as quoted by Gilligan from her interviews with Sarah (ibid.).

37. Ibid., p. 100.

38. See Carroll Smith Rosenberg, "The Female World of Love and Ritual: Relations between Women in Nineteenth Century America," *Signs* 1, no. 1 (1975): 1–29.

theless depends profoundly on the labors of women who are sustained by such networks.[39] Care ethics unfortunately replicates this omission. Care ethics, in addition, ignores the sense of solidarity or commonality that most women share with at least some other women. It neglects those relationships among women that foster political consciousness and, thereby, enable some of them to resist the societal subordination of women and to work to improve the lot of women's lives on a broader scale.

One might say that the caring perspective as advanced by Gilligan and Noddings treats relationships *too individualistically*. Although human individuals are understood in terms of their relationships to other human individuals, those relationships themselves are abstracted from the wider social context of governmental, economic, and familial institutions and practices of which they are a part. "Atomistic" or abstractly isolated relationships are as much a theoretical misrepresentation as are atomistic (human) individuals. Removing relationships from their institutional settings obscures the way relationships are defined, structured, sustained, limited, and domesticated by those institutions and practices.

In light of the risks posed by promoting care ethics as a distinctively female ethic, we can retain the theory but work to modify its counterfeminist implications, or we can jettison the theory altogether and start anew. At the most general level, the key question is whether a female-associated care ethic in its current rudimentary state of development does more harm than good or more good than harm to the liberatory interests of diverse groups of women.

In light of how recently care ethics was articulated in moral theory—Gilligan's most famous statement of it was published in 1982, Nodding's in 1984, and Ruddick's book on maternal thinking in 1989—it seems premature to seek definitive answers to those questions now. A tentative compromise stance, however, is already available to us. In the previous chapter, I suggested that even if there is no gender gap between women and men in their moral perspectives, nevertheless, ethical theory should take account of

39. See the illuminating discussion of these networks in Adrienne Rich, "Compulsory Heterosexuality."

the different voice represented by care ethics. Recent moral theory has neglected the moral activities and experiences involved in caring and nurturing, both the caring by mature persons for those dependent on them[40] and the caring that can and should go on among morally competent adults. These themes are worth developing for contemporary moral theory even if care ethics is not a distinctively female moral orientation.

In addition, it may be premature to conclude that care ethics cannot expand to encompass such concerns as violence and oppression in personal relationships. As Card puts it, we need an understanding of "the capacity for love" that is "comparable in sophistication to Immanuel Kant's understanding of the capacity for acting on principle," an understanding that would illuminate the ways that "not every passionate attachment to persons is valuable" while still recognizing the ethical worth of those attachments that are valuable.[41] Thus, a conception of what we can call "enlightened care" should enable us to grasp that, in close personal relationships with morally competent adults, women deserve as much care and nurturing as we provide. Furthermore, enlightened care should enable women to discern appropriate ways to modify, refuse, or end those relationships that threaten to neglect our interests or to harm us. In the next section, I begin to explore the sorts of care that women, as care givers, should seek for ourselves.

2. CARE FOR WOMEN AS CARE GIVERS

A fully liberatory feminist ethic must legitimate a woman's care for herself and her pursuit of caring and nurturing from others. From the standpoint of care ethics, it is important to recognize that women, who are normally relied upon to provide the bulk of nur-

40. This way of emphasizing what is missing from modern moral theory is particularly prominent in the work of Sara Ruddick, *Maternal Thinking*; and Virginia Held, for example, in her "Non-Contractual Society," in Hanen and Nielsen, *Science, Morality, and Feminist Theory*, pp. 111–37.

41. "Gender and Moral Luck," p. 215. In Chapters 2 and 3, I explore some ways of distinguishing valuable from worthless close personal relationships.

turant care for others, are vulnerable in various ways. The forms of care that women need are not vouchsafed in the course of our caring for others. Even though women's caring for others sustains networks of interpersonal relationships, the existence of these relationships does not guarantee women's safety or equality of social status with men. Caring remains a risky business for women.

The care that can make a moral difference to a woman's life is roughly twofold. On the one hand, there is the kind of care involved in resisting our own devaluation, denigration, harassment, marginalization, exclusion, exploitation, subordination, domination, or openly violent abuse. Systematic attempts to overcome such harms may take the form of petitioning or pressuring societal institutions either to alter their own structures toward greater gender equity or to intercede more effectively on behalf of women in so-called private affairs, as in woman-battering cases. But rescue is not always available, and some of the problems in question arise out of social institutions and practices that are culturally sanctioned and widely tolerated. To protect ourselves, we as women must often rely on our own self-assertive efforts against oppressive practices. Thus, one major form of care for oneself concentrates on the variously necessary ways of protecting oneself against harm by others.

The second major category of care for self that a fully liberatory feminist ethic should offer involves positive flourishing, self-development that goes beyond merely resisting subordination or oppression. To be fully liberatory for women, such an ethic must develop ideals for a variety of personal achievements and excellences (other than those that center around self-protection). Care ethics does, of course, glorify the virtue of caring for and nurturing others. But this is not the only sort of human excellence that women can attain. Thus, a fully liberatory feminist ethic, with an eye toward the lives of women as typical care givers, should idealize forms of personal flourishing in addition to excellent care giving.[42]

42. I do not have in mind asocial concepts of human flourishing. In my view, no distinctively human excellence is possible apart from a human social context. The reference to excellences as "personal" indicates merely that the

The sort of care for oneself involved in flourishing is significantly different from the sort that concentrates on protecting oneself from harm. The familiar criticisms that the women's movement in the United States concentrates on the needs of middle-class, white women and ignores the needs of low-income women or women who are not white have much to do with this distinction. Many women in our culture lack access to the resources for forms of personal development that extend beyond self-protective and survival needs. To sue the Rotary Club for barring female applicants from membership is a different sort of feminist project from volunteering support services at a battered women's shelter.[43] Yet each is, in its own way, a quest by women to care for themselves and for some other women, a quest to surmount some facet of subordination or oppression facing some women and to live as well as conditions permit.[44] Both of these wide-ranging sorts of concerns, self-protection as well as personal flourishing, require moral anchorage in a notion of care for oneself.

On Nodding's formulation of care ethics, not much primary importance is attached to caring for oneself.[45] As Hoagland ob-

---

traits are ascribed to persons. In their origin, development, meaning, and manifestation, such traits are (I would argue) necessarily social.

43. I am not suggesting that domestic violence is a problem to which only low-income women or women of color are subject. The point is that low-income women, with few resources of their own and few alternative support systems available to them, are the ones who need special battered women's shelters to protect them from domestic violence. Women with more money can check into motels and, later, can afford to leave their abusive relationships.

44. As many feminist writers have emphasized, it is crucial that women with greater social privileges and advantages not presume that their experiences universally typify those of all women or exemplify woman's lot in life. It is also crucial that battles for the opportunities for (some) women's flourishing not be waged at the expense of other, less-advantaged women or articulated as if they were currently relevant for all women, or thought to be the only changes that women in general need in their lives. For an important philosophical discussion of how, in practice, to give due recognition to the cultural and ethnic differences among women, see Elizabeth V. Spelman, *Inessential Woman: Problems of Exclusion in Feminist Thought* (Boston: Beacon Press, 1988).

45. Noddings, *Caring*, p. 100.

serves,[46] the responsibility to care for oneself is derivative in Noddings's system; it derives from the responsibility to maintain one's capacity to care for others, a goal that requires staying in good, care-giving shape. Caring for oneself as such appears to have no intrinsic value.

Hoagland has noticed a unidirectional nature to Noddings's care ethics. Noddings explores what she herself calls "the logic of caring" as it flows from a care giver to one who is cared for. Someone in the role of care giver is not to seek or expect reciprocal care giving from the one for whom she cares. The only reciprocity that should be sought by the one who renders care is that of mere "recognition" by the recipient of the care.[47] In Noddings's view, the sole "major contribution" made by the care *recipient* to the relationship is a "willing and unselfconscious revealing of self."[48]

Such a conception of caring is inappropriate for intimate relationships among morally competent adults. On Hoagland's view, such unidirectional caring threatens to devolve into self-sacrificing care.[49] This problem arises whether or not the relationship between the adults is oppressive in any way. An oppressive relationship, however, worsens the problem. It is difficult to see how someone can strive to overcome oppressive conditions facing her unless, at the very least, she has begun to feel intrinsically entitled to care for herself and to demand reciprocal caring in return for the care she provides others.

Noddings has recently made it clear that her care ethic formulates a call for each person to foster caring relations in which the care giver is a recipient as well as a giver of care. No one is supposed to be "stuck" in a position of being one or the other.[50] Nevertheless, on Noddings's view, the relationship, and not the care giver, remains primary. Noddings has not yet explored, to the same depth or level of complexity as she has examined the attitude of caring for others, an adult care giver's own need for care. Con-

46. Hoagland, "Some Thoughts about 'Caring,' " p. 255.
47. Noddings, *Caring*, p. 71.
48. Ibid., p. 73.
49. Hoagland, "Some Thoughts about 'Caring,' " pp. 253–59.
50. Noddings, "A Response," p. 123.

trary to care giving, ensuring that one is well cared for by others does not appear to constitute a major moral problem for Noddings—not even under historical conditions of women's cultural subordination or other sorts of vulnerability. Noddings's recent clarification thus leaves caring and relationship as the central foci of care ethics while relegating the caring self to a status of only derivative importance. The risk of self-sacrifice remains present.

In Gilligan's formulation of care ethics, the threat that care might devolve into self-sacrifice is somewhat ameliorated. Gilligan regards self-sacrificing care as a manifestation of conventional femininity, a mode of behavior that is surmounted by the postconventional caring that at least some women manage to attain. Postconventional caring involves the recognition that self and other are equally deserving of care. In the school of developmental moral psychology out of which Gilligan's work initiated, postconventional moral reasoning of any sort is thought to be more morally adequate than conventional moral reasoning.[51] Gilligan's formulation of a mature caring perspective has the advantage, then, of making a woman's care for herself intrinsically valuable, and not valuable merely in so far as it derives from the responsibility to care for others or to foster caring relationships.

Gilligan's mature care ethic thus permits the care giver to grasp the legitimacy of including herself in the scope of her own caring. Gilligan's formulation, however, does not go far enough. Gilligan's mature, postconventional care ethic leads someone to "include herself among the people whom she considers it moral not to hurt" but does not afford the insight that she deserves to be cared for in return by those she loves.[52]

This is not, of course, to argue that there should be a quid pro quo accounting of services in personal relationships. Something is amiss, however, if a close personal relationship between morally competent adults lacks an overall approximate reciprocity in the

51. See Lawrence Kohlberg, *The Philosophy of Moral Development: Moral Stages and the Idea of Justice* (San Francisco: Harper & Row, 1981), e.g., pp. 147–73.

52. Gilligan, *In a Different Voice*, pp. 149, 165.

diverse ways of caring. This mutuality seems, on the face of it, to be a moral requirement for those morally competent persons who genuinely care for each other.[53] A care ethic such as Gilligan's, which does not illuminate caring as a mutual relationship, seems, in that respect, still to be incomplete. In close relationships among such morally competent adults, it is critical for a woman to avoid exploitation and to be nurtured herself by the relationship and by those for whom she cares.[54]

The gendered nature of our caretaking practices means that women are held accountable for continuing to provide care even under conditions in which women are mistreated by those for whom they care. The pressures on a woman to forgive and forget her injuries, to kiss and make up, for example, in those wife-battering cases that manage to reach family court, are infamous.[55] And it is in relationships with male peers, especially intimate relationships, that women have historically encountered substantial subordination and much of the abuse to which they are subject.

In Noddings's view, the perspective of caring calls upon us to

53. My generalization is intended to allow for exceptional cases; sometimes one partner is infirm or otherwise deeply needful of care and unable to reciprocate this care for a prolonged period of time. This notion introduces the concept of reciprocity into an understanding of care. Reciprocity is one of the formal features that define justice reasoning on a Kohlbergian model; see Kohlberg, *Philosophy of Moral Development*, pp. 147–67. Perhaps "mutuality" is a more appropriate term than "reciprocity" for the realm of personal interrelationships. "Reciprocity" suggests that specific actions are met with corresponding actions as repayments; "mutuality" suggests, in addition, the sharing of interests or concerns. "Mutuality" identifies a richer relationship than that of mere repayment for good turns rendered. Nevertheless, reciprocity is not irrelevant to personal relationships; it would seem to be a part, even though only a part, of what mutuality involves.

54. Ann Ferguson investigates the physical-social interaction that sustains human sexuality, parenting, family relationships, and other nurturant social relationships. She construes the sustaining interactions as a form of labor which, like the productive labor of the marketplace, may be exploited. The exploitation of women's sexual and caregiving labor is the system of male dominance; see her *Blood at the Root: Motherhood, Sexuality, and Male Dominance* (London: Pandora, 1989), pp. 7–8 and passim.

55. See Rhode, *Justice and Gender*, p. 239.

stop abuse and "nothing in the ethic of caring . . . disables" a woman from asserting that she will "not allow" it. Noddings also concedes that sometimes the need for self-protection might make "physical withdrawal" necessary. Physical withdrawal, however, is not the same thing as severance of the relationship, and Noddings opposes severance. Noddings's only other counsel to an abused woman is that she and her supporters "surround the abusive husband with loving models who would not tolerate abuse in their presence and would strongly disapprove of it whenever it occurred in their absence."[56] Aside from the difficulty a battered woman faces in orchestrating such a collective response, there is no reason why a care reasoner must settle for nothing more than "loving" moral persuasion when challenging men who beat up women. Care ethics, in my view, should begin by taking seriously the intrinsic worth of care-giving individuals (as well as that of individual care receivers) and the intrinsic value of whatever protects all of them from violence and violation.

Contemporary statements of care ethics figure prominently in the recent trend in moral theory to conceive of individuals as fundamentally social beings, relationally and communally defined. An ethics of care thus incorporates into its conception of personhood a much-needed recognition of the role of the social at the constitutive level of human identity and agency. Such an approach is a welcome challenge to those forms of individualism that treat only individual persons, abstracted from social connection, as the loci for moral agency and obligation. This virtue of care ethics is, however, also a source of one notable weakness. Care ethics neglects the well-being of individual persons to the extent that *it can* be conceptualized separately from that of other persons and the relationships with which the individual is nevertheless deeply intertwined.

My emphasis on the importance of caring for oneself and of being cared for in return by those for whom one cares introduces into care ethics an emphasis on self that is lacking in Noddings's formulation and that appears only in undeveloped form in Gilli-

56. Noddings, "A Response," p. 125.

gan's version. On the approach I am recommending, the self is still defined, at least in part, by her relationships. My approach, however, incorporates the recognition that the care-giving self is herself someone who needs care and that her needs as such make legitimate moral demands on those to whom she is close.

There is room in care ethics for a cautious strain of individualism, one that is consistent with a theoretical emphasis on interconnection and the social nature of persons. Responsibilities to care should not eclipse those features of the care giver that constitute her as an individual, nor should they obscure those dimensions of meaning in her life that are independent of her care-giving role. Subordination, exploitation, abuse, and oppression occur to individuals—individuals in relationships,[57] to be sure, but individuals nevertheless. Care ethics requires a notion of individuality (together with an adequate conception of human groups) in order to illuminate who is subordinated, who is oppressed, and why and how this occurs on a daily piecemeal basis.

A moral concept of individual personhood need not isolate the individual from social context and need not view individuals merely as mutually disinterested rational contractors. A person's needs and wants may well be social constructions arising out of relationships. Nevertheless, when a relatively mature person enters a new relationship, she brings with her needs and wants that were forged in the context of prior relationships. Such needs and wants give her an identity and a perspective that are, at the outset, independent of the new relationship. It is not inconsistent with an ontology of human relationships to recognize our relative independence of newcomers in our lives or to suppose that our preexistent needs and wants may remain stable and persistent through the vicissitudes of new relationships. This concept of relative mutual independence (on the parts of relatively mature adults) may be of special relevance to women entering relationships that threaten to subordinate or engulf them. Thus, the notion of caring for oneself is

57. For an in-depth development of the ontology and morality of individuals in relationships outside the context of care ethics, see Larry May, *The Morality of Groups* (Notre Dame, Ind.: University of Notre Dame Press, 1987).

a conceptual hybrid, exemplifying both relationality and individuality.

More so than Noddings and Gilligan, then, I construe the needs, wants, hopes, fears, and so forth of the care-giving self as legitimately helping to set the moral agenda for her relationships with other adults. The caring self, in such relationships, should care for herself and should expect her loved ones to reciprocate the care that she provides for them to the extent that they are able to do so. Self-assertion is not inimical to caring but, rather, helps to ensure that caring is mutual and undefiled by subordination of the care-giver.

In the next section, I turn to a different problem raised by actual caring practices. These practices impose greater responsibilities for care giving on women than on men and call for greater personal sacrifices by women in the provision of that care. A sufficiently liberatory care ethic should presume at the outset that these gender differences are morally unacceptable.

3. WOMEN WHO DON'T . . . CARE

Bernard Williams, in developing his conception of moral luck, offers a provocative discussion of how it might, in retrospect, be justified to have abandoned one's caretaking responsibilities to one's close family members.[58] His discussion provides a useful backdrop for exploring the full social significance of women's caretaking roles.

Williams's discussion of moral luck pertains to a theoretical matter not directly relevant to our present concern. Williams was seeking to challenge a background assumption of modern ethical theory, namely, that one's morally significant choices are either justified or not depending only on one's intentions and on other

58. Bernard Williams, "Moral Luck," in his *Moral Luck* (Cambridge: Cambridge University Press, 1981), pp. 20–39. This example was discussed in Chapter 3 to show the limitation it exposes in Williams's commitment to partiality toward beloved wives. On the general relevance of Williams's notion of moral luck to matters of gender and morality, see Card, "Gender and Moral Luck."

matters that are, in some sense, under one's control. Williams argues, contrary to this, that the actual outcomes of one's actions and projects—whether or not they are successful—also matter for the justification of one's choices. Such a view makes justification depend on factors beyond one's control and, from the agent's standpoint, makes justification a function of luck.

Although the notion of moral luck is paradoxical from the perspective of modern ethical theories, nevertheless, our daily moral (and legal) practices of holding people responsible for their actions do incorporate considerations of the (lucky or unlucky) outcomes of those actions. An actual murder, for example, is legally treated as a more serious offense than an unsuccessful attempt. Outcomes are partly determined by the nature of the situations that one faces, the circumstances that are not fully known, foreseen, or predictable (what Williams calls "incident" moral luck), and partly by the kind of person one is, one's abilities and temperament (what Williams calls "constitutive" moral luck).

Williams originally discussed incident moral luck in relation to moral dilemmas, situations in which one must unavoidably do harm in order to attain some good; his concern was with the justification for doing such harm. The famous quasi-hypothetical case study explored by Williams involved a man who turned away "from definite and pressing human claims on him" in order to be an artist and who later produced works of singular artistic merit.[59] The historical Gauguin is the model for Williams's study. Paul Gauguin deserted his wife and five children and embarked on a style of life which was to involve sojourns across France, close contact with other young artists of the day, and travels to the exotic islands of Martinique and Tahiti in search of artistic inspiration.[60] Gauguin, in other words, abandoned those persons for whose care he was most of all responsible, his five children among them, in order to paint pictures.

59. Williams, *Moral Luck*, p. 22. In the ensuing discussion, I consider artwork to be a metaphor for any project other than caring for one's intimates and for the sake of which one might abandon those care-giving responsibilities.

60. See Yann le Pichon, *Gauguin: Life, Art, Inspiration* (New York: Harry N. Abrams, 1987).

Williams encourages us to regard the (lucky) achievement of great art as an outcome that sufficiently justifies a man's forsaking the "definite and pressing human claims" of his wife and children.[61] Williams is subtle enough to sense the complexity that characterizes justification in such a case. Those who have been harmed by the artist do continue to have justified complaints against him, in Williams's estimation, and are not bound to regard the artist's choice as justified.[62] By contrast, Williams, who was *not* harmed by the artist, does consider that the success of Gauguin's project justifies the injury to Gauguin's family. After all, it is the sort of project, in Williams's estimation, that "can yield a good for the world."[63]

61. Williams's discussion evokes what Linda Nochlin has disparagingly called the "myth of the Great Artist—subject of a hundred monographs, unique, godlike—bearing within his person since birth a mysterious essence, rather like the golden nugget in Mrs. Grass's chicken soup, called Genius or Talent, which, like murder, must always out, no matter how unlikely or unpromising the circumstances." See her "Why Have There Been No Great Women Artists?" (originally published in 1971), in her *Women, Art, and Power* (New York: Harper & Row, 1988), p. 153. Nochlin recounts the way this conception of "the apparently miraculous, nondetermined, and asocial nature of artistic achievement" was "elevated to hagiography in the nineteenth century," as art historians and critics came to view the artist as someone who "struggles against the most determined parental and social opposition [those 'pressing human claims'], suffering the slings and arrows of social opprobrium like any Christian martyr, and ultimately succeeds against all odds . . . because deep within himself radiates that mysterious, holy effulgence: Genius" (p. 155). Williams's illustration of moral luck evokes this romantic notion of artistic talent.

62. Williams, *Moral Luck*, p. 37.

63. Ibid., p. 37. This justification sounds a surprisingly utilitarian note in Williams's writings. Tangentially, we might also note that the notion of justification becomes extraordinarily complex on the supposition that distinct standpoints might warrant mutually contradictory judgments and attitudes. To speak, then, of justification in a sense that is independent of standpoint requires either the sort of omniauthoritative impartial standpoint that Williams himself rejects (see ibid., "Persons, Character and Morality," pp. 1–19), or it requires identifying certain sorts of partial standpoints as morally more authoritative than others—a suspect theoretical maneuver. (From what standpoint would the ranking itself be justified?)

Williams does not clarify just how good the resultant art must be in order to justify the desertion of wife and children. If it is only works of the canonical stature of Gauguin's paintings that justify the abandonment of pressing human claims, then Williams's notion of justification in virtue of the luck of great subsequent accomplishment becomes a mere theoretical curiosity in ethics, having virtually no commonplace moral relevance. Only a few individuals in any generation would ever have such prodigious moral luck—although many more might be willing to sacrifice the welfare of their loved ones in the hope of attaining it. Williams's discussion, on that interpretation, has little practical relevance for people in general.

On the other hand, if one need not attain the rank of the Great Masters but need merely attain a more accessible level of excellence in one's subsequent accomplishments in order to justify abandoning one's loved ones, then Williams's notion has wide relevance for people of more ordinary talents. They need merely have some ambition and a willingness to shirk their own responsibility for the "pressing human claims" that weigh upon them.

If Williams's example is to constitute a moral examplar of the sort of justification he has in mind, then it is a troubling example for several reasons. First, the moral risk undertaken by the would-be artist imposes definite costs on those human beings whose pressing claims are thereby abandoned. In terms of a care ethic, the pressing human claims forsaken by Williams's artist were precisely those of close family relations for whose care the artist was responsible. For these persons, there is no risk of good or bad luck but rather a near certainty of suffering and, possibly, of tragedy. (Gauguin's wife was able to ameliorate her family's hardship by obtaining financial support from her own family of origin,[64] but the average mother who is abandoned with five dependent children is not so comfortably situated.)

Second, a would-be artist may never personally have to acknowledge the possible failure of his artistic endeavor or accept final responsibility for abandoning his loved ones. So long as the artist manages to eke out a living, he can sustain a life centered

64. Le Pichon, *Gauguin,* p. 25.

around the production of his art. Even if the artist does not find artistic acclaim in his lifetime, the continuing absence of great success or reward need not reveal the artistry to be mediocre, the project to have failed. After all, many historically revered artists achieved their acclaimed reputations only posthumously, following a lifetime's neglect, even ridicule, of their works. Conversely, success during the artist's lifetime can also be ephemeral and inconclusive; it does not always foreshadow enduring artistic repute.

The artist may, thus, endlessly defer a final accounting, a final assessment of the overall (moral as well as artistic) justifiability of his abandonment of wife and children. Only history will render the final accounting, and, by the time it does so, the artist, the wife, and the children will all be dead. No moral rectification will then be possible for the failure of artistic ambition. The artist can, thus, in a kind of perpetual moral adolescence, endlessly defer coming to terms with the ethical significance of his life.[65]

The two problems raised above are not specifically feminist in perspective. In turning to my more specifically feminist concern, I may seem to be reversing my attitude toward Williams's notion of incident moral luck. Having just pointed out some moral problems with it, I may seem now to be endorsing it by arguing that it should simply be extended to women. This is not my view. Let us proceed cautiously, then, for the terrain is uncertain.

The third problem with Williams's example is that the different genders have very unequal access to the sort of moral luck Williams describes. On the one hand, the success of artistry depends on more than mere talent; it also depends on how others respond to one's art. Such responses are "intrinsic," in Williams's term, to the success of the project.[66] Great art is, in important ways, a social construction; art critics and historians, art dealers and investors,

---

65. Williams fails to consider the fads and fancies of critical veneration or neglect that often delay the final accounting of artwork beyond an artist's own lifetime. This feature of art criticism and of other forms of cultural assessment complicates Williams's reflections on how a moral-risk-taking life might be assessed in retrospect from the (still-living) standpoint of the risk taker: ibid., pp. 34–37.

66. Ibid., p. 36.

the public at large, and other artists enable the production of great art and constitute its greatness in part through their reactions to it. (Can a painting be genuinely great if it does not profoundly stir other human beings?) In their readiness to view, purchase, display, emulate, find significance in, and derive creative inspiration from an artist's work, the people of a culture constitute the historical greatness of that work and of that person as a would-be great artist.

Careful assessment of Williams's quasi-hypothetical example and its full significance for matters of gender and moral theory calls for a brief digression, an excursion into some art history. Though limited to the field of pictorial art, this history is typical of a vast and pervasive problem, one that has yet to be entirely solved.

Until recently, no women achieved the enduring artistic acclaim afforded to some men. Linda Nochlin argues that the reason for this difference "lies not in the nature of [women's] individual genius or the lack of it, but in the nature of given social institutions and what they forbid or encourage in various classes or groups of individuals."[67] From the time of their inception in the late sixteenth century until the late nineteenth century, British and European art academies barred women from life-drawing classes (except as models) and, thus, from critically important formal training in drawing the nude. Until the twentieth century, this deprivation alone virtually precluded women from creating major works of art by consigning women "to the 'minor' fields of portraiture, genre, landscape, or still life."[68] In nineteenth-century France, where a surprising one-third of all artists were female, women were, nevertheless, not admitted to the Ecole des Beaux Arts until the end of the century, by which time the academic system had lost importance.[69] As late as the mid-nineteenth century, in addition, to attain any success as a painter, a woman required, without exception, the moral good luck of having been born to and raised by an artist father.[70]

67. Nochlin, *Women, Art, and Power*, p. 158.
68. Ibid., pp. 159–60.
69. Ibid., pp. 162–63.
70. Ibid., p. 169. The moral luck of personal origins—the kinds of caretakers one has, their degree of wealth or poverty, etc.—does not fit either of

Most cultures, furthermore, have not been sanguine about the possibility that a *woman's* subsequent art or other public achievement could justify her abandonment of the pressing claims of husband and children. In Europe, the nineteenth century witnessed the birth of the image of the "lady painter," someone who was permitted to be a proficient amateur but whose artistry would not interfere with the major caring work for husband and children that she was expected, on all sides, to undertake.[71] To attempt to be an artist, a woman had to defy all these restrictions and suffer grave personal costs. Barred from formal study of the human nude, for example, the nineteenth-century French painter Rosa Bonheur turned to livestock: "at a certain period," she once wrote, "I spent whole days in the slaughterhouses. Indeed, you have to love your art in order to live in pools of blood."[72]

Contemporary American culture is nearly unanimous in condemning a mother who turns away from familial responsibilities, no matter what she does afterward, while at the same time entertaining the possible justification of a father's similar desertion. Indeed, abandoning fathers often do not have to produce great art (or anything else great) at all in order, nevertheless, to win sympathy, even approval, for abandoning their families. The flight of men from familial responsibilities has long been a tolerated motif of American fiction.[73] In addition, as Barbara Ehrenreich contends, this theme began to attain great cultural prominence in the 1950s with the advent of several major trends.[74] One was the rise of the

---

Williams's categories; it is not incidental moral luck, nor is it, in itself, constitutive moral luck, although it has a great bearing on the development of character and talents.

71. Ibid., p. 164.

72. Quoted in ibid., p. 174.

73. See Judith Fetterley, *The Resisting Reader: A Feminist Approach to American Fiction*, Bloomington: Indiana University Press, 1978, esp. pp. 1–12.

74. Barbara Ehrenreich, *The Hearts of Men: American Dreams and the Flight from Commitment* (New York: Anchor Press/Doubleday, 1983), esp. chaps. 4 and 5. Ehrenreich suggests that the masculine-oriented trends of the 1950s did more to promote the current breakdown of "the" American family than anything the feminist movement is accused of perpetrating. She contrasts this period with earlier decades of the twentieth century in the United States, during

beat generation, which made a virtue out of cutting domestic ties and hitting the road. Another trend was the proliferation of what can be called "coffee table pornography," particularly *Playboy* magazine, which glamorized a model of male sexuality utterly devoid of marital or familial commitment.[75]

Thus, women and men have had radically different degrees of access to the artistic and other successes that can, on Williams's view, justify their having foresaken the pressing moral claims of those for whom they are supposed to care. It is a woman's moral luck to be expected by our culture to devote herself to the care of her family even at substantial personal cost to herself. In the case of a woman who deserts husband and children altogether, the justificatory stakes are raised appreciably.

Gauguin once wrote that "one man's faculties can't cope with two things at once, and I for one can do *one thing only:* paint. Everything else leaves me stupefied."[76] The woman who deserts her husband and children because caring for them left her "stupefied" can expect condemnation, no matter how great her subsequent achievements. Unlike Gauguin, she will not be canonized; she would be lucky to be remembered.

For all we know, of course, Williams himself might willingly accept a revision in his example, a female artist who takes the moral risk of abandoning husband and five children to pursue her art. The gender configuration of Williams's original example, however, remains an apt illustration of a widespread and gender-asymmetric cultural attitude. In those cases in which the meaning or success of our projects lies in awakening certain receptive attitudes in others, what Williams calls "moral luck" discloses a form of social control that we exercise over the outcomes of one another's project—a control that is deployed differently across lines of gender.

Claudia Card has investigated the way our genders determine the sorts of virtues open or closed to us in a hierarchical gender

---

which the adult male role of breadwinner supporting wife and children was much more widely honored; see chap. 2.

75. Ibid., chap. 4.
76. Le Pichon, *Gauguin,* p. 26.

system.[77] Furthermore, we might add, they determine how much weight our projects will have when weighed in the balance, and they determine how much gravity will be assigned to the familial obligations over against which these projects are set.

Why do we have such difficulty forgiving women for deserting their families for the sake of art or other projects of singular achievement while tolerating men who do so for lesser reasons? The feminist aim of equality for women has never sought the opportunity for women to be as villainous as men have been permitted to be. Still, it challenges moral thinking to say why, if women are to attain cultural and moral equality with men, they should be denied the moral excuses that men are permitted to use. Of course, one can always argue that men should not be so readily forgiven for their excuses, that feminist equality entails holding men to as high a moral standard as women. But what are the practical implications of such a view? Gauguin will hardly be dethroned; his artistic acclaim will not be rescinded. His cultural eminence remains an exemplar of what men—but not women, it seems—can attain who free themselves from the pressing human claims of their dependent families, those for whom they are supposed to care.

Our cultural practices hold mothers to a higher standard of accountability than fathers for the nurturant and attentive day-to-day labor of child care. Part of what this difference means in its full significance is exemplified by the justifiability that Williams finds in Gauguin's desertion of his family. What moral conception will sustain this gendered moral differentiation? What moral notions would undergird the view that the responsibilities for care, especially for dependents, fall more heavily on women than on men? Perhaps we fear that if women stop caring for children and the infirm, then *no one* will care for them. However realistic this observation may be, it yields a strategy of practical compromise but not a moral insight.

Care giving, especially when women's caretaking labors are in question, is not usually construed as a constraint but rather as a moral opportunity and a personally fulfilling venture. It is some-

77. Card, "Gender and Moral Luck," passim.

times thought sacrilegious, toward motherhood in particular, to contest this view. One sure way to derogate feminism is to portray it, contrary to its most representative formulations, as a theory that recommends that women abandon their familial responsibilities.[78] In these antifeminist maneuvers, the notion of profound responsibilities toward children, with which most of us would agree wholeheartedly, are used as an umbrella to shield other relationships of female care giving, especially those toward husbands, from careful scrutiny. Besides misrepresenting feminism, such positions seem to presume without argument that traditional conceptions of women's overriding caretaking responsibilities are virtually unassailable, no matter what the circumstances are.

How will a gender difference in caretaking responsibilities be handled by a care ethic? (Notice that this is not to ask how a gender difference in actual caretaking practices can be *explained*.)[79] Most recent moral philosophy aspires to gender neutrality. Contemporary ethics does not offer theoretical resources to sustain a differentiation of moral duties grounded in gender per se. In this respect, academic ethics diverges radically from popular morality, which features distinct gender differentiations. The gender-differentiated standards of care giving responsibility in close personal relationships are but one example of gender differences in the popular morality of care. Even in the workplace, typically female occupations are more likely than typically male occupations to call for friendly behaviors and pleasing attitudes toward those who are

78. Christina Hoff Sommers, "Philosophers against the Family," in George Graham and Hugh LaFollette, eds., *Person to Person* [Philadelphia: Temple University Press, 1989], pp. 82–105) portrays feminists, along with contractarians, as showing a "hostility to family morality" (p. 83) and contributing to the growing divorce rate. Sommers's main argument against divorce is that children are hurt by it (pp. 98–102), an argument that, in the context of Sommers's paper, preposterously suggests that feminists are unconcerned about the welfare of children.

79. The most familiar explanation is to be found in the work of Nancy Chodorow (*The Reproduction of Mothering* [Berkeley: University of California Press, 1978]), who offers an account of differences in female and male personalities which would explain why women, more than men, identify themselves in relational terms and seek nurturant affiliation with others.

served by the occupations in question.[80] What is it that so appalls or frightens us in women who do not care, who do not nurture us or greet us with a ready smile?

Can tradition per se constitute the rationale for gender-differentiated caretaking roles? If so, changes in tradition or legitimate moral criticisms of those traditional practices will undermine their moral authority and that of the corresponding gender differentiation.[81] Can utility be the rationale, that is, the sheer utilitarian value of the traditional practices and not their status as tradition? If so, changing circumstances, the economic transformations of our times, for example, may readily upset the relevant calculations and call for altogether new, possibly nongendered, arrangements. The notion of universalizability does not offer much help, nor do those of virtue or human flourishing, unless essentialist gendered natures are tacitly, question-beggingly assumed in specifying what is to be universalized or what is to count as a virtue.

It seems that not only care ethics but also moral theory as a whole still owe an accounting of the moral difference that gender makes in determining moral responsibilities—or, failing such an account, a critique of popular morality for its continued gender-based, moral differentiation.

4. INSTRUMENTAL CARE AND SOCIAL EMPOWERMENT

Care ethics attracts the attention of feminist philosophers because it appears to introduce typically female moral concerns into moral theory. This view of the importance of care ethics reflects an assumption that women do the bulk of caring work in our culture, a view I took for granted in the foregoing discussion. Common experience appears to support this assumption. Women, it seems, are still the primary caretakers for infants and young

80. See Arlie Hochschild, *The Managed Heart: The Commercialization of Human Feeling* (Berkeley: University of California Press, 1983).

81. See Chapter 9 below for a critique of certain communitarian writings and their inadequate treatment of the cultural traditions surrounding women's caretaking roles in marriage and family.

children as well as for elderly and infirm persons, whether non-professionally for their own family members or professionally in the capacity of child-care workers, nurses, and so forth. Women still find themselves defined in terms of their intimate relationships; witness the continued use of "Miss" and "Mrs."

Women are still widely expected to need and desire relationships in which they will be primary carers for others, particularly for husbands and children. It continues to be assumed without question that women who do not have such caring responsibilities have failed to find fulfillment in their lives.[82] In addition, the prospect of living a life devoid of family relationships is used as a threat to scare women away from challenging the traditional patriarchal family.[83] The underlying presumption of such threats is that women are desperate for marriage and babies regardless of the costs. Such threats are seldom made to men who avoid or criticize the institutions of marriage and family. Caring, it seems, is *the* presumptive domain of women. Or is it?

We care about and for others in various ways. To care *about* someone is to take an interest in her, be concerned about her, have regard for her. To care *for* someone is to protect her and attend to her needs, to take responsibility for her well-being, perhaps by providing material sustenance or emotional support and nurturance. Care may involve feelings of affection and solicitude for someone, as well as respect and esteem. Protecting someone may include watching over her, defending her against dangers, and tending to her wounds and infirmities. Care may also include formal guardianship, involving custody and managerial control.

82. For a wide-ranging survey of various contemporary media and the endless ways they promote this assumption, see Susan Faludi, *Backlash: The Undeclared War against American Women* (New York: Crown, 1991), e.g., chap. 2, "Man Shortages and Barren Wombs: The Myths of the Backlash."

83. Christina Hoff Sommers, for example, warns that those who avoid or divorce themselves from the patriarchal family "often" suffer harm and "might" feel "betrayed by the ideology" that led them to this state: "Feminist Philosophers Are Oddly Unsympathetic to the Women They Claim to Represent," *Chronicle of Higher Education*, October 11, 1989, p. B3. These veiled threats are unexplained and unsupported.

The ways of caring are diverse. When we consider the wide variety of modes of caring, it becomes clear that much of the positive support that men provide to their intimates, the traditional breadwinning, for example, also falls under the rubric of care. In addition to earning income support for the family, the traditional husband and father may fix the car or the plumbing when it needs repair, do most of the tedious driving on long trips, undertake home carpentry projects, and, weapon in hand, venture forth to investigate suspicious nighttime noises in the home. From these examples, it begins to appear that women have no society-wide monopoly over caring practices.

On the one hand, this insight is good news; men indeed are capable of the practices and moral orientations of care. On the other hand, this insight obscures the distinctive nature of the care that men provide. Most important, I contend, the sort of care men typically provide for women manifests, consolidates, and perpetuates male power with respect to women. In heterosexual relationships, men do reciprocate the care that women provide, but in forms that preserve their dominant and privileged social positions.

Francesca Cancian's exploration of typical female and male patterns of loving in the context of heterosexual relationships helps to illuminate a wide-ranging and complex conception of care and the way its practice by both women and men promotes female subordination.[84] Speaking of love, Cancian differentiates expressive from instrumental forms. Expressive love has to do with intimate self-disclosure and the expression of feelings. Instrumental love pertains to protection and material forms of help. In the context of adult heterosexual relationships, argues Cancian, women tend to prefer and to be more skillful than men at expressive love while instrumental forms of love appear to be more distinctively the domain of men.[85]

84. Francesca M. Cancian, "The Feminization of Love," *Signs* (Summer 1986): 692–709.

85. Ibid., pp. 692–96, 699–705. Male philosophers who defend partiality tend to exhibit a preference, in their discussions, for illustrations of love or care of the instrumental variety, especially those that exhibit the resources or prowess of the care giver. Their most common examples of defensible partiality

The gentleness, tenderness, emotional revelation, and talka-tiveness of expressive love are sterotyped as feminine in our cul-ture. In Cancian's view, "both contemporary scholarship and public opinion" are dominated by a definition of love that tends to treat these modes of interaction as paradigmatic of love per se.[86] By contrast, instrumental ways of loving are not widely recognized as love. Cancian refers to this interrelated complex of ideas as the "feminization of love." Women are, accordingly, regarded as better at loving than men, a view that is bolstered by psychological studies following the works of Gilligan and of Nancy Chodorow which treat love and attachment thus feminized as fundamental to wom-en's personalities in ways not typical of men.[87]

Cancian challenges the feminization of love. In her view, it works to devalue and exploit women. Among other problems, it reinforces an ideology of separate spheres by continuing to ster-eotype female and male modes of intimate interrelationship along a conventional expressive-instrumental dichotomy. In Cancian's view, these stereotypes obscure the way (men's) helping behaviors are genuinely loving and they obscure the fact that women, too, provide instrumental forms of support to their loved ones.[88]

Most intriguing, Cancian observes that, in the context of het-erosexual relationships, the differences between women's and men's typical ways of loving put women at a relative social dis-advantage. In part, this is because men's instrumental ways of loving "reinforce men's power over women." Much of what men do as love "involves giving women important resources, such as money and protection that men control and women believe they need." Cancian states that women control resources on which men depend. This reliance, however, is not widely grasped as a form of dependency; being covert and unrecognized, it does not result

---

are those of saving a loved one, rather than a stranger, who is in danger and of providing financial and material resources to a loved one rather than to a stranger; see my discussion of this literature in Chapter 2.

86. Ibid., pp. 694–95.

87. Gilligan, *In a Different Voice;* Chodorow, *Reproduction of Mothering;* see Cancian's discussion of this literature: "Feminization of Love," p. 696.

88. Cancian, "Feminization of Love," pp. 705–8.

in empowering women.[89] In addition, the "intimate talk about personal troubles that appeals to women" requires or manifests "vulnerability, a willingness to see oneself as weak and in need of support." Thus, the expressive forms of women's love "involve admitting dependency and sharing or losing control."[90]

Women, too, provide instrumental love for others; cooking and doing laundry are common examples. Cancian argues, however, that because love is conceptualized in terms of its expressive manifestations, these activities are not viewed as love. The result is to ignore women's instrumentality. Since our culture "glorifies instrumental achievement," the net effect is that love is devalued for not being instrumental and women are accordingly devalued for their preoccupation with (supposedly noninstrumental) love.[91]

Cancian's suggestion that women's instrumental behavior toward loved ones is not viewed as love by our culture is puzzling. If instrumental achievement per se is highly valued in our society, then it would be valued wherever it were to be found, whether done by women or men, whether labeled as "love" or not. Upon more careful inspection, it appears that women's instrumental efforts for the sake of love are indeed often recognized as love. Women used to be routinely advised that the way to a man's heart is through his stomach; and, as the old Pillsbury commercial put it, "nothin' says lovin' like somethin' from the oven." The problem, it seems to me, is not that our culture fails to grasp women's instrumental support as love. Rather, the problem is that women's traditional caretaking instrumentalities are *ranked lower* than those of men, laundry and housecleaning, for example, as compared to, say, home carpentry and auto repair. More on this below.

Cancian's conclusion is to call for what she (qualifiedly) refers to as an androgynous conception of love.[92] Her analysis, outlined above, supports this call with two major overall observations. The important point about women is that, in loving relationships, they

89. Ibid., pp. 705–6; Cancian does not specify the resources controlled by women.
90. Ibid., p. 706.
91. Ibid.
92. Ibid., pp. 692, 708–9.

actually provide both expressive interaction and instrumental assistance. The important point about men, however, is not that they provide both expressive and instrumental love. Rather, the instrumental help that men provide, in Cancian's view, should be seen as genuinely loving, contrary to the feminized conception of love.

Overall, Cancian's observations suggest that the bulk of what men provide to women in loving relationships is instrumental help, whereas instrumental help is a part, but only a part and perhaps the lesser share, of what women provide to men. These combined revelations appear to suggest that men provide women with more instrumental love than they receive from women in return. If women's labors of love are already socially devalued relative to whatever it is that men are thought to do, then Cancian's recommendation will not help to correct that imbalance. Given our culture's esteem for instrumental achievement, the net result of recognizing that instrumental love is genuinely love would be to raise esteem somewhat for women's ways of loving, but to raise esteem for men's ways of loving even more. It seems that the mere alteration of our view of love to admit instrumentality will do little by itself to prevent the devaluation of women.

Despite this drawback, some features of Cancian's analysis seem right. There are varied ways of loving, and protection and material help should count among them as well as emotional expressiveness and intimate self-disclosure. A class bias, as Cancian suggests, may well lie behind the tendency to omit instrumental help from the contemporary conception of love as emotional intimacy; "poorer people [women as well as men] are more likely [than affluent people] to see practical help and financial assistance as a sign of love."[93] Applied to the larger domain of caring connections, of which heterosexual love relationships are but one example, this insight seems even more plausible. Instrumental ways of caretaking, such as feeding or sheltering someone and protecting her from harm, are obviously of critical importance in care overall. It may well be true that "man" does not live by bread alone; still less will an infant survive on her caretaker's emotional expressiveness

93. Ibid., p. 695; also see p. 704.

alone, however critical it may be for her later psychological maturation.

Cancian's concept of instrumental love bears further exploration. She has discerned that instrumental love is more socially powerful than expressive love in virtue of manifesting, consolidating, and perpetuating greater control of social resources, privileges, and status. Cancian does not appear to notice that there are power differences among the various forms of instrumental assistance. Although Cancian ranks preparing meals as instrumental, this form of assistance, especially on a routine daily basis, is, in important respects, far less powerful than, say, fixing someone's car.

One important difference among forms of instrumental care has to do with the extent to which the activity is governed by the desires and tastes, the subjective viewpoint, of the recipient of the care. The subjective viewpoint of the recipient may play a major, minor, or nonexistent role in determining the details, even the overall aim, of what the caretaker does. The difference is one of relative autonomy in the rendering of care. In a culture obsessed with autonomy and self-reliance, it seems that a great dependence on the desires, the mere whims, of the recipient of care reduces the status of the care rendered and the corresponding power of the care giver.

Consider the difference between fixing someone's car and feeding her. Fixing someone's car depends on relatively independent standards of car functioning, the principles of auto mechanics. The person whose car I fix may be entirely ignorant of those principles, even while the help I render her and on which she thereby depends is governed by (my apprehension of) them. Her desires and tastes will have relatively little to do with how I help her. As the person with greater car expertise, I will have substantial control over the assistance I render; my judgment, in the main, will ground what I decide to do and will determine whether or not I have done it well. I will not have to please her or cater to her tastes; my aim is to get her car running again.

Providing food for someone who is old enough to express her eating preferences is an altogether different matter. This sort of instrumental care is supposed to be especially attendant on the expressed desires of the one being cared for. It is true that independent standards of both culinary arts and good nutrition do apply to food preparation. A mother cooking for her family, for example, must master numerous cooking techniques and is not supposed to feed her children only junk food. A gourmet cook may become relatively autonomous in her gastronomic caretaking activity. Nevertheless, in the realm of everyday cooking, the mother who keeps serving the tuna casserole that her family detests, however nutritious or well prepared it is, does not earn wide esteem as a cook and will seem a bit cranky, to boot. Even a gourmet cook will not be a successful care giver if her exotic creations displease her family's palates.

At the extreme end, caretaking that is driven largely by the expressed desires and tastes, the very whims, of those who are cared for, devolves into servility. Servile behavior has never been much respected, either by philosophers or by people in general. Women's traditional forms of instrumental caring for husbands include numerous activities in which she is supposed to defer to his preferences, from what she cooks to how she looks. The more deferential the caretaking is supposed to be, deferential to the subjective viewpoint of the one cared for, the less autonomous is the caretaker and the less powerful she becomes with respect to the recipient of her care.

Another key to the social ranking of forms of instrumental care is the extent of the formal training that is publicly recognized as required to perform the care in question. Income-producing labors in the marketplace, traditionally assigned as the primary caretaking responsibility of men with families, usually require either formal education or special on-the-job training. Although much of women's traditional domestic work also requires training (e.g., cooking), nevertheless, many domestic chores (e.g., laundering clothes, cleaning house) are widely regarded as menial forms of labor needing little or no special instruction.

Sometimes, the facility and preparation required to perform women's traditional care-giving labor is quite high but, for various reasons, it goes unacknowledged. Most girls in our culture have engaged extensively in forms of socialization that prepare them to care for children, typically, playing with dolls, playing house, babysitting, and caring for younger siblings under maternal supervision. This training goes on in the private realm, however, and is not publicly recognized as training; it is simply child's "play." In addition, the educative role of this girlhood socialization has been effectively eclipsed by the concept of a "maternal instinct." Thus, the undeniably advanced level of proficiency engaged by child care and the training required to attain it are masked by a cultural stereotype that treats the adult competence in question as a spontaneous and innate propensity.

Protection against external dangers and enemies is another culturally revered form of instrumental caretaking. In our society, it seems that men do most of the physical dirty work of defending against "enemies" and contending with dangers, whether prowlers in the stairwell, rodents in the cellar, or storms on the horizon.[94] Contemporary films elevate the man furiously avenging his wife's rape to the status of cultural demigod. To be able to protect someone is a powerful stance with respect to her. It manifests one's greater capacity for discerning and guarding against danger, one's greater strength and cunning for fighting enemies. Protectiveness may carry with it the privilege of managing the affairs of the protected one, even to the point of dictating what she must do "for her own good." Displays of superior strength or practical intelli-

---

94. Protecting women against sexual violence by other men is also a traditional form of protective care men render to women in heterosexual relationships. Feminists, however, have discerned disturbing complications in this form of care. It is a form of protection that arises when sexual violence by some men drives women into the arms of other men. Many heterosexual men thus benefit from sexual violence by some among them. The unsettling result is to give most heterosexual men a kind of stake in the societal perpetuation of male sexual violence against women. (That stake obviously does not impute the conscious desires or motives of any particular man.) At any rate, my aim in this chapter is not to uncover either covert or unconscious hypocrisy at the heart of men's care-giving practices but, rather, to show how men's *genuine and sincere* forms of traditional care giving nevertheless subordinate women. Thus, I avoid delving into the complicated topic of men protecting women from sexual violence by other men.

gence consolidate greater relative social status. To save a damsel in distress is, after all, to be a hero, an achievement with clear masculine connotations.

Thus, both women and men provide care for others and, in heterosexual relationships, for each other. As Cancian has illuminated, both women and men provide instrumental forms of care, having to do with food, clothing, shelter, protection, and the other material bases of life. The forms of instrumental care that men typically provide, however, reflect and promote their more powerful social positions. The particular forms of instrumental care that a man traditionally renders, in the context of heterosexual relations and family life, manifest and promote his autonomy and expertise. In return, a woman provides her male partner with both expressive care and forms of instrumental care that tend to subordinate her activities to his desires. The overall effect of this exchange of care is to reinforce his, but not her, independent personhood. The consequence is a promotion of women's continued subordination to men, even in the domain of genuinely mutual care.

To subvert this caretaking hierarchy, we could challenge it along at least three different lines. We could call for a more equitable distribution of instrumental (and expressive) caretaking labor between women and men. Or we could try to show that women's expressive and instrumental forms of caring are really more powerful (more autonomous, expertise-based, or physically protective) than is commonly thought. Or we could challenge the higher status of the more powerful forms of care. We could also combine elements of all three strategies.

An awareness of class differences should govern our approach. A low-income woman might willingly accept some subordination to a husband-provider if he could ensure the material well-being of her children and herself. Given her precarious conditions, she may view this exchange as an attractive bargain. It is important not to underestimate the critical importance of protection and material well-being to those whose circumstances make such security elusive.[95]

95. See, however, bell hooks's discussion of the importance to low-income

The fact that a woman might accept subordination under such circumstances, however, does not indicate that there is nothing wrong with the social conditions that require a woman to make such a sacrifice in exchange for her security. Nor does it indicate that subordination made comfortable and alluring is thereby morally vindicated. To cover such cases, our best theoretical strategy might involve challenging the higher status of protective care and trying to raise esteem for the counterbalancing caretaking values which women, as traditional care givers, provide in return. The most important practical strategy, with respect to low-income women, must surely be to challenge the economic and social arrangements that make it necessary for many women to relinquish a substantial degree of personal autonomy in exchange for material support.

However we respond to this assessment of caretaking practices, it seems that we can no longer take a wholly benign view of the role of caring in women's lives, especially in the context of heterosexual relationships. If my analysis is correct, then it, together with the other feminist criticisms of care ethics outlined at the beginning of this chapter, yields a complex portrait of care. On the one hand, care is essential for the survival and development of both individuals and their communities, and care giving is a noble endeavor as well as being often morally requisite. On the other hand, care is simultaneously a perilous project for women, requiring the sacrifice of other important values, its very nobility part of its sometimes dangerously seductive allure. An ethic of care, to be fully liberatory for women, must not fail to explore and reflect this deep complexity.

---

women of equally shared parenting, where feasible: *Feminist Theory: From Margin to Center* (Boston: South End Press, 1984), pp. 140–41. If a man's participation in a heterosexual family relationship is explicitly defined at the outset in terms of his sharing child caretaking responsibilities equally, then, even in a low-income household, a woman would not have to bargain away her autonomy in order to secure a man's care for the children.

PART III

Friendship

7

Friendship and
Moral Growth

What are friends for? What does friendship add to our moral lives? In a time of widespread decline in the role of extended kinship networks and pitched battles over the role of sexual relationships in our lives, friendship may emerge, in our culture, as the least contested, most enduring, and most satisfying of all close personal affiliations. Virtue theorists and feminist philosophers are among those who have recently given a good deal of philosophical attention to the moral dimensions of friendship.[1] These investi-

1. A virtue-theoretic approach to friendship appears in the following, among many others: Lawrence Blum, *Friendship, Altruism, and Morality* (London: Routledge & Kegan Paul, 1980); Michael Stocker, "Values and Purposes: The Limits of Teleology and the Ends of Friendship," *Journal of Philosophy* 78 (December 1981): 747–65; and Michael Slote, "Morality Not a System of Imperatives," *American Philosophical Quarterly* 19 (October 1982): 331–40. The feminist literature on relationships is extensive. The following deal specifically with friendship: Martha Ackelsberg, " 'Sisters' or 'Comrades'? The Politics of Friends or Families," in Irene Diamond, ed., *Families, Politics, and Public Policy* (New York: Longman, 1983), pp. 339–56; Mary Dietz, "Citizenship with a Feminist Face: The Problem with Maternal Thinking," *Political Theory* 13 (February 1985): 19–37; Claudia Card, "Gender and Moral Luck," in Owen Flanagan and Amélie Oksenberg Rorty, eds., *Identity, Character, and Morality* (Cambridge, Mass.: MIT Press, 1990), pp. 199–218; and Janice Raymond, *A Passion for Friends* (Boston: Beacon Press, 1986).

Other noteworthy discussions of friendship, that do not exemplify either

gations have yet to scale the full heights of value and richness that friendship can afford to our lives.

Part 1 of this book deals with the challenge posed by the partiality of personal relationships to the scope and adequacy of traditional impartialist moral theories. In Part 2, I investigate the significance for ethical theory of a moral orientation focused primarily on care and relationships. Those discussions tend to be general, not differentiating among the variety of personal relationships. When I do focus on particular sorts of relationships, my examples, in the earlier chapters, are usually of familial or intimate heterosexual bonds. Such relationships certainly may, but do not necessarily, constitute friendships. In Part 3, I turn to friendship in particular. I seek a richer understanding of this relationship, in which there has been a recent revival of philosophical interest.

In the first section of this chapter, I reiterate and expand a discussion from Chapter 5 about the ways commitment to particular persons differs from commitment to abstract moral values, principles, and rules. Then I suggest, in section 2, that commitments to persons, in particular to our friends, offer us important possibilities for moral growth and for transformation of the abstract moral guidelines to which we are committed. Finally, in section 3, as a brief counterpoint, I reflect on some of the risks involved in relying on our friends to inspire the sort of moral change discussed in section 2.

1. The Nature of Commitment to Particular Persons

Relationships vary considerably. We can relate to others in ways that approach equality and mutuality; or we can relate to

---

a feminist or a virtue-theoretic perspective can be found in Elizabeth Telfer, "Friendship," *Proceedings of the Aristotelian Society*, 1970–71, pp. 223–41; Jane English, "What Do Grown Children Owe Their Parents?" in Onora O'Neill and William Ruddick, eds., *Having Children* (New York: Oxford University Press, 1979), pp. 351–56; Marcia Baron, "The Alleged Moral Repugnance of Acting from Duty," *Journal of Philosophy* 81 (April 1984): 197–220; and Laurence Thomas, "Friendship," *Synthese* 72 (1987): 217–36. Still other sources appear in subsequent notes.

others in ways that involve forms of dependency or hierarchies of power and authority. The sort of relationship I explore here is friendship, that is, a relationship that is based on approximate equality (in at least some respects) and a mutuality of affection, interest, and benevolence.[2] Friendship, in this sense, can occur between or among lovers or familial relations as well as between or among people not otherwise affiliated with one another. To a greater or lesser extent, one can be friends with one's parents or children, siblings or spouse.[3]

The important sort of equality in friendship is not a matter of formal equality in some measurable or quantifiable dimension, such as age or years of schooling. The important sort of equality has to do with personality, attitudes, emotions, and overall character. Friends should be able to respect and take an interest in one another's perspectives. One friend's superiority in one area, for example, in breadth of life experience, need not give that friend a privileged place in the relationship if it is balanced by the other friend's superiority in some other area, for example, in vitality of imagination.

Relationships that lack this sort of balance and mutuality would

2. For Aristotle, as is well known, there are three forms of friendship, which originate in three different sorts of attraction to other persons: recognition of moral goodness of character, pleasure seeking, and seeking of personal advantage. The best sort for Aristotle is, of course, friendship based on recognition of moral goodness (*Nichomachean Ethics*, 1156a6–1157b5). See John Cooper, "Aristotle on the Forms of Friendship," *Review of Metaphysics* 30 (June 1977): 619–48. My own discussion does not depend on the nature of the friendship in question. The notion of moral growth that I discuss in this chapter requires only that there be a sharing of personal experiences between the friends, whatever the motivation for this sharing, and that each friend trust the other to be what I call a "reliable moral witness," the reliability in question having as much to do with epistemic capacity as with moral goodness.

3. Mary Lyndon Shanley argues that the most important thesis in John Stuart Mill's *The Subjection of Women* is that friendship must be made possible in marriage if marriage is to offer the possibility of a genuinely moral relationship for women and men. In turn, friendship between women and men requires female-male equality. For Shanley's discussion of the strengths and weaknesses of Mill's proposals, see her "Marital Slavery and Friendship: John Stuart Mill's *The Subjection of Women*," *Political Theory* 9 (May 1981): 238–44.

seem to reduce to something too hierarchical to constitute genuine friendships. They would seem, instead, to take on a master-apprentice or mentor-student quality. In those instances in our lives in which mentor-student relationships and so forth do become genuine friendships, it is likely that the formal inequality of social position is balanced by excellences in the student which inspire the mentor's respect and from which the mentor might even learn something.

Being a friend to someone usually involves being committed to her in at least some important respects and trusting her in at least some important respects, even if not in all respects. In countless ways, from the trivial to the monumental, friendship invites us to marshal the greater part of the scarce resources of our care, attentiveness, and trust in the selective support of our friends, even though other human beings have similar needs or qualities. This is not equivalent to saying that friends have claims on our personal resources, although I would defend that view. My suggestion here is instead psychological rather than morally normative and pertains to the way friendship invites us to feel about our friends.

Commitment to a friend can easily be an example of the sort of commitment to a person in her unique particularity that I first explored in Chapter 5. In my estimation, friendship typically provides some of the best examples of particularized person-based commitment. Commitment to a person as such, to reiterate, is unlike commitment to an abstract moral guideline, such as the moral rules that dictate right or wrong action, the moral values that encompass desirable goals or aspirations, and the moral principles that define methods by which we justify rules and values. These abstract moral guidelines structure modes of reasoning from which one derives specific judgments governing the situations and choices faced in daily life. Abstract moral guidelines are general and make no reference to particular persons or occasions. They presume to hold across all relevantly similar situations unless there are exceptional circumstances or overriding considerations.

By contrast, commitment to a person in her unique particularity, a friend, for example, takes as its primary focus the unique concatenation of wants, desires, identity, history, and so on of a

particular person. It is specific to that person and is not generalizable to others.[4] It acknowledges the uniqueness of the friend and
can be said to honor or celebrate that uniqueness.[5] The interests
and *best* interests of the friend become central, though not exclusively so, to determining which of one's own actions are right or
wrong and which goals and aspirations are worthwhile. A friend's
successes become occasions for our own joy; her judgments may
provoke our reflection or, even, deference; her behavior may encourage our emulation; and the causes that she champions may
inspire our own devotion. We show partiality for our friend by
attending selectively to her particularity in all its detail and variety.[6]

Just how we care for a particular friend depends on her specific
needs, interests, and values. In some cases, one might feel called
upon to provide a great deal of support or nurturance for a friend.
In other cases, because the friend wishes to struggle independently
with the burdens in her life, one will find it fitting to resist the
inclination to help or comfort her. One's behavior toward the friend
takes its appropriateness, at least in part, from her goals and aspirations, her needs, her character—all of which one feels prima
facie invited to acknowledge as worthwhile just because they are

4. This point has been made by, for example, Telfer, in "Friendship,"
p. 224.
5. This point has also been made by Howard Kamler, in "Strong Feelings,"
Journal of Value Inquiry 19 (1985): 6–8.
6. Blum (*Friendship, Altruism, and Morality*, p. 49) argues that it is morally
legitimate to show such partiality as helping our own friends when they are
stuck in the snow before helping others who are also stuck. Charles Fried (*An
Anatomy of Values* [Cambridge: Harvard University Press, 1970]) argues (p. 27)
that it is permissible for a man to choose to save his wife if several people are
drowning and he cannot save them all. The present chapter explores some of
the positive value that arises from the admittedly partial support and nurturance which friends provide selectively for each other. In Chapter 2, by contrast,
I discuss the inadequacies of caretaking that result from our common practices
of being partial to relatives and friends in a context of radical inequalities of
resources. I do not regard partiality as a moral wrong in itself, but only a
complex moral problem under conditions of scarcity or maldistribution of caretaking resources. Unfortunately, these conditions seem virtually inescapable
in human life, and this chapter is not intended to diminish the importance of
the problem.

hers. None of these responses (necessarily) accords with one's moral rules, values, or principles. Partiality for a friend involves being motivated by the friend as an individual, by who she is and not by the principled commitments of one's own which her circumstances happen to instantiate.

Of course it is possible to regard one's friend and her needs, interests, and values as morally worthy according to some moral rule, value, or principle.[7] One might, for example, act to serve her needs because those needs seem important, in some general sense. One might emulate her behavior because that behavior appears justifiable in accord with moral rules that one holds. And one might resist the inclination to serve her needs or defer to her judgment just in case one's principled commitments or values compel doubt about the worth of those attitudes. Evaluations such as these are implicitly governed by general moral standards of some sort and, thereby, reflect more than simply a commitment to the friend whose needs or behavior are in question. They also reflect commitment to the relevant standards for assessment—standards, in the light of which any person, not merely the friend, might have occasioned such consideration.

For one's response clearly to reflect a commitment to another person in her particularity, as such, it must be prompted, at least in part, by a readiness to act on exactly her behalf or as determined by precisely who she is even when one's general moral values and principles do not support such action. One's general, abstract moral commitments might entail uncertainty or doubt about the worth or justifiability of whatever it is about her that now incites one's response. If I act on her behalf despite that generalized uncertainty, then I manifest a commitment to the particular friend herself.

Friendship provides us with an inclination or invitation to *take our friends seriously* and to take seriously what our friends care

7. Various philosophers dissent from a view they attribute to Aristotle, namely, that we need to think of our friends as good people; see Telfer, "Friendship," pp. 227–28; Kamler, "Strong Feelings," p. 5; and Ferdinand Schoeman, "Friendship and Testimonial Privilege," in Frederick Elliston and Norman Bowie, eds., *Ethics, Public Policy, and Criminal Justice* (Cambridge, Mass.: Oelgeschlager, Gunn & Hain, 1982), p. 264.

about. Supposing that, at the beginning of my relationship with a friend, I did not share with my friend all her values or principles; then friendship beckons me to consider those unshared values and principles as new moral possibilities for myself and to consider my previously held values and principles in a new light—admittedly without predetermining what will result from the consideration. We may find that we have reasons for rejecting what our friend values and abides by, but we may also find that our reasons weaken in the face of what we learn about how our friend's life manifests her values.

My notion of commitment to a particular person can be made clearer by considering the difference between affection and respect.[8] Friendships, in practice, normally seem to exhibit both of these dimensions of human involvement. Affection encompasses the fond and tender feelings of liking and love with which we respond to (some) other persons. Affection need not involve any judgmental or evaluative component. It can consist of no more than affective responsiveness to the one who is liked or loved.

Respect contrasts with affection in this regard. There are at least two different sorts of respect for persons, and both sorts are grounded on evaluative considerations that presuppose commitments to abstract moral guidelines. The first sort of respect to consider is respect for persons as moral equals. According to the usual formulations of certain deontological moral principles, this form of respect is owed to all persons, regardless of whether or not we like them or think well of them. It has nothing to do with individual merit or moral qualities. Thus, the respect one shows to other persons in virtue of their moral equality to oneself, their equal membership in the moral community, is based, not on a commitment to them in their unique particularity, but rather on a

8. Claudia Card discusses the distinction between respect for persons in general and cherishing, which is a way of valuing persons in their particularity: "Gender and Moral Luck." In my discussion, I try to differentiate affection from what I have, following common usage, called "respect," which is a type of positive attitude we might feel for particular persons in light of their merits. Card does not distinguish different sorts of cherishing and, as she uses the term, it seems to cover both respect in the particularized sense and affection.

commitment to a principle about the inherent moral worth of persons.

In addition to the generalized form of respect for persons as equal members of the moral community, there is another form of respect, one that does take into account the particularity of persons. It is the sort of respect that is involved when someone is admired specifically for her worthwhile qualities, her excellences. Respect in this sense is not owed to all persons and is usually something that must be earned or merited. It may involve affection or fond feelings, but it need not. What is most important about this particularized sort of respect is that, although it differs from abstract respect for a moral equal in that it takes account of someone's uniqueness, nevertheless it is like respect for a moral equal in its commitment to abstract standards. Respect for a particular person's excellences is based on positive assessments in terms of standards of worth.

Thus, respect for a person's worth, although it is indeed focused on a person's particularity, nevertheless, still contrasts with affection for a particular person, in that the former is not merely oriented toward the particular person in question. It exemplifies in addition a commitment to certain abstract moral guidelines by which to judge the worth of particular persons—values or standards pertaining, for example, to personality traits, behavior patterns, or human virtues. A person earns our respect, in this particularized sense, by measuring up to standards we consider worthwhile. To the extent that our commitment to someone is contingent upon our high regard for her, then to that extent our commitment to that person is subordinate to our commitment to the relevant moral standards and is not intrinsically a commitment to that person.

Parenthetically, it should be noted that even affection for someone need not constitute, in the full sense, a commitment to her. Commitment to a particular person involves some readiness to be attentive to her, to take her seriously, and to act on her behalf. One's behavioral tendencies as well as one's feelings are engaged by commitment to a person, in the full sense. When affection does generate commitment and the commitment is based on affection alone, the resulting attachment seems rather more akin to a taste for certain foods than to the generality-based attitude involved in either form of respect. Affection, on my view of it, does not necessarily of itself involve evaluations of personal worth or even assumptions about the inherent moral worth of the personhood of the one who is the object of the affection. More than either sort of respect, it exemplifies attentiveness to someone's unique particularity.

Commitments to friends that are based on judgments of their personal worth are obviously not wrong. I am concerned, however, to explore certain moral possibilities that inhere in the nature of commitment to a person, as such, whether or not either form of generality-based respect is also present. These moral possibilities might be constricted, or even absent, when commitment to a friend is wholly derived from commitment to abstract moral guidelines. My proposal is that our commitments to particular persons are, in practice, necessary counterbalances to our commitments to abstract moral guidelines and may, at times, take precedence over them. I turn now to a consideration of the sort of moral growth that is made possible by our capacity to commit ourselves to particular persons, such as our friends.

2. FRIENDSHIP AND MORAL GROWTH

Various contemporary philosophers have explored many of the values provided by friendship. Elizabeth Telfer suggests that friendship promotes consideration of the welfare of others, makes possible unique services not otherwise available, is pleasant and life enhancing, increases our stake in the world and our capacity for emotions, intensifies our absorption in many of our activities, and enlarges our knowledge. John Rawls emphasizes the way friendship and other forms of mutual trust, in human associations already characterized by just rules, generate the feelings of trust and confidence that are necessary for the growth of a moral perspective in new members of the association. Ferdinand Schoeman focuses on the reciprocated intimate sharing of one's self in friendship. For Lawrence Blum, friendship is a locus of altruistic emotions and can attain a morally worthwhile level of "deep caring" that involves genuine understanding of the other person while allowing a grasp of her separateness from oneself. Mary Dietz proposes that friendship offers, to citizens of a polity, a model for a type of civic bond which emphasizes democratic values, participatory citizenship, and egalitarianism. Jane Mansbridge offers a detailed analysis of the sort of political process that is based on the friendship relationship.[9]

These discussions together lay a rich groundwork for appreciating friendship. Even so, they do not exhaustively explore its varied forms of moral worth. Here, I call attention to one important good made possible by friendship that seems to have been neglected in these and other contemporary discussions. This good is moral growth—of a certain particular sort. Let us recall that one's first values and moral rules are learned in the course of the moral socialization that most people receive from their early caretakers, usually parents or family. Against the background of these earliest learned moral abstractions, many of us find ourselves undergoing remarkable changes of commitment in later life. Friendship can be an invaluable source of such moral transformation.

The sort of moral growth that most interests me is the profound sort that occurs when we learn to grasp our experiences in a new light or in radically different terms. It is the kind that involves a shift in moral paradigms, in the basic values, rules, or principles which shape moral thought and behavior. In general, abstract moral guidelines are "tested" by concrete human lives. The more

9. Sources for the views surveyed in this paragraph are Telfer, "Friendship," pp. 238–40; John Rawls, *A Theory of Justice* (Cambridge: Harvard University Press, 1971), p. 470; Schoeman, "Friendship," p. 263; Blum, *Friendship, Altruism, and Morality,* pp. 43, 70; Dietz, "Citizenship," pp. 31–32; and Jane Mansbridge, "The Limits of Friendship," in J. Roland Pennock and John W. Chapman, eds., *Participation in Politics,* Nomos XVI (New York: Lieber-Atherton, 1975), pp. 246–75. For a discussion of Aristotle's views on the goods provided by friendship, see John Cooper, "Friendship and the Good in Aristotle," *Philosophical Review* 86 (July 1977): 290–315.

we know about real lives lived according to, or under the influence of, various abstract moral guidelines, the more we gain insight into the living realities of those guidelines. Our everyday experiences can seem to confirm or to disconfirm our abstract moral guidelines, or they can seem inconclusive or irrelevant. Widening the experiential base against which we make our assessments promotes our more adequate evaluation of those guidelines. Because we might comprehend our own personal experiences in limited terms, or because the range of our own experience might be narrow in virtue of the restricted opportunities of our own lives, we do not always have the experiential or conceptual resources on our own to gain new moral insights or to surpass our prior moral outlook.

Such deep transformations can undoubtedly occur in virtue of a wide range of experiences. Friendship offers one potential pathway toward such transformations, and even though it is not the only such route, it is one that is widely available and accessible. The needs, wants, fears, experiences, projects, and dreams of our friends can frame for us new standpoints from which we can explore the significance and worth of moral values and standards. In friendship, our commitments to our friends, as such, afford us access to whole ranges of experience beyond our own. Friendship offers such access in virtue of the shared trust that underlies friendship. This trust manifests itself in a variety of forms. There is the obvious trust in the friend's goodwill and good intentions with respect to one's own well-being. But a rather different sort of trust is even more important for the moral growth I am considering.

In friendship, there is a substantial measure of trust in the ability of our friends to bear what I call reliable "moral witness" to their own experiences. Among friends, there is generally a mutual sharing of stories about past and present experiences. Friendship enables us to come to know the experiences and perspectives of our friends from their own points of view. So long as our friends confide their experiences authentically, sensitively, and insightfully, we can gain knowledge of lives lived in accord with moral rules and values that differ from our own. Based on this "empirical" grasp of the morally relevant features of the experiences of our friends, we broaden and enrich our own empirical base for evaluating both the abstract moral guidelines we already hold and alternatives we might consider.

Tangentially, it is worth emphasizing the moral empiricism underlying my approach. This approach rests on the presumption that experience makes a relevant epistemological contribution to the process of critical reflection by which we determine and reconsider our moral principles and values. At the very least, experience provides irreplaceable evidence about the consequences of our behavior; it, therefore, contributes importantly to the consequentialist dimensions of moral reasoning. But, in general, the difference experience makes resists easy explication. The problems here are nothing short of intractable. We are, after all, confronted with all the problems and uncertainties of induction.

At any rate, the alternative to moral empiricism is to shield moral reasoning altogether from experiential confrontation, as if it did not matter how our moral values and principles fared in practice. We do not let the problems of induction discourage us from relying on experience in nonmoral realms; why, then, should we do so in the moral realm? Of course, descriptions and accounts of morally relevant experiences do not by themselves suffice to yield conclusive moral knowledge. Nevertheless, as conceptualized and understood in everyday terms, they counterbalance large-scale moral and social theories in a process of reflective equilibrium[10] that my moral empiricism leads me to favor.

What distinctive contribution does friendship make to moral experience? Friendship is a close relationship in which trust, intimacy, and disclosure open up for us whole standpoints other than our own. Through seeing what my friend counts as a harm done to her, for example, and seeing how she suffers from it and what she does in response, I can try on, as it were, her interpretive claim and its implications for moral practice. I can attend to what happens as a result of her acquiescence and accommodation or as a result of her resistance and rebellion.

10. This is, of course, Rawls's familiar notion: *Theory of Justice*, pp. 20–21, 48–51, 120–21.

Because we come to know, in minute and intimate detail, so much of what is happening to a good friend, those experiences live for us with narrative specificity and richness. Because a friend is other than oneself and, pace Aristotle, rarely simply "another self,"[11] a friend will differ from oneself in some ways. Usually she conceptualizes experience and comprehends its significance in terms that are at least somewhat different from one's own. Because of those differences, the narratives and judgments she shares will implicitly reveal a moral perspective that is, to at least some extent, unlike one's own. The stories she tells will be informed by her conceptualizations, values, and standards; these stories will, thus, live for us in the terms that reflect our friend's perspective, one that we do not necessarily share.

Obviously, moral induction is not limited to relationships of friendship. A dependent child whom I nurture, for example, becomes a touchstone for assessing the success of my own behavior in meeting the child's needs and also for determining the appropriate societal arrangements for enabling those needs to be met. My principles about social justice, no less than my principles about how I should nurture, are brought into question when I confront the hunger of a child I cannot adequately feed. Other relationships, as well, inform us of experiences that test various moral guidelines. Nevertheless, friendship, that is, a relationship of some degree of mutual intimacy, benevolence, interest, and concern, strongly promotes trust and the sharing of perspectives, a kind of mutuality that, in turn, fosters vicarious participation in the very experience of moral alternatives.

What does my friend consider important in the situations she faces? What harms her? What offends her? What gives her hope and courage? How does she respond? How does she feel about what happens to her? When does she take the initiative? When does she let go? How does she explain, in her reflective moments, what she has done? As she narrates her stories, she reveals her own moral conceptions and principles in practice: her conceptions for discerning what happens to her and her principles for deter-

11. Aristotle, *Nichomachean Ethics*, 1166a, 29–32.

mining her own behavior. In virtue of understanding the experiences of our friends in their own terms, we not only widen our inductive basis for moral assessment but, as well, we enrich the range of conceptual resources we can use for interpreting and evaluating all the morally significant experience we can comprehend.

There are at least two different kinds of "inductive" moral knowledge one can gain from one's friends. First, one can see how a friend is affected by the various social arrangements in which she lives and by the behavior of others toward her. These effects reveal something about the adequacy of the standards that shape the social arrangements and the human actions that impinge upon her.

Second, one can observe how the course of her life tests the moral guidelines by which she herself lives. One can reflect on what motivates, guides, or affects her. One will be inspired to take those motives and guides seriously because one takes *her* seriously. It becomes a living option for oneself. Through intimate knowledge of one's friend, one participates vicariously in the living that embodies and realizes her divergent values. One learns what life is like for someone who is motivated by springs of action different from one's own, and one sees how the moral abstractions that inform and affect her life fare in practice.

Because of these opportunities for growth in our moral knowledge, friendship permits us to orient ourselves in times when we doubt our own moral rules, values, or principles. When we do not know exactly what to believe, we can try to determine *whom* to believe. Trusted friends offer us one important sort of guide through our uncertainties. Even if we have not yet doubted our own moral standards, commitments to particular persons may still surprise us with the inspiration to consider new values and principles. Thus, when we least expect it, our friendships may stimulate our moral transformation.

One might wonder whether the only role played by friendship in broadening our moral understanding is merely to help us draw out the implications of moral views we already hold.[12] The fuller

12. This question was posed by David Solomon in his commentary on an

articulation of our preexistent moral commitments is certainly one thing that is facilitated and promoted when we learn about the morally relevant experiences of our friends. My main concern here, however, is to explore a more profound sort of moral change that friendship can inspire. Friendship can open up the very possibility of growth in our deepest moral values, rules, and principles and not simply their fuller articulation. In this sense, friendship gives us a point of view that may well be external to the principled moral commitments we already hold. What a friend may provide for us is a viewpoint informed by an alternative set of principled moral commitments.

Moral growth is clearly made possible by sources other than friendship. Novels, biographies, and autobiographies may do as well and, sometimes, even better than friendship to promote our moral growth. The transformative power of literature as a whole is undeniable. Its educative value in particular cases, of course, depends on who the writer is, just as the transformative potential of friendship depends on who the friend is.

Nevertheless, the access to the new standpoint is interestingly different in these two cases. The literary work may be more articulate than my friend, but I can talk to my friend and she can answer me in her own terms, directly responsive to what I say and what I ask her. By contrast, I may have to extract "responses" from the fixed number of sentences in a literary work and I am limited to interpreting those responses in my own, possibly uncomprehending, terms. Moreover, my friend's life continues to unfold in new directions that may surprise even her; while she lives, her life is still an open book whose chapters she does not wholly author as a mere self-confirmation of her own preexisting moral commitments. Thus, the lived experiences of friends have the potential for a kind of authenticity and spontaneity not available in novels,

---

earlier version of this chapter when it was read at the American Philosophical Association meetings, Central Division, Chicago, Ill., April 1987. Solomon also raised other important points to which I am grateful to have been able to respond, including the suggestion, immediately following in the text, that works of literature can inspire the same sort of moral transformation that I attribute to friendship.

leaving only biography and autobiography as relevant analogues. To reiterate, however, I certainly do not preclude the possibility that all of these sources and more, not solely friendship, may contribute to moral transformation.

Moral change obviously offers the possibility of enabling us to improve the moral quality of our lives. It may facilitate our moral autonomy as well. Autonomy is promoted when one acquires a plurality of standpoints from which to assess one's choices, one's values and principles, one's very character.[13] The greater the diversity of perspectives one can adopt for assessing rules, values, principles, and character, the greater the degree of one's autonomy in making moral choices. People to whom we are affiliated, especially our friends, afford us standpoints from which to comprehend, in their experiential significance, alternative perspectives on our own abstract moral guidelines. Through fostering our moral growth, our friends may, thus, occasion our moral autonomy.

People generally befriend those who are close to them, whether in interests, attitudes, needs, or circumstances.[14] (Birds of a feather flock together.) If friends are, thus, like each other to begin with, then what becomes of the possibility that they can provide for each other alternative and new perspectives from which to view the moral problems and situations of daily living? Does the potential for radical moral transformation through friendship diminish in virtue of the typically extensive similarity among friends? It would seem that friends who are very akin to each other could not stimulate each other's *wholesale* rethinking of deep moral values or principles.

Part of the answer to these questions is to recognize that deep-level moral growth through friendship is a potentiality in friendship, but not one that is realized all the time. The more alike friends

13. For a discussion of the way autonomy is fostered by access to a plurality of perspectives, see my "Autonomy in Social Context," in James Sterba and Creighton Peden, eds., *Freedom, Equality, and Social Change* (Lewiston, N.Y.: Edwin Mellen, 1989), pp. 158–69. See also Diana T. Meyers, *Self, Society, and Personal Choice* (New York: Columbia University Press, 1989).

14. See Lois Verbrugge, "The Structure of Adult Friendship Choices," *Social Forces* 56, no. 2 (1977): 576–97.

are, the less likely they are to afford each other radically divergent moral perspectives in which to participate vicariously. This is not to belittle the richness and value of friendship among very similar persons. Far from it. Nor is it to deny any possibility of moral growth through friendship with those who are like oneself; such a denial would be absurd. In case friends are extremely similar, however, the moral growth that occurs through vicarious participation in the friend's perspective is less likely to amount to radical transformation of deep-level, abstract moral commitments and more likely to amount to a fuller articulation of the moral values both friends already have in common.

Still, even when friends are very similar, differences remain. This is another part of the answer to the problem posed by similarity among friends. We should not underestimate the importance of the differences that do obtain. It seems that there may be an important moral interplay between the similarities and the differences. A range of similar traits, interests, or circumstances between persons may be exactly what facilitates trust between them as the whole individuals they are. This trust is essential if either friend is to rely on the moral witnessing of the other. It is a kind of wholesale trust in the friend that opens one up to entertaining and embracing the friend's perspective as such, not simply in regard to those values one already shares, but in its full complexity, including its divergences from one's own prior point of view. Thus, radical, deep-level moral transformation is a possibility even among friends who are very similar to each other, since similarity in many respects does not preclude important differences.

3. The Risks of Commitment to Particular Persons

The moral growth made possible by access to a friend's experience as she lives it depends crucially on the reliability of our friend as a witness to the events and circumstances of her life. When we commit ourselves to someone by relying on the authenticity and legitimacy of what she tells us about her life, we take certain risks. In this last section, I outline some of these risks. I hope to make clear the important challenge involved in trying to minimize these risks while still remaining open to the influence of a friend.

If a commitment to one's friend is largely a commitment to her as a person, that is, if it is based on affection, attraction, or interest that is not itself informed by values or principles, then one may be as likely to follow a sinner as a saint. When one's moral commitments are shaped in accord with the example set by another person's standpoint, as defined by her interpretations, her rules, or her values, then one is vulnerable to affiliating with someone who, on some *principled* moral grounds or other, does not deserve one's deference or trust.[15]

When we depend on a friend to bear authentic and reliable witness to her moral experience, we are trusting not only her good intentions; we are also trusting the quality of her sensitivity and insightfulness into her own life. We rely on the friend to have noticed what is significant about the circumstances she faces, and we rely on her to have conceptualized that significance in appropriate terms. We are, thus, trusting her epistemic capacities as a moral witness and, moreover, as an involved witness who is affected by those circumstances and who, in turn, refashions them, to some extent, in accord with her own purposes.

If one genuinely recognizes that someone's intentions or values are profoundly unworthy or her perspective seriously flawed, then, unless there are good reasons of an overriding sort, one should not rely on that person's account of her own experience.[16] The problem is to determine which of our disapprovals of another person's perspective are reliable and which are not. Resolving such

---

15. Insightful discussions of the problems of unfounded loyalties and unfounded trust, respectively, can be found in Marcia Baron, *The Moral Status of Loyalty* (Dubuque, Iowa: Kendall Hunt, 1984); and Annette Baier, "Trust and Antitrust," *Ethics* 96 (January 1986): 231–60.

16. For a discussion of the problems involved in uncritical deference to the principles of another, see my "Moral Integrity and the Deferential Wife," *Philosophical Studies* 47 (1985): 141–50; and Sandra Bartky, *Femininity and Domination* (New York: Routledge, 1990), chap. 7.

questions of trustworthiness is a complex matter. Even the standards by which we decide, in the first place, that our friends are reliable moral witnesses might themselves be questionable. We can be as mistaken about values and principles as about particular persons. If our friends are to provoke changes in our standards, by bearing witness either to the inadequacy of those very standards or to the worth of alternatives, then our commitments to our own standards must be somewhat tentative—and this must include the standards by which we decide whose judgment and discernment are reliable and whose are not. Our own standards must permit us the flexibility to subordinate them on occasion to our commitments to our trusted friends. Determining exactly when and how to do this is a profoundly complex matter.

It seems utterly foolish to trust someone who is not estimable in any way, given one's current values, even more so if that person is morally corrupt, again according to one's current values. I suggested at the end of the previous section that the similarities among friends may be what fosters the sort of trust that leads them to welcome and embrace one another's moral differences. When similarities are not recognizable, then in order sensibly to trust someone as a friend, one may need to find her worthwhile in terms of one's preexisting moral values. If the resultant trust however, does not extend beyond those of the friend's qualities that pass the test, then one forecloses the possibility that the friend herself, as the whole person she is, might inspire one to reconsider even those standards the friend had to meet in order to be considered trustworthy.

If my commitment to my friends is based entirely on their exemplifying what I already believe to be good or right, if I abandon any friend who departs from the values I already hold dear, then I close myself off from what my friends might reveal about the need to transform my deepest abstract moral concerns. Keeping open the possibility of deep-level moral change seems to require that one sustain an uneasy, although vital, balance between commitments to one's abstract moral values and principles, on the one hand, and on the other, commitments to persons such as one's friends in their unique, whole particularity.

My goal in this chapter has been to identify a neglected potential benefit of special relationships, particularly of friendship. Our friends offer us perspectives alternative to our own from which we can assess abstract moral guidelines. In that way, they may offset our own prior commitments and stimulate growth in our moral lives. Commitments to particular persons afford both an important counterbalance to our commitments to moral principles and a means to achieve the critical distance necessary to put our own principles in doubt. This potential is not without moral risks. Nevertheless, at its best, friendship can provide us with invaluable and underestimated foundational resources out of which to construct, and reconstruct, our moral lives.

8

Friendship, Choice, and Change

Friendship, in our culture, is a notably voluntary relationship: as adults, we choose our own friends; and, together with our friends, we generate relationships that, more than most other close personal ties, reflect our choices and desires. This voluntariness, a trait historically so remarked in other contexts, also merits serious consideration in the moral exploration of friendship.[1] In that spirit, I present in this chapter a quasi-voluntarist account of friendship: the special moral requirements of friendship, the loyalty, support, care, and intimacy we owe to friends but not necessarily to others, are best regarded as morally grounded partly on the voluntariness that underlies particular friendships in our culture.

In the previous chapter, I explored the potential of friendship to promote radical transformation in individual moral perspectives. In this chapter, I explore a related notion, the capacity of friendship to inspire and support unconventional values, deviant life-styles, and, ultimately, social change. Friendship offers personally as well as socially transformative possibilities usually lacking in other important tradition-based close relationships, such as family ties. Thus, the potential of friendship to foster social change provides

---

1. In the growing contemporary literature on friendship, relatively little has been said about the voluntary nature of the relationship. A brief discussion appears in David Annas, "The Meaning, Value, and Duties of Friendship," *American Philosophical Quarterly* 24, no. 4 (1987): 349–56. A more extensive discussion appears in Laurence Thomas, "Friendship," *Synthese* 72 (1987): 217–36, esp. pp. 217–21.

a central theme for my quasi-voluntarist account of our friendship practices. I aim, as well, to show that a quasi-voluntarist account of friendship avoids some of the major difficulties that commonly attend voluntarist moral and political theories.

I explore the voluntary nature of friendship in the first section of this chapter. I outline a quasi-voluntarist account of the responsibilities in, and value of, friendship in section 2. In section 3 I differentiate this voluntarism from that of liberal contractarianism.

1. THE NATURE OF FRIENDSHIP

In our culture, friendship is a voluntary relationship:[2] no particular people are assigned by custom or tradition to be a person's friends. Friends are supposed to be people one selects on one's own to share activities and intimacies. Friendship is voluntary in at least two ways: we usually choose the particular people we try to befriend from among the larger number of our acquaintances; and we evolve with our friends the particular ways in which we will interact, the extent of mutual support and nurturance, the depth of shared intimacy, and so forth.

To say that something is "voluntary" is typically to say that it lacks external coercion or constraint. In the context of personal relationships, however, this definition is not wholly appropriate. On the one hand, it is too narrow. The sense in which we have no choice over, for example, family ties has more to do with the fact that most of those relationships are unavoidably ascribed to us than with coercion or constraint. Biological and legal facts become the basis for societal ascriptions of certain kinship ties among people. Thus, the voluntariness of friendship must also encompass the notion that it is not a socially *ascribed* relationship.

2. Across cultures, there is variation in the way the practice is carried on. My discussion pertains only to friendship within our own culture. Even within our culture, there is certainly variation, given that our culture is really a heterogeneous mixture of many distinct cultural traditions. To simplify my discussion, I ignore this variation, mindful of the perils of doing so.

On the other hand, voluntariness as an absence of external constraint is too *broad* a notion to characterize friendship. Our choices of friends are indeed constrained, both by the limited range of our acquaintances and by the responses of others to us as we extend gestures of friendship toward them. Thus, friendship is voluntary only within the limits imposed by certain external constraints.

Even within these limits, friendship is still more voluntary than most other close personal relationships. Family ties, for example,[3] are constituted by consanguineal and legal connections, and active family relationships are sustained by a large number of people participating in a variety of traditional social practices and rituals with defined roles and duties. Most people are simply identified, usually from birth, in terms of certain familial relationships to certain particular others; I am the daughter of Florence and Edward, the niece of Eileen and Al, and so forth. With the exception of marital relationships (in some cultures), people generally do not choose their kinfolk. Whether we like them or not, our aunts, uncles, siblings, nieces, and so forth remain tied to us by family connections. The duties of kinship, as well, are often socially ascribed.

Friendship receives far less formal recognition in our rituals and conventions, including legal conventions, than do familial relationships and is maintained by fewer of those formalities. If kinship is a form of ascribed status, then friendship is a kind of achievement. Those who would be friends must exert themselves actively to sustain their relationship.[4] Indeed, outsiders to a friendship may create barriers to its maintenance by recognizing only kin as "related" to the friends; after all, only kinfolk are called "relations." Thus, friends must take the initiative to share activities, communicate with one another, and provide mutual positive self-affirmation. Friends must also take care to avoid the sorts of dis-

3. This point is discussed by Lillian Rubin in chapter 2, "On Kinship and Friendship," of her *Just Friends* (New York: Harper & Row, 1985), esp. pp. 22–24. Thomas also compares friendship to what he calls the more "structured" relationships of family: "Friendship," pp. 218–19.

4. See Rubin, *Just Friends*.

loyalties and betrayals that would create distrust or disaffection. These forms of engagement with a friend must be reasserted with some frequency over time if a friendship is to endure.

Friendship is a culturally idealized relationship. Equality, mutuality, and trust are among the ideals commonly associated with friendship.[5] These ideals have an important bearing on the voluntariness of friendship, a point I shall expand below. First, it should be noted that the realities of actual friendships often fall short of these ideals.[6] Affection may be complicated by envy; positive regard for another may mask the gratification of merely self-regarding needs; mutuality and equality may be infringed by tendencies to defer or to dominate; and trust may be compromised by betrayal. So long as people regard each other as friends and spend some minimal time in activities that are shared in some sense, their relationship is prima facie a friendship.[7] When the ideals of friendship are not realized in an actual friendship, they are nevertheless the relevant values toward which the friendship should aim and in terms of which it is properly assessed.

To the extent that actual friendships realize the ideals of equality, mutuality, and trust, to that extent the voluntariness of the relationships is enhanced. The mutual interestedness of friends is reinforced by egalitarianism in friendship, by an approximate overall equivalence of status and authority of the friends, and by an approximate equivalence in their mutual confidences and disclosure of vulnerabilities.[8] One's involvement in a particular friend-

5. These qualities are cited as popular ideals of friendship in various sociological studies of the relationship. See John Reisman, *Anatomy of Friendship* (New York: Irvington, 1979), p. 6. For Aristotle's discussion of the role of equality in friendship, see *Nichomachean Ethics*, 1058b–1059a.

6. Aristotle discusses the way "even unequals can be friends,": *Nichomachean Ethics*, 1058b, 1059b.

7. It can make sense to tell someone that a person she has considered to be a friend is not "really" her friend. The presumption that someone who is regarded as a friend is (thereby) a friend holds only prima facie and can be challenged in any particular case.

8. On the importance of self-disclosure between friends, see Thomas, "Friendship," esp. pp. 223–27.

ship and the extent of one's commitment to it should be affected by how the other party responds to one's efforts, for example, to share different activities, intensify the emotional intimacy, or extend the level of nurturance and mutual support. What each friend wants should not be self-contained but, over time, should come to recognize and incorporate what the other friend wants from the relationship. Also, hierarchy and domination should be relatively absent. Domination and subordination in a relationship are conditions that override the consent of one or both parties and, thereby, undermine the voluntariness of the relationship. Thus, voluntariness in friendship seems to require, overall, a measure of roughly equal and mutual adaptation, a synergism achieved through the combined and mutually interested adjustments of those who are becoming, or are already, friends.

The voluntariness of friendship also requires some measure of trust.[9] This trust may manifest itself in a variety of forms. One may trust and rely on a friend's intellectual or emotional capacities.[10] Most important, perhaps, is trust in the friend's goodwill and good intentions with respect to one's well-being. Friendship inspires us to let down our defenses, to reveal our deeper selves, and we do this voluntarily only if we trust the friend not to take advantage of a knowledge of our vulnerabilities.[11]

Thus, voluntary choice plays an important role in the creation and maintenance of friendship in our culture. Its fullest possible realization in that context requires, as supporting conditions, affection and positive regard, mutuality, equality, and trust. This point, in turn, suggests the viability of a quasi-voluntarist account of friendship. It is, therefore, to an explication of voluntarism and what it offers us in an account of friendship that I now turn.

9. On the importance of trust in friendship, see ibid., pp. 223–26; and R. E. Ewin, *Liberty, Community, and Justice* (Totowa, N.J.: Rowman & Littlefield, 1987), pp. 77–78. A more general discussion of trust appears in Annette Baier, "Trust and Antitrust," *Ethics* 96, no. 2 (1986): 231–60.

10. For an expanded discussion of this point, see Chapter 7 above.

11. Thomas's discussion of this point is illuminating: "Friendship," pp. 223–27 and 230–31.

2. Voluntarism and Friendship

A moral or political theory is "voluntarist" to the extent that it holds moral or political obligation to arise only insofar as it is freely self-assumed by individuals, that is, is grounded on personal choice, commitment, or consent.[12] I propose an account of friendship that is voluntarist to a significant extent, although, for reasons to be mentioned later, it is not exclusively voluntarist—hence, the label "quasi-voluntarist."

My account has two central themes. First, the special sorts of care, loyalty, or support that any particular set of friends may come to share and, probably, to expect and rely on from one another are moral requirements for them because they have voluntarily committed themselves to one another as friends. Second, there is important social value to the practice of basing friendship on choice—both the choice of whom one will befriend and the choices friends make as they evolve the very character of their relationship.

To elaborate the first theme: Voluntary commitment to someone as a friend is a sufficient condition for being prima facie morally required to treat the friend in certain special ways, according to the shared understandings between the friends regarding their needs and desires.[13] Friendship requires one to show care, loyalty, assistance, and so on, at some inconvenience to oneself, surpassing what is owed to others in general. The special requirements of friendship also include (within limits) partiality, that is, special attention to one's friends even though there may be others with comparable need or desire, particularly when circumstances preclude one's showing care and support to more than a few.[14]

---

12. The concepts of choice, commitment, and consent are not identical in meaning; for the purposes of this discussion, however, the differences can be disregarded.

13. Obviously, a quasi-voluntarist account of the duties in certain special relationships, such as friendship, does not presuppose that voluntary commitments are the only bases for duties of partiality or special regard for another person.

14. Neither a friend nor a relative should be given priority when her needs

In case there are several friends, or other loved ones, who simultaneously need one's care or support and one is incapable of helping all of them, the notion of special duties to friends does not, by itself, decide the order that one's priorities should take. Other morally relevant circumstances in the situation at hand must also be considered. I do not presume that special duties to friends necessarily override, or are necessarily subordinate to, comparable duties arising out of other nonvoluntary (or voluntary) close relationships, for example, kinship. In such cases of conflicting duties (my friend and my sister both need my help now), the particularities become crucial: Whose need is the greatest? Who has fewer means of alternative support? To whom do I owe the greatest debt of gratitude for care and protection previously rendered to me? And so on.

The special requirements of friendship derive from such considerations as the particularities of those who are friends, the circumstances of friends' lives, and the special infirmities of friends. In this respect, friendship is no different from other special relationships whose special requirements bid us take account of the context of someone's life and of her own specific needs and desires in determining what we might or should do for her.

Friendship differs, however, from other special relationships in that it does not even exist as a special relationship unless so chosen by the participants. By contrast, most other special relationships are grounded in various forms of unavoidable connection or dependency. The special duties one has in most of those other close relationships have something to do with features of the relationship and of the participants that are not mutually voluntary, for example, the fact that a being is someone one has brought into the world, or someone by whom one was nurtured during the time

---

are minor and one is in a position to help strangers with substantially greater needs, or when one is duty-bound to show no favoritism to one's own, for example, because one holds a relevant public office. See the discussion of this point in Blum, *Friendship, Altruism and Morality* (London: Routledge & Kegan Paul, 1980), chap. 3. Beware, however, of the excessive and misleading philosophical attention paid in such discussions to hypothetical disasters in which loved ones compete with strangers for sheer survival.

of one's own childhood dependency. These considerations create prima facie nonvoluntary moral responsibilities to particular others. Since friendship is not, either by definition or by idealization, a relationship based on one-way dependency, the circumstances of non-voluntary dependence do not generally determine that one ought to show the special consideration *of a friend* to any particular others.

Furthermore, a friend is supposed to show not simply the mechanical features of caring behavior but positive concern as well; not simply the techniques of loyalty but also personal commitment. What is owed to a friend has as much to do with one's underlying motivations that prompt one to be attentive and responsive to the friend as with the specific behaviors that are needed or desired by the friend.[15] Since friendship is a relationship sustained by such motivations, it makes sense to suppose that one is required to show special consideration for the friend because of those friendly feelings and that commitment toward the friend. And these are the very attitudes that constitute *voluntary* commitment to someone who is not otherwise related to one.

The sort of close relationship in which personal choice and commitment ought to determine (a substantial part of) what is morally required is a relationship whose circumstances facilitate the most authentic expression of choice and commitment. Friendship is precisely a relationship that provides for the morally unimpaired expression of personal commitment. This is far less true of personal relationships that lack equality and mutuality. Family relationships, for example, frequently feature great differences in status and power between family members. Age differences are often a cause of this, as well as gender inequality, which continues to make its dreary contribution to status and power disparities. Under the influence of such disparities, the choices and commitments that one makes to help or care for a close partner may be the product of subtle forms of influence or pressure.

15. This point has been made by many others; see Michael Stocker, "Values and Purposes: The Limits of Teleology and the Ends of Friendship," *Journal of Philosophy* 78 (December 1981): 747–65.

A quasi-voluntarist account of friendship has still other advantages. It endorses an admirable conception of the self. Voluntarism in general presumes the prima facie legitimacy of subjective preference and personal commitment, and the context of friendship corrects the tendency of voluntarist theories to consider only isolated hyperautonomous subjectivity. It is decisively important that the voluntariness of friendship be mutual. The mutual commitments between and among friends should evolve together. The voluntariness of friendship can bring us out of isolated choice into shared commitment. Thus, friendship invites us to consider our friends in certain ways, namely, as selves whose preferences and commitments should be respected by us equally with our own and accorded their due in our conduct. The friend may be another self, as Aristotle wrote,[16] but she is still ineliminably an *other* self. Friendship engages us in the interest of persons other than ourselves but in a way that does not leave our own interests behind. Friendship motivates us to a shared attentiveness to self. This joint consideration of myself as a choosing person in interaction with another choosing person with whom I share attentiveness, both to myself and to her, is an important kind of mutual respect.

In friendship, motivated as it is by affection, we are inspired to practice this respect for another in a nonthreatening context, where the risks we take in letting ourselves be influenced by someone else's choices and desires are mitigated by the affection and concern the other feels for us. The practice of respecting the preferences, choices, and commitments of others in general can be psychologically reinforced by early success in doing so in friendship, where respect can be a cooperative and mutually rewarding endeavor. Thus, the voluntariness of friendship can be a significant part of the development of a moral attitude of respect for persons, respect for the preferences and commitments of others, which can later be generalized to people for whom one has no affection and with whom one is not even acquainted.

My quasi-voluntarist account of friendship does not entail that friendships are not governed by any nonvoluntary special require-

---

16. *Nichomachean Ethics*, 1166a, 29–32.

ments. There are certain nonvoluntary moral boundaries that pertain to any friendship. Not all features of friendship are open for individual voluntarist negotiation; and not all the moral requirements of friendship, at whatever level of generality or abstraction, are grounded on nothing more than the shared agreement negotiated by the friends. If they were, then subordination, exploitation, and abuse would be legitimate possibilities in friendship, so long as they are mutually agreed upon—a position I find morally unacceptable.

Real friendships in the real world may be far from ideal. It seems desirable to seek an account of the special requirements of friendship that does not license harms done to friends, even to misguidedly consenting friends. For this reason, I do not consider individual voluntary choice to be an exhaustive account of the requirements of friendship. For one thing, friends owe one another all the usual moral duties that each of us owes to persons in general regardless of the presence or absence of consent. Thus, among other things, friends owe one another nonmalevolence, respect as moral equals, and a rectification of wrongs done.

But even some of the special requirements that arise in virtue of the special relationship of friendship are best thought of as nonvoluntary in origin. That is, they are voluntary only in the limited sense that they do not pertain to a relationship unless it is one of friendship, and we do (in our culture, especially as adults) choose our friends. Having committed ourselves to someone else as a friend, however, we now fall under certain special but nonvoluntary requirements that we are not at liberty to negotiate away.

Such nonvoluntary requirements for friendship follow from the nature of friendship and its ideally defining attributes. Thus, the nonvoluntary special requirements of friendship call upon us, for example, to enhance the conditions that promote the voluntariness of the relationship. This requires of each friend a respect for the other's preferences and choices regarding the relationship. It also requires efforts to augment the mutuality, equality, and trust that are part of the ideals of friendship and that themselves promote its voluntariness. Some of the nonvoluntary requirements of friendship are expressed in well-worn clichés; a friend in need is certainly a friend in/deed. To fail to provide the care, assistance, or support needed by a friend is to fail to be a genuine friend, a friend indeed.

The voluntary special requirements of friendship might well be considered analogous to promises in their moral force, while the nonvoluntary special requirements of friendship are more like rules of the game. In both cases, we can opt not to participate. Having elected to be friends with someone, one does so only by exemplifying the relevant nonvoluntary, defining norms. Only with regard to the voluntary requirements are we at liberty to redefine what we commit ourselves to do.

The second thesis that forms the core of my voluntarist account of friendship is that there is important social value to a voluntary friendship practice. Most notably, voluntary friendship has the potential to support unconventional values and deviant lives, themselves a source of needed change in our imperfect social practices. Alasdair MacIntyre's views about the nature of social practices[17] form a convenient springboard for discussing this issue.

MacIntyre has praised the nonvoluntary traditions and practices that embed the self, as a role-defined member of communities, in social networks of expectations and assigned duties that give an individual life "its moral starting point."[18] But many of these starting points, many of the traditional institutions and practices MacIntyre has in mind, are problematic, in one way or another, for many of their participants. Extensive research has documented the gender hierarchies and inequalities of traditional family relationships. Subordinate status, economic dependence, denial of economic rights, rape within marriage, and wife battering are just some of the past and still-current examples of problems that family relationships have posed for women.[19]

Thus, at least some traditional practices merit our distrust.

17. *After Virtue* (Notre Dame, Ind.: University of Notre Dame Press, 1981), p. 30 and passim.

18. Ibid., pp. 204–7.

19. Obviously, to emphasize the problems in traditional family relationships is not to deny that any positive value ever arises in such relationships. Reciting the positive values of relationships, however, does not contribute much to their improvement.

MacIntyre acknowledges this point. He concedes that "there *may* be practices . . . which simply *are* evil," but qualifies this immediately by writing, "I am far from convinced that there are."[20] Perhaps MacIntyre's disagreement on this point stems from his focusing only on "evil," a term that suggests thoroughgoing moral corruption, with no redeeming value. Most of the evils of the world, however, including those of traditional practices, are "mixed curses," to vary a familiar phrase. They are evil in their effects on some persons, beneficial in their effects on others, clearly wrong to some persons, ambiguous or even clearly right to others. Most of the evils of our traditional practices, in other words, involve some uncertainty, ambiguity, or even aspects of positive value; this, in my view, explains why those practices find supporters and adherents. If a traditional practice has elements of moral worth, however, this does not entail that there is nothing seriously wrong with it. Even MacIntyre concedes that his appeal to the notion of a practice to define and explain virtues does not entail "approval of all practices in all circumstances," nor does it obviate the need for "moral criticism" of some actual practices at some times.[21]

In an imperfect world, it is of the greatest importance to retain social traditions of critical moral reflection that can generate criticism and transformation of any social practices that promote or facilitate harm, exploitation, or oppression of persons. It matters not whether the practices be those of state, economy, or religion, whether marriage, family, or sexuality. The options of withdrawing from those institutions, resisting their alleged authority, and transforming them in progressive ways rest comfortably on the notion that traditional practices and institutions do not have an a priori morally decisive authority.

It is not difficult to locate practices that claim to support and

20. MacIntyre, *After Virtue*, p. 186.
21. Ibid., p. 187. In *After Virtue*, MacIntyre's reference point for a socially critical perspective on practices such as family traditions is "the good life for man" (p. 204). In that work, this notion is still undeveloped; however, the neo-Aristotelian account of the notion that MacIntyre anticipates does not promise to respond to feminist concerns.

promote critical reflection on all of our social institutions. We like to consider philosophy as one such practice, along with academic life in general and the arts, to name a few. But besides the traditions for critical *thought,* we also need practices that can inspire people, when necessary, to unconventional or disloyal *action.* It is here that our voluntary friendship practice makes a distinctive contribution. Friendships can support unconventional values, deviant life-styles, and other forms of disruption of social traditions. The voluntariness of friendship permits friends to evolve idiosyncratic values and life-styles or to find others who support and affirm the idiosyncratic values and life-styles that they have already evolved. As the political theorist Horst Hutter has written, "Every friendship is . . . a potential culture in miniature and also a potential countercul-ture."[22]

As mentioned earlier, friendship largely lacks the crusty rigidity of such formalized institutions as kinship. In this informality of friendship lies the option for sets of friends to go their own distinctive ways. The mutually voluntary way that friends evolve their relationship and their shared commitment allows them latitude for experimentation. Through shared affection and mutual support, which contribute to self-esteem, friendship enables the cultural survival of people who deviate from social norms and who suffer hostility and ostracism from others for their deviance.

The evolution of distinctive values and pursuits may lead friends to shared perspectives that generate disloyalties to existing social institutions. This gives friendship disruptive possibilities within society at large. Out of these disruptions may emerge beneficial social change. To be sure, the disloyalties and disruptions that friendship can promote may as easily foster change for the worse. But this is no less true of any practice that allows for experimentation. Friendship is, at least, democratic in its accessibility; the experimental possibilities are widely shared, since most people have friends and most people realize some degree of voluntariness

22. *Politics as Friendship* (Waterloo, Ont.: Wilfrid Laurier University Press, 1978), p. 19.

in the friendships they can form and, therefore, in the options they have for countering convention through the support of their friends.

It is true that people are somewhat free to evolve new shared values and pursuits in other relationships besides friendship. But those other relationships are often bound up with socially defined purposes that transcend what the individuals, as individuals, might want or need. Marriages, and the families that result have the socially defined purpose of the reproduction and rearing of children, and this may circumscribe the options and opportunities for participants to sustain socially disruptive activities. By contrast, friendships seem to have no socially defined purpose other than those that friends themselves evolve. These relationships are, in an important way, self-focused. They center on the affections, wants, needs, and commitments of the participants. Thus, the context that friendship provides for the development and support of unconventional attitudes and behaviors constrains the participants far less than the contexts provided by other close personal ties.

This flexibility of friendship as we know it is hardly a virtue in MacIntyre's estimation. By contrast, he upholds what he portrays as an Aristotelian conception of friendship: a network of relationships that unifies a political community in virtue of a "shared recognition of and pursuit of the good" and a "common project of creating and sustaining the life of the *polis*."[23] MacIntyre decries the weakness that he attributes to what he calls "modern" friendship derived from its consignment to "private life," in contrast to the "social and political" friendship of the ancients. Equally he disparages the basis of modern friendship in emotion and affection and regards it as, at best, "that inferior form of friendship which is founded on mutual advantage."[24]

23. Aristotle's actual view seems to be more complex than MacIntyre acknowledges. In Aristotle's view, for example, friendship plays a role in sustaining the various smaller communities that aim at their own special advantage even while comprising the larger polis; Aristotle, *Nichomachean Ethics*, 1159b–1160a.

24. MacIntyre, *After Virtue*, pp. 146–47.

For MacIntyre, the virtues of the right sort of friendship will cement the political bonds of the community. He, thus, grasps the political possibilities of friendship in general but misses the political dimension of specifically modern friendship, that is, friendship based on shared choice. Of course, had he recognized it for what it is, he would have rejected it. For modern friendship is not necessarily nonpolitical; rather it is, as a practice, politically unaffiliated. Modern friends have the option of evolving their own shared values since they are not bound by friendship rituals to participate in a community-wide allegiance to, and pursuit of, a communally defined good. It is precisely this unaffiliated nature of modern friendship that gives it the potential for supporting independent standpoints and unconventional pursuits, which may, in turn, disrupt other social institutions in progressive ways.

I have sketched a voluntarist account of friendship, emphasizing, first, that the special moral requirements among friends are grounded in the voluntary nature of the relationship; and, second, that the voluntary nature of the relationship, as a practice, is justified, in part, by its potential for supporting unconventionality and, in turn, for promoting social change. The two themes of my quasi-voluntarist account of friendship are interconnected: the social value I have attributed to a voluntary friendship practice is enhanced if the special requirements of friendship are viewed, by the participants in the practice, as grounded in their voluntary consent. The conviction that their own mutually evolved special friendship requirements are morally legitimate should bolster the self-esteem and personal enhancement they derive from their friendships, and this, in turn, can reinforce whatever socially transformative potential their lives hold.

It is now time to allay various possible objections to my account.

3. Dissociating Voluntarism from Liberal Contractarian Presuppositions

The most distinctive modern example of a voluntarist theory is liberal contractarianism. In Hobbes's extreme version of this theory, there is "no Obligation on any man, which ariseth not from some act of his own."[25] Feminist and other theorists who discern the moral and political importance of close personal relationships generally eschew such theoretical strategies as contractarianism for making sense of any of these relationships.[26] Objections are raised, for example, to the contractarian tendency to model all human interactions on market relationships and on the competition and conflict facing "economic man."[27] Criticism is leveled at the contractarian disregard of the ongoing, precontractual, social relationships and trust that the very possibility of sustainable contracts presupposes.[28] Feminist thought decisively rejects the liberal split between public and private realms that constituted only male human beings as free rational public citizens capable of consent and constituted women, by contrast, as unfree, nonrational members of the private, domestic realm.[29] And feminists denounce the inconsistent practice, in liberal societies, of falsely presuming wom-

25. *Leviathan*, ed. C. B. McPherson (Harmondsworth, U.K.: Penguin, 1968), p. 268.

26. See Virginia Held's writings on parental obligations, especially the responsibilities and responses of mothers, for example, "Non-Contractual Society: A Feminist View," in Marsha Hanen and Kai Nielsen, eds., *Science, Morality, and Feminist Theory, Canadian Journal of Philosophy* suppl. vol. 13 (1987): 111–37.

27. See Virginia Held, "Feminism and Moral Theory," in Eva Feder Kittay and Diana T. Meyers, eds., *Women and Moral Theory* (Totowa, N.J.: Rowman & Littlefield, 1987), p. 116.

28. See Carole Pateman's discussion of promising as a social practice, *The Problem of Political Obligation* (Berkeley: University of California Press, 1979) p. 26–30; and Virginia Held, *Rights and Goods* (New York: Free Press, 1984), chap. 5, "The Grounds for Social Trust."

29. The literature on this issue is extensive; see Pateman, *The Problem of Political Obligation*, pp. 189–94; and Seyla Benhabib, "The Generalized and the Concrete Other: The Kohlberg-Gilligan Controversy and Moral Theory," in Kittay and Meyers, *Women and Moral Theory*, pp. 154–77. For additional feminist criticism of voluntarist liberalism, see Alison Jaggar, *Feminist Politics and Human Nature* (Totowa, N.J.: Rowman & Allanheld, 1983); and Linda Nicholson, *Gender and History: The Limits of Social Theory in the Age of the Family* (New York: Columbia University Press, 1987).

en's consent when convenient to protect male privileges, for example, in rape litigation.[30]

If legitimate, these objections reveal that certain versions of voluntarism are unacceptable from a feminist standpoint.[31] They do not show, however, that voluntarism as such is inherently antifeminist. The sort of voluntarism that (partly) accounts for friendship need not be analogous to the voluntarism of liberal contractarianism in these troubling respects. The following four features, at least, differentiate the two approaches.

(1) For contemporary versions of social contract theory, persons are not to rely on their affection for other persons or the interest they might take in the well-being of others in their deliberations over the merits of social institutions or forms of social cooperation.[32] Friendship voluntarism, by contrast, has no theoretical need for the typical liberal contractarian presupposition of mutual disinterest among persons and can accommodate the recognition of their (varying degrees of) mutual interest.

Most human beings care about some persons other than themselves. The liberal contractarian assumption of mutual disinterest

30. Legal practice in this area has assigned to female victims of rape the burden of proving nonconsent, and the evidentiary requirements for such proof have been demanding. For a discussion of these issues in the context of liberal voluntarism, see Carole Pateman, "Women and Consent," *Political Theory* 8 (May 1980): 149–68, esp. pp. 156–62. Only recently have these practices been modified somewhat in the United States; see Leigh Bienen, "Rape III—National Developments in Rape Reform Legislation," *Women's Rights Law Reporter* 6 (Spring 1980): 170–213.

31. I am skeptical about the argument that the public-private split necessarily constitutes women as incapable of rational consent. But that is a discussion for another time.

32. Thus, contemporary social contract theorists such as John Rawls and David Gauthier each restrict the standpoint from which social institutions are to be assessed by limiting what are to count as acceptable reasons for consenting to certain social institutions or forms of social cooperation. For Rawls, the relevant limitation is expressed as the assumption of mutual disinterest: *A Theory of Justice* (Cambridge: Harvard University Press, 1971), esp. pp. 127–30; for Gauthier, it is called "mutual unconcern," or, more colorfully, "nontuism": *Morals by Agreement* (Oxford: Oxford University Press, 1986), esp. pp. 328–29.

is meant to make it theoretically inappropriate for us to *appeal* to those interests in justifying social institutions or forms of social cooperation. Liberal contractarianism is about foundational choices that pertain to the overall organization of society and government. It is not about the choices we make as particular individuals facing the specific circumstances of our daily lives. My quasi-voluntarist account of friendship is, by contrast, concerned with those everyday circumstances in which our interests in particular other persons are of paramount concern. The relationship of friendship is motivated by mutual affection and positive regard. Without such a mutual interest, a relationship would simply not constitute a friendship.

Moreover, concern for a friend may well change the nature of the self's own interests. The mutual interest of friendship is a complex, interconnected, reciprocal process. One's own preferences may be modified by the preferences of the friend so as to produce shared values and purposes. The friendship becomes fashioned over time by the, ideally mutual, adjustments of the parties to the relationship.

Because the other friend is a friend, what she wants from the friendship matters to me. If I initially want to participate in certain activities with her but discover that she would prefer to avoid them, I do not simply search for a bargaining advantage to force her to yield. Since she is already, or is becoming, my friend, I am, by definition, interested in her and in what she wants. Against my own needs and desires, I now have a countervailing inclination to attend to her needs and desires, even when they conflict with my own. Her response has altered, and added complexity to, the nature of *my desire*, to the nature of what I want and expect from our friendship.

If this account of the mutual adjustment of interest is correct, then an interest in someone else's well-being would not constitute a mere variety of self-interest but would interact with, and influence, self-interest rather more like a separable dimension of motivation. Theoretical accounts of voluntary friendship practices should not disregard the mutual concern on which such relationships are based. In establishing cooperative arrangements with someone one cares about, one does not merely want to bargain for a "good deal" in which one minimizes the concessions one makes.[33] Thus, a voluntarist account of friendship would tie its notion of consent, at the outset, to the conception of persons who are other-interested as well as self-interested.[34]

(2) A second difference between friendship voluntarism and liberal contractarian voluntarism is that friendship is genuinely, and not simply hypothetically, voluntary. In contemporary philosophical versions of contract theory, the social contract generally becomes the rational reconstruction of a hypothetical agreement[35] that was never entered into at all by most of the persons on whose behalf the theory is advanced—persons who may not even be rational by conventional philosophical criteria. Certain choices are theoretically determined to be appropriate for all of us to make in our capacity as, perhaps, "free and equal persons" or "utility-maximizers."[36] The voluntariness presumed by such reconstructions is, of course, admittedly hypothetical.

It is clear why such an approach might seem necessary in regard to contractarian theories of the state. There is, as yet, no workable process by which all the members of a political community may share their reflective deliberations over basic institu-

33. Gauthier uses this wording to characterize the process of accommodation that constitutes the basis of social cooperation: *Morals by Agreement*, pp. 137–45.

34. At a more developed stage, such a theory would also take account of both the particularized concern we have for others of our acquaintance that we care for and the generalized, abstract concern some might feel for large numbers of humankind who are not known in particular.

35. The expression "hypothetical voluntarism" is used by Pateman in *The Problem of Political Obligation*, p. 15. She adapted it from Hanna Pitkin's expression "hypothetical consent"; see Hanna Pitkin, "Obligation and Consent," in P. Laslett, W. G. Runciman, and Q. Skinner, eds., *Philosophy, Politics, and Society*, 4th ser. (Oxford: Blackwell, 1972).

36. John Rawls now appeals to "the nature of democratic citizens viewed as free and equal persons"; see his "Justice as Fairness: Political Not Metaphysical," *Philosophy and Public Affairs* 14, no. 3 (1985): 227. Gauthier develops his theory of impartial morality as part of the theory of rational choice, according to which rationality is identified with the "maximization of utility" and utility is a measure of preference: *Morals by Agreement*, pp. 2–4 and 22.

tions or the fundamentals of social cooperation in one grand civic dialogue. Given this current impossibility, some other means must be found of theoretically representing all the members of a political community in the deliberative process that is to justify their constitution as a state. Hypothetical consent, as rationally reconstructed, is an interpretation of social contract that aims at representing somehow the participation, in some sense, of *all* citizens in the scope of the so-called shared agreement. (Of course, whether or not actual citizens are in any way bound by a theoretical hypothetical consent represented on their behalf without their actual participation is quite another matter.)[37]

At any rate, the unwieldiness of the process of shared agreement is not a problem in friendship. In accounting for the constitution of friendship in our culture, there is no need for a concept of hypothetical consent. Friends generally talk to each other. Actual friends can usually share their thoughts about the nature of their friendship. Those persons who never convey to friends their thoughts or feelings about their friendship might be exhibiting their own idiosyncrasies of personal style in intimacy. Or they might be withholding their deepest thoughts in order to protect themselves against friends of more privileged social stature who might turn out to be untrustworthy after all. Or they might be men, and might have been raised to avoid emotional expressiveness and intimate self-disclosure even in close personal relationships. Such patterns of noncommunicativeness in close relationship seem not to be part of the cultural conception or idealization of friendship but to derive instead from other contingently related social conditions, such as the practices of masculinity. Nothing about friendship as such in our culture mitigates against communication between or among friends about the nature of their relationship. In light of the mutual communicative possibilities of friendship, a voluntarist account of friendship could accept at face value the mutual commitments friends actually make or tacitly understand in their relationship with each other. If people's express (or tacit)

37. See Jeffrey Paul, "Substantive Social Contracts and the Legitimate Basis of Political Authority," *Monist* 66, no. 4 (1983): 513–28.

[226]

friendship commitments are to be disregarded by moral theory, the reasons for doing so must be defended carefully, and the explanation for doing so cannot be that the process of achieving shared agreement is unmanageable.[38]

Parenthetically, we should note that the concept of choice is hardly without difficulties. Acquiescent behavior, and even expressed consent, does not in general necessarily indicate genuine consent. Consent may occur as a strategy for accommodating to difficult or coercive circumstances; in those cases it is not voluntary in the requisite sense. However, the coercion may not be obvious to others or even well understood by those who are its victims; a person may misunderstand her situation, her needs, her self.

Choices of economic relationships, for example, are often made under significant constraints; a person being hired in a particular job may be under constraints of economic necessity that undermine the voluntariness of her choice to join that company and that lead her to choose not so much these particular co-workers as any job offer here and now. In that respect, such choices may not be equally voluntary on all sides and are usually not mutual choices to share a relationship but are instead choices aimed at other ends, choices that result in certain relationships when they are enacted. Friendship, by contrast, is supposed to be a mutually voluntary commitment to another particular person and to the relationship with

38. Empirical studies suggest that among the large number of acquaintances one might have, friendships typically arise with those who are similar along such dimensions as age, sex, class, and race. See Lois Verbrugge, "The Structure of Adult Friendship Choices," *Social Forces* 56, no. 2 (1977): 576–97. All these characteristics and more play some role in determining whether we enter into relationships of equality, mutual trust, reciprocal concern, or intimacy with particular others. Of course, these factors do not determine who our friends are in any strict sense; they are not inexorable, and we do find frequent exceptions. Still, the existence of such widespread patterns of similarity among friends suggests that what seems like voluntary choice in one's movement toward a closer relationship with someone may have strong elements of attraction in it that are not within the range of volitional control and may even fall outside the scope of one's reflective self-awareness. As noted in the text, however, it does not seem to me that these psychological influences are relevant to the sense in which friendship is, or should be, voluntary.

that person. Even though there might be circumstances which lessen the voluntariness of friendship, our commonly accepted ideals of friendship seem to be reasonably approximated in case the relationship rests on a commitment that was not coerced, imposed, or ascribed.

(3) A third differentiating feature of my quasi-voluntarist account of friendship is that it is concerned with certain nongovernmental moral requirements. By contrast, for liberalism, voluntarism was thought to have solved the problem of so-called *political* obligation, that is, the problem of justifying obedience to the *state*.[39] This endeavor has a noteworthy ambiguity. A liberal contract theory may merely defend the legitimacy of certain idealized political institutions. At the same time, the institutions of actual societies that call themselves "liberal" may not fit the conceptual model. Yet the theoretical contractarian exercise may seem, to many, to show the legitimacy of actual societies which identify themselves as liberal. Because of this penumbra of seeming legitimation which liberal contract theories cast, many theorists who are critical of actual "liberal" societies may become suspicious of any voluntarist theoretical strategies.

However, this legitimation spillover is not inherently bound up with the voluntarist component of liberal contractarian theories. There is nothing intrinsic to the notion of moral requirements being based on voluntary choice that causes the hypothetical representation of consent to an idealized state to be misconstrued as the consensual justification of actual states.

Furthermore, a quasi-voluntarist account of friendship is not even focused on the problem of obligations toward governments. Instead, it is centered on certain problems pertaining to very small-scale relationships, in particular, the problem of accounting for the special requirements that specific sets of friends have to treat one another in certain ways.

39. See the discussion by A. John Simmons in chap. 3, "The Consent Tradition," of his *Moral Principles and Political Obligations* (Princeton: Princeton University Press, 1979).

(4) A fourth difference between the two sorts of voluntarisms is that a quasi-voluntarist account of friendship does not utilize the conception of an atomistic or presocial self. Indeed, this is not a necessary difference between friendship voluntarism and contemporary social contract theory since this classical presupposition has already been explicitly disavowed by some contemporary contractarians. But it is a point worth mentioning since various communitarian critics of liberal and contractarian theories still consider it to be a philosophical underpinning of those theories.[40]

I am inclined to agree, for example, with Jean Hampton when she argues that a contractarian account of political obligation does not need Hobbes's radical individualism, a conception of human selves as prior to their socially constituted identities.[41] Hampton's alternative contractarian underpinning is what she calls "moderate individualism," the view that conceptualizes individuals as prepolitical, that is, as having natures that are independent of the particular *governments* under which they live, although not as having presocial natures. Tangentially, we might notice that this view does not provide an account of the constitution of social life as such, and, thus, it renders the expression *"social* contract theory" obsolete. The resulting theory should be called *"state* contract theory" instead.[42]

At any rate, a quasi-voluntarist account of friendship similarly has no use for the conception of a presocial self. Participation in specific friendships is clearly also not the constitution of social life as such, and there is no reason to imagine that the basis for one's

40. See Michael J. Sandel, *Liberalism and the Limits of Justice* (Cambridge: Cambridge University Press, 1982). For further discussion of the contractarian criticism of the atomistic self and its limited relevance to the goals of feminist practice, see Chapter 9.

41. Jean Hampton, *Hobbes and the Social Contract Tradition* (Cambridge: Cambridge University Press, 1986), pp. 6–11 and 270–72.

42. Some contemporary versions of contractarianism remain more ambitious than this. In Gauthier, *Morals by Agreement*, voluntarism is connected with an account of moral obligation generally, across the whole range of social and political life.

commitment to a friend must originate wholly within the emotional or cognitive resources of an atomistically conceived individual self.[43]

Thus, a quasi-voluntarist account of friendship can easily avoid various objectionable features of liberal contractarianism that disturb feminist, communitarian, and other philosophers. It does so by presupposing mutual interest among friends, avoiding the notion of hypothetical voluntariness, ignoring the problem of duties toward the state, and shunning the conception of an atomistic presocial self.

To conclude: I explored the nature of friendship as a voluntary relationship (in this culture) and proposed a quasi-voluntarist moral account of friendship which avoids some of the troubling features of liberal contractarian voluntarism. According to this account, first, the special requirements of friendship are justified, to a significant extent, by the voluntary nature of the relationship. And, second, the voluntary nature of the relationship, as a practice, is justified, among other things, by its potential for supporting unconventionality and, in turn, for promoting social change. In the next chapter, I delve more deeply into the ways friendship may facilitate changes in communal traditions.

43. For a discussion of the social conception of the self and a summary of its importance to contemporary moral theory, see Chapter 3 above.

9

Feminism and
Modern Friendship:
Dislocating the Community

A predominant theme of much recent feminist thought is the criticism of the abstract individualism that underlies some important versions of liberal political theory.[1] Abstract individualism considers individual human beings as social atoms, abstracted from their social contexts, and disregards the role of social relationships and human community in constituting the very identity and nature of individual human beings. Sometimes the individuals of abstract individualism are posited as rationally self-interested utility-

1. See Carole Pateman, *The Problem of Political Obligation: A Critique of Liberal Theory* (Berkeley: University of California Press, 1979); Zillah Eisenstein, *The Radical Future of Liberal Feminism* (New York: Longman, 1981); Nancy C. M. Hartsock, *Money, Sex, and Power* (Boston: Northeastern University Press, 1983); Alison M. Jaggar, *Feminist Politics and Human Nature* (Totowa, N.J.: Rowman & Allanheld, 1983); Naomi Scheman, "Individualism and the Objects of Psychology," in Sandra Harding and Merrill B. Hintikka, eds., *Discovering Reality* (Dordrecht: D. Reidel, 1983), pp. 225–44; Jane Flax, "Political Philosophy and the Patriarchal Unconscious: A Psychoanalytic Perspective on Epistemology and Metaphysics," in Harding and Hintikka, *Discovering Reality*, pp. 245–81; and Seyla Benhabib, "The Generalized and the Concrete Other: The Kohlberg-Gilligan Controversy and Moral Theory," in Eva Feder Kittay and Diana T. Meyers, eds., *Women and Moral Theory* (Totowa, N.J.: Rowman & Littlefield, 1987), pp. 154–77.

maximizers.[2] Sometimes, also, they are theorized to form communities based fundamentally on competition and conflict among persons vying for scarce resources, communities that represent no deeper social bond than that of instrumental relations based on calculated self-interest.[3]

Against this abstractive individualist view of the self and of human community, many feminists assert a conception of the self as inherently social. This conception, as discussed earlier,[4] acknowledges the fundamental role of social relationships and human community in constituting both self-identity and the nature and meaning of the particulars of individual lives.[5] The modified conception of the self carries with it an altered conception of community. Conflict and competition are no longer considered to be the basic human relationships; instead they are being replaced by alternative visions of the foundation of human society derived from nurturance, caring attachment, and mutual interestedness.[6] Some feminists, for example, urge that the mother-child relationship be recognized as central to human society, and they project major changes in moral theory from such a revised focus.[7]

As noted earlier, some of these anti-individualist developments emerging from feminist thought are strikingly similar to other theoretical developments which are not specifically feminist. Thus,

2. See David Gauthier, *Morals by Agreement* (Oxford: Oxford University Press, 1986).

3. See George Homans, *Social Behavior: Its Elementary Forms* (New York: Harcourt, Brace and World, 1961); and Peter Blau, *Exchange and Power in Social Life* (New York: Wiley, 1974).

4. See Chapter 3.

5. See Drucilla Cornell, "Toward a Modern/Postmodern Reconstruction of Ethics," *University of Pennsylvania Law Review* 133 (January 1985): 291–380.

6. See Annette Baier, "Trust and Antitrust," *Ethics* 96, no. 2 (1986): 231–60; and Owen Flanagan and Kathryn Jackson, "Justice, Care, and Gender: The Kohlberg-Gilligan Debate Revisited," *Ethics* 97, no. 3 (1987): 622–37.

7. See Hartsock, *Money, Sex, and Power*, pp. 41–42; and Virginia Held, "Non-Contractual Society: A Feminist View," in Marsha Hanen and Kai Nielsen, eds., *Science, Morality, and Feminist Theory, Canadian Journal of Philosophy* suppl. vol. 13 (1987): 111–38.

the "new communitarians," to borrow Amy Gutmann's term,[8] have also reacted critically to various aspects of modern liberal thought, including abstract individualism, rational egoism, and an instrumental conception of social relationships. The communitarian self, or subject, is also not a social atom but is instead a being constituted and defined by its attachments, including the particularities of its social relationships, community ties, and historical context. Its identity cannot be abstracted from community or social relationships.

With the recent feminist attention to values of care, nurturance, and relatedness—values that psychologists call "communal"[9] and which, as documented in Chapters 4 and 5 above, have been amply associated with women and women's moral reasoning[10]—one might anticipate that communitarian theory would offer important insights for feminist reflection. There is considerable power to the model of the self as deriving its identity and nature from its social relationships, from the way it is intersubjectively apprehended, from the norms of the community in which it is embedded.

However, communitarian philosophy as a whole is a perilous ally for feminist theory. Communitarians invoke a model of community that is focused particularly on families, neighborhoods, and nations. These sorts of communities have harbored numerous social roles and structures that lead to the subordination of women, as much recent research has shown. Communitarians, however, seem oblivious to those difficulties and manifest a troubling complacency about the moral authority claimed or presupposed by those communities in regard to their members. By building on uncritical references to those sorts of communities, communitarian philosophy can lead in directions feminists should not wish to follow.

8. Amy Gutmann, "Communitarian Critics of Liberalism," *Philosophy and Public Affairs* 14 (Summer 1985): 308–22.
9. See Alice H. Eagly and Valerie J. Steffen, "Gender Stereotypes Stem from the Distribution of Women and Men into Social Roles," *Journal of Personality and Social Psychology* 46 (1984): 735–54.
10. See Carol Gilligan, *In a Different Voice* (Cambridge: Harvard University Press, 1982).

This discussion is an effort to redirect communitarian thought so as to avoid some of the pitfalls it poses, in its present form, for feminist theory and feminist practice. In the first section, I develop some feminist-inspired criticisms of communitarian philosophy as it is found in writings of Michael Sandel and Alasdair MacIntyre.[11] My brief critique of communitarian thought has the aim of showing that communitarian theory, in the form in which it condones or tolerates traditional communal norms of gender subordination, is unacceptable from any standpoint enlightened by feminist analysis. This does not preclude agreeing with certain specific communitarian views, for example, the broad metaphysical conception of the individual, self, or subject as constituted by its social relationships and communal ties, or the assumption that traditional communities have some value. But my aim in section 1 is critical: to focus on the communitarian disregard of gender-related problems with the norms and practices of traditional communities.

In the second section, I delve more deeply into the nature of certain sorts of communities and social relationship that communitarians largely disregard. I suggest that modern friendships, on the one hand, and urban relationships and communities, on the other, offer an important clue for developing a model of community that usefully counterbalances the family-neighborhood-nation complex favored by communitarians. With that model in view, we can begin to transform the communitarian vision of self and community into a more congenial ally for feminist theory.

1. The Social Self, in Communitarian Perspective

Communitarians share with most feminist theorists a rejection of the abstractly individualist conception of self and society so prominent in modern liberal thought.[12] This self—atomistic, pre-

11. In particular, Michael Sandel, *Liberalism and the Limits of Justice* (Cambridge: Cambridge University Press, 1982); and Alasdair MacIntyre, *After Virtue* (Notre Dame, Ind.: University of Notre Dame Press, 1981).

12. Contemporary liberals do not regard the communitarians' metaphys-

social, empty of all metaphysical content except abstract reason and will—is allegedly able to stand back from all the contingent moral commitments and norms of its particular historical context and assess each of them in the light of impartial and universal criteria of reason. The self who achieves a substantial measure of such reflective reconsideration of the moral particulars of her life has achieved autonomy, a widely esteemed liberal value.

In contrast to this vision of the self, the new communitarians pose the conception of a self whose identity and nature are defined by her contingent and particular social attachments. Communitarians extol the communities and social relationships, including family and nation, that comprise the typical social context in which the self emerges to self-consciousness. Thus, Michael Sandel speaks warmly of "those loyalties and convictions whose moral force consists partly in the fact that living by them is inseparable from understanding ourselves as the particular persons we are— as members of this family or community or nation or people, as bearers of this history, as sons and daughters of that revolution, as citizens of this republic."[13] Sandel continues:

> Allegiances such as these are more than values I happen to have or aims I "espouse at any given time". They go beyond the obligations I voluntarily incur and the "natural duties" I owe to human beings as such. They allow that to some I owe more than justice requires or even permits, not by reason of agreements I have made but instead in virtue of those more or less enduring

---

ical claims (discussed below) as a threat to liberal theory. The liberal concept of the self as abstracted from social relationships and historical context is now treated, not as a metaphysical presupposition, but, rather, as a vehicle for evoking a pluralistic political society whose members disagree about the good for human life. With this device, liberalism seeks a theory of political process that aims to avoid relying on any human particularities that might presuppose parochial human goods or purposes. See John Rawls, "Justice as Fairness: Political Not Metaphysical," *Philosophy and Public Affairs* 14, no. 3 (1985): 223–51; and Joel Feinberg, "Liberalism, Community, and Tradition," excerpted from *Harmless Wrongdoing*, vol. 4 of *The Moral Limits of the Criminal Law* (Oxford: Oxford University Press, 1988).

13. *Liberalism and the Limits of Justice*, p. 179.

attachments and commitments which taken together partly *define the person I am.*[14]

Voicing similar sentiments, Alasdair MacIntyre writes:

> We all approach our own circumstances as bearers of a particular social identity. I am someone's son or daughter, someone else's cousin or uncle; I am a citizen of this or that city, a member of this or that guild or profession; I belong to this clan, that tribe, this nation. Hence what is good for me has to be the good for one who inhabits these roles. As such, I inherit from the past of my family, my city, my tribe, my nation, a variety of debts, inheritances, rightful expectations and obligations. These constitute the given of my life, my moral starting point. This is in part what gives my life its own moral particularity.[15]

It is remarkable that neither writer mentions sex or gender as a determinant of particular identity. Perhaps this glaring omission derives not from a failure to realize the fundamental importance of gender in personal identity—could anyone really miss that?—but rather from the aim to emphasize what social relationships and communities contribute to identity, along with the inability to conceive that gender is a social relationship or that it constitutes communities.

For communitarians, at any rate, these social relationships and communities have a kind of morally normative legitimacy; they define the "moral starting points," to use MacIntyre's phrase, of each individual life. The traditions, practices, and conventions of our communities have at least a prima facie legitimate moral claim upon us. MacIntyre does qualify the latter point by conceding that "the fact that the self has to find its moral identity in and through its membership in communities such as those of the family, the neighborhood, the city and the tribe does not entail that the self has to accept the moral *limitations* of the particularity of those forms of community."[16] Nevertheless, according to MacIntyre, one's

14. Ibid.; italics mine.
15. *After Virtue*, pp. 204–5. This passage was quoted earlier, in Chapter 3.
16. Ibid., p. 205.

moral quests must begin by "moving forward from such particularity," for it "can never be simply left behind or obliterated."[17]

Despite feminist sympathy for a conception of the self as social and an emphasis on the importance of social relationships, at least three features of the communitarian version of these notions are troubling from a feminist standpoint. First, the communitarian's metaphysical conception of an inherently social self has little usefulness for normative analysis; in particular, it will not support a specifically feminist critique of individualist personality. Second, communitarian theory pays insufficient regard to the illegitimate moral claims that communities make on their members, linked, for example, to hierarchies of domination and subordination. Third, the specific communities of family, neighborhood, and nation so commonly invoked by communitarians are troubling paradigms of social relationship and communal life. I discuss each of these points in turn.

First, the communitarian's metaphysical conception of the social self does not support feminist critiques of ruggedly individualist personality or its associated attributes: the avoidance of intimacy, non-nurturance, social distancing, aggression, and violence. Feminist theorists have often been interested in developing a critique of our cultural norm of the highly individualistic, competitive, aggressive personality type, seeing that personality type as more characteristically male than female and as an important part of the foundation for male domination throughout society and culture.

Largely following the work of Nancy Chodorow, Dorothy Dinnerstein, and, more recently, Carol Gilligan,[18] many feminists have theorized that the processes of psycho-gender development, in a society in which early infant care is the primary responsibility of women but not men, result in a radical distinction between the genders in the extent to which the self is constituted by, and identifies with, its relational connections to others. Males are theorized

17. Ibid.
18. Dorothy Dinnerstein, *The Mermaid and the Minotaur: Sexual Arrangements and Human Malaise* (New York: Harper & Row, 1976); Nancy Chodorow, *The Reproduction of Mothering* (Berkeley: University of California Press, 1978); and Gilligan, *In a Different Voice*.

to seek and value autonomy, individuation, separation, and the moral ideals of rights and justice that are thought to depend on a highly individuated conception of persons. By contrast, females are theorized to seek and value connection, sociality, inclusion, and moral ideals of care and nurturance.[19]

Highly individuated selves seem to be a problem. They appear incapable of human attachments based on mutuality and trust, unresponsive to human needs, approaching social relationships merely as rationally self-interested utility maximizers, thriving on separation and competition, and creating social institutions that tolerate, even legitimize, violence and aggression.

However, a metaphysical view that all human selves are constituted by their social and communal relationships does not itself entail a critique of these highly individualistic selves or yield any indication of what degree of psychological attachment to others is desirable. On metaphysical grounds alone, there is no reason to suppose that caring, nurturant, relational, sociable selves are better than more autonomous, individualistic, and independent selves. According to a conception of selves as inherently social, all selves, whatever their personality or character, are equivalently constituted as social at a metaphysical level.

On this view, abstract individualism's failure is not that it has produced asocial selves, for, on the communitarian view, such beings are metaphysically impossible. Rather, the mistake in abstract individualism is simply to have failed theoretically to *acknowledge* that selves are inherently social. On the basis of a metaphysical conception of the self as social, it follows that autonomy, independence, and separateness are merely alternative ways of being socially constituted, no worse or better than heteronomy, dependence, and connectedness.

The communitarian conception of the social self, if it is simply

19. In Chapter 5, I question the empirical authenticity of this view of female-male difference, suggesting that it might reflect the influence of mistaken gender stereotypes. The present passage concerns feminist worries about aggressively individualistic personalities. My point about such personalities is independent of whether or not gender stereotypes mistakenly bias us toward attributing such personalities to men more than to women.

a metaphysical view about the constitution of the self (which is what it seems to be), thus provides no basis for regarding nurturant, relational selves as morally superior to those who are highly individualistic. For that reason, it appears to be of no assistance to feminist theorists seeking a normative account of what might be wrong or excessive about competitive self-seeking behaviors or aggressively individualistic character traits. The communitarian social self, indeed, any merely metaphysical account of the self as inherently social, is largely irrelevant to the array of normative tasks that many feminist thinkers have set for a conception of the self.

My second concern about communitarian philosophy has to do with the legitimacy of the communal norms and traditions that are supposed to define the moral starting points of community members. As a matter of moral psychology, it is certainly common for people to take for granted the moral legitimacy of the norms, traditions, and practices of their communities. However, this point about moral psychology does not entail that those norms and practices really are morally legitimate. It leaves open the question of whether, and to what extent, those claims might really be morally binding. Unfortunately, the new communitarians seem sometimes to go beyond the point of moral psychology to a stronger view, namely, that the moral claims of communities really are morally binding, at least as "moral starting points." MacIntyre refers to the "debts, inheritances, *rightful* expectations and obligations"[20] that we "inherit" from family, nation and so forth.

But such inheritances are enormously varied. In light of this variety, MacIntyre's normative complacency is quite troubling. Many communities practice the disturbing exclusion and suppression of non–group members, especially outsiders defined by ethnicity and sexual orientation.[21] In addition, there surely are "rightful expectations and obligations" that cross community lines, some of them involving the rectification of past wrongs that also

20. *After Virtue,* p. 205; italics mine.
21. A similar point is made by Iris Young in "The Ideal of Community and the Politics of Difference," *Social Theory and Practice* 12 (Spring 1986): 12–13.

crossed community lines. Did Jews, Gypsies, Poles, Czechoslovakians, among others, not have "rightful expectations" that Germany would not practice military conquest and unimaginable genocide? Did Germany not owe reparations to non-Germans for those same genocidal practices? If the new communitarians do not recognize legitimate "debts, inheritances, rightful expectations and obligations" across community lines, then their views also have diminished relevance for our radically heterogeneous modern society. Our society intermixes an array of smaller communities which often retain a substantial degree of cohesive separation from the rest. If there are intercommunity obligations that override communal norms and practices, then moral particularity is not accounted for by communal norms alone. In that case, the community as such, that is, the relatively bounded and local network of relationships which forms a subject's primary social setting, would not singularly determine the legitimate moral values or requirements that rightfully constitute the self's moral commitments or self-definition.

Besides excluding or suppressing outsiders, the practices and traditions of numerous communities are exploitative and oppressive toward many of their own members. This problem is of special relevance to women. The traditions and practices that create, promote, emphasize, or rely on gender differentiation often lead to the subordination, exploitation, or abuse of women. Many of these traditions are located in the sorts of communities invoked uncritically by communitarians, for example, family practices and national political traditions. The communitarian emphasis on communities unfortunately dovetails too well with the current emphasis on that mythic idealization known as "the family." It harkens back to the world of what some sociologists call communities of "place," the world of family, neighborhood, school, and church, which rested on a morally troubling politics of gender. Any political theory that lends support to the cultural hegemony of such communities and that supports them in a position of unquestioned moral authority must be viewed with grave suspicion. I will come back to this issue when I turn to my third objection to communitarian philosophy.

It is eminently plausible to admit into our descriptive notion of the self the important constitutive role played by social and communal relationships. It does not thereby follow, however, that the moral claims made by a community on any particular subject who is a member or who identifies herself in its terms are necessarily morally authoritative for her. The moral claims or imperatives of the community that constitutes or defines someone are not morally binding on her simply in virtue of being the moral claims of her constitutive communities. To evaluate the moral identities conferred by communities on their members, we need a theory of communities, of their interrelationships, of the structures of power, dominance, and oppression within and among them. Only such a theory would allow us to assess the legitimacy of the claims made by communities upon their members by way of their traditions, practices, and conventions of "debts, inheritances, . . . expectations, and obligations."

The communitarian approach appears to celebrate the attachments in which any person finds herself unavoidably embedded, the familial ties and so forth. Even apart from the questionable moral authority of communities, the issue of communal loyalty is not so easily decided. In our heterogeneous society, we may find ourselves embedded in several communities simultaneously. Some communities and relationships compete with others, and some relationships provide standpoints from which other relationships appear threatening or dangerous to oneself, one's integrity, or one's well-being. In such cases, simple formulas about the value of community provide no guidance. The problem is not simply to appreciate community per se but rather to reconcile the conflicting claims, demands, and identity-defining influences of the variety of communities of which one is a part.

It is worth recalling that liberalism has always condemned, in principle if not in practice, the norms of social hierarchy and political subordination based on inherited or ascribed status. While liberals historically have usually applied this tenet only to the public realm of civic relationships,[22] feminism seeks to

22. John Stuart Mill's *Subjection of Women* is a noteworthy exception. My

extend it more radically to the "private" realm of family and other communities of place. In particular, those norms and claims of local communities that sustain hierarchies based on gender have no intrinsic legitimacy from a feminist standpoint. A feminist interest in community aims for social institutions and relational structures that diminish and, finally, erase gender subordination.

Reflections such as these characterize the concerns of the modern self, the self who acknowledges no a priori loyalty to any feature of situation or role and who claims the right to question the moral legitimacy of any contingent moral claim.[23] We can agree with the communitarians that it would be impossible for the self to question all her contingencies at once, but at the same time, unlike the communitarians, still emphasize the critical importance of morally questioning various particular communal norms and circumstances one at a time.

A third problem with communitarian philosophy has to do with the sorts of communities evidently endorsed by communitarian theorists. Human beings participate in a variety of communities and social relationships, not only across time but at any one time. However, when people think of community, the examples they commonly call to mind are primarily those of family, neighborhood, school, and church.[24] These paradigms of community are also the ones most commonly invoked by Sandel and MacIntyre. These most familiar examples of community fall largely into two groups. First, there are political, or government-based, communities which constitute our civic and national identities in a public world of nation-states. MacIntyre mentions city and nation, while Sandel writes of "nation or people, . . . bearers of this history, . . . sons and daughters of that revolution, . . . citizens

thanks to L. W. Sumner for reminding me of the relevance of this work to my discussion.

23. See Cornell, "Toward a Modern/Postmodern Reconstruction of Ethics," p. 323. Such reflections among feminists often reflect a postmodern, rather than modern, standpoint. Fortunately, that topic exceeds the scope of this book.

24. This point is made by Young in "Ideal of Community," p. 12.

of this republic."[25] Second, there are local communities centered around families and neighborhood, which some sociologists call "communities of place." MacIntyre and Sandel both emphasize family, and MacIntyre also cites neighborhood along with clan and tribe.[26]

But where, one might ask, is the International Ladies Garment Workers' Union, the Teamsters, the Democratic party, Alcoholics Anonymous, or the National Organization for Women? Although MacIntyre does mention professions and, rather archaically, "guilds,"[27] these references are anomalous in his work, which, for the most part, ignores such communities as trade unions, political action groups, and even associations of hobbyists.

Some of the communities cited by MacIntyre and Sandel have indeed figured prominently in the historical experiences of women, especially the inclusive communities of family and neighborhood. By contrast, political communities form a particularly suspect class from a woman's perspective. We all recall how political communities have, until only recently in recorded history, excluded the legitimate participation of women. It would seem to follow that they have accordingly *not* historically constituted the identities of women in profound ways. As "daughters" of an American revolution spawned parthenogenetically by the "fathers" of our country, we find our political community has denied us the self-identifying heritage of our cultural mothers. In general, the contribution made to the identities of various groups of people by political communities is quite uneven, given that they are communities to which many are subject but in which far fewer actively participate.

At any rate, there is an underlying commonality to most of the communities that MacIntyre and Sandel cite as constitutive of self-identity and definitive of our moral starting points. Sandel himself explicates this commonality when he writes that, for people "bound

25. MacIntyre, *After Virtue*, p. 204; Sandel, *Liberatism and the Limits of Justice*, p. 179.
26. MacIntyre, *After Virtue*, p. 204; Sandel, *Liberalism and the Limits of Justice*, p. 179.
27. MacIntyre, *After Virtue*, p. 204

by a sense of community," the notion of community describes "*not a relationship they choose (as in a voluntary association) but an attachment they discover*, not merely an attribute but a constituent of their identity" (italics mine).[28] Not voluntary, but "discovered," relationships and communities are what Sandel takes to define subjective identity for those who are bound by a "sense of community." The communities to which we are involuntarily bound are those to which Sandel accords metaphysical pride of place in the constitution of subjectivity. What are important are not simply the "associations" in which people "co-operate" but the "communities" in which people "participate," for these latter "describe a form of life in which the members find themselves commonly situated 'to begin with', their commonality consisting less in relationships they have entered than in attachments they have found."[29] Thus, the social relationships one finds, the attachments that are discovered and not chosen, become the points of reference for self-definition by the communitarian subject.

For the child maturing to self-consciousness in her community of origin, typically a complex of family, neighborhood, school, and church, it seems uncontroversial that "the" community is found, not entered; discovered, not created. But this need not be true of an adult's communities of mature self-identification. Many communities are, for at least some of their members, communities of choice to a significant extent: labor unions, philanthropic associations, political coalitions, and, if one has ever moved or migrated, even the communities of neighborhood, church, city, or nation-state may have been chosen to an important extent. One need not have simply discovered oneself to be embedded in them in order for one's identity or the moral particulars of one's life to be defined by them. Sandel is right to indicate the role of found communities in constituting the unreflective, "given" identity that the self discovers when first beginning to reflect on herself. But for mature self-identity, we should also recognize a legitimate role for com-

28. *Liberalism and the Limits of Justice*, p. 150.
29. Ibid., pp. 151–52.

munities of choice, supplementing, if not displacing, the communities and attachments that are merely found.

Moreover, the discovered identity constituted by one's original community of place may be fraught with ambivalences and ambiguities. Our communities of origin do not necessarily constitute us as selves that agree or comply with the norms that unify those communities. Some of us are constituted as deviants and resisters by our communities of origin, and our defiance may well run to the foundational social norms that ground the most basic social roles and relationships upon which those communities rest.

Poet Adrienne Rich writes about her experiences growing up with a Christian mother, a Jewish father who suppressed his ethnicity, and a family community that taught Rich contempt for all that was identified with Jewishness. In 1946, while still a high school student, Rich saw, for the first time, a film about the Allied liberation of Nazi concentration camps. Writing about this experience in 1982, she brooded: "I feel belated rage that I was so impoverished by the family and social worlds I lived in, that I had to try to figure out by myself what this did indeed mean for me. That I had never been taught about resistance, only about passing. That I had no language for anti-Semitism itself."[30] As a student at Radcliffe in the late forties, Rich met "real" Jewish women who inducted her into the lore of Jewish background and customs, holidays and foods, names and noses. She plunged in with trepidation: "I felt I was testing a forbidden current, that there was danger in these revelations. I bought a reproduction of a Chagall portrait of a rabbi in striped prayer shawl and hung it on the wall of my room. I was admittedly young and trying to educate myself, but I was also doing something that *is* dangerous: I was flirting with identity."[31] Most important, Rich was consolidating her identity while separated, both geographically and psychologically, from the family community in which her ambiguous ethnicity originated.

30. "Split at the Root: An Essay on Jewish Identity," in Adrienne Rich, *Blood, Bread, and Poetry* (New York: W. W. Norton, 1986), p. 107.
31. Ibid., p. 108.

For Sandel, Rich's lifelong troubled reflections on her ethnic identity might seem compatible with his theory. In his view, the subject discovers the attachments that are constitutive of its subjectivity through reflection on a multitude of values and aims, differentiating what is self from what is not self. He might say that Rich discriminated among the many loyalties and projects which defined who she was in her original community, that is, her family, and discerned that her Jewishness appeared "essential"[32] to who she was. But it is not obvious, without question begging, that her original community really defined her as essentially Jewish. Indeed, her family endeavored to suppress loyalties and attachments to all things Jewish. Thus, one of Rich's quests in life, so evidently not inspired by her community of origin alone, was to reexamine the identity found in that original context. The communitarian view that found communities and social attachments constitute self-identity does not, by itself, explicate the processes by which we reconsider and revise, often through tortured struggles, our originally given identities. It seems more illuminating to say that Rich's identity became, in part, "chosen," that it had to do with social relationships and attachments she sought out rather than merely found, created as well as discovered.

Communities of place are relatively nonvoluntary; one's extended family of origin, for instance, is given or ascribed, and the relationships are found as one grows. The commitments and loyalties of our found communities, our communities of origin, may harbor ambiguities, ambivalences, contradictions, and oppressions that complicate as well as constitute identity and that have to be sorted out, critically scrutinized. In these undertakings, we are likely to use resources and skills derived from various communities and relationships, both those that are chosen or created and those that are found or discovered. Thus, our theories of community should recognize that resources and skills derived from communities that are not merely found or discovered may equally well contribute to the constitution of identity. The constitution of identity and moral particularity, for the modern self, may well require

32. This term is used by Sandel in *Liberalism and the Limits of Justice*, p. 180.

the contribution of radically different communities from those invoked by communitarians.

The whole tenor of communitarian thinking would change if we opened up the conception of the social self to encompass chosen communities, especially those that lie beyond the typical original community of family-neighborhood-school-church. No longer would communitarian thought present a seemingly conservative complacency about the private and local communities of place which have so effectively circumscribed, in particular, the lives of most women.

In the next section I explore more fully the role of communities and relationships of choice, which point the way toward a notion of community more congenial to feminist aspirations.

2. Modern Friendship, Urban Community, and Beyond

My goals are twofold: to retain the communitarian insights about the descriptive contribution of communities and social relationships to self-identity, yet open up for critical reflection the moral particulars imparted by those communities and identify the sorts of communities that provide nonoppressive and enriched lives for women.

Toward this end, it will be helpful to consider models of human relationship and community that contrast with those cited by communitarians. I believe that modern friendship and urban community can offer us crucial insights into the social nature of the modern self. It is in moving forward from these relationships that we have the best chance of reconciling the communitarian conception of the social self with the longed-for communities of feminist aspiration.

Modern friendship and the stereotypical urban community share an important feature that is either neglected or deliberately avoided in communitarian conceptions of human relationship. From a liberal, or Enlightenment, or modernist standpoint, this feature would be characterized as voluntariness: these relationships are based partly on choice.

Let's first consider friendship as it is understood in this culture. I have already argued[33] that friends are supposed to be people one chooses on one's own to share activities and intimacies. No particular people are assigned by custom or tradition to be a person's friends. From among the larger number of one's acquaintances, one moves toward closer and more friendlike relationships with some of them, motivated by one's own needs, values, and attractions. No consanguineal or legal connections formally establish or maintain ties of friendship. As this relationship is widely understood in our culture, its basis lies in voluntary choice.

In this context, "voluntary choice" refers to motivations arising out of one's own needs, desires, interests, values, and attractions, in contrast to motivations arising from what is socially assigned, ascribed, demanded, or coercively imposed. Because of its basis in voluntary choice, friendship is more likely than many other relationships, such as those of family and neighborhood, to be grounded and sustained by shared interests and values, mutual affection, and possibilities for generating reciprocal respect and esteem.

In the preceding chapter, I also argued that friendship is more likely than many other relationships to provide social support for people who are idiosyncratic, whose unconventional values and deviant life-styles make them victims of intolerance from family members and others who are unwillingly related to them. In this regard, friendship has socially disruptive possibilities. Out of the unconventional living it helps to sustain there often arise influential forces for social change. Friendship has had an obvious importance to feminist aspirations as the basis of the bond that is (ironically) called "sisterhood."[34] Friendship among women has been the cement not only of the various historical waves of the feminist movement but also of numerous communities of women throughout history who defied the local conventions for their gender and lived

33. See Chapter 8.
34. Martha Ackelsberg points out the ironic and misleading nature of this use of the term "sisterhood" in " 'Sisters' or 'Comrades'? The Politics of Friends and Families," in Irene Diamond, ed., *Families, Politics, and Public Policy* (New York: Longman, 1983), pp. 339–56.

lives of creative disorder.[35] In all these cases, women moved out of their given or found communities into new attachments with other women by their own choice, that is, motivated by their own needs, desires, attractions, and fears, rather than, and often in opposition to, the expectations and ascribed roles of their found communities.

Like friendship, many urban relationships are also based more on choice than on socially ascribed roles, biological connections, or other nonvoluntary ties. Urban communities include numerous voluntary associations, such as political action groups, support groups, associations of cohobbyists, and so on. Yet friendship is almost universally extolled, while urban communities and relationships have been theorized in wildly contradictory ways. Cities have sometimes been taken as "harbingers" of modern culture per se[36] and have been particularly associated with the major social trends of modern life, such as industrialization and bureaucratization.[37] The results of these trends are often thought to have been a fragmentation of real community and the widely lamented alienation of modern urban life: people seldom know their neighbors; population concentration generates massive psychic overload;[38] fear and mutual distrust, even outright hostility, generated by the dangers of urban life may dominate most daily associations. Under such circumstances, meaningful relationships are often theorized to be rare, if even possible.

Does this portrait of urban life sufficiently represent what cities offer their residents? It is probably true, in urban areas, that communities of *place* are diminished in importance; neighborhood plays a much less significant role in constituting community than it does

35. See Janice Raymond, *A Passion for Friends* (Boston: Beacon Press, 1986), esp. chaps. 2 and 3.

36. Claude Fischer, *To Dwell among Friends* (Chicago: University of Chicago Press, 1982), p. 1.

37. See Richard Sennett, "An Introduction," in Richard Sennett, ed., *Classic Essays on the Culture of Cities* (New York: Appleton-Century-Crofts, 1969), pp. 3–22.

38. See Stanley Milgram, "The Experience of Living in Cities," *Science* 167 (1970): 1461–68.

in nonurban areas.[39] This does not entail, however, that the social networks and communities of urban dwellers are inferior to those of nonurban residents.

Much evidence suggests that urban settings do not, as commonly stereotyped, promote only alienation, isolation, and psychic breakdown. The communities available to urban dwellers are different from those available to nonurban dwellers but not necessarily less gratifying or fulfilling.[40] Sociological research has shown that urban dwellers tend to form their social networks, their communities, from people who come together for reasons other than geographical proximity. Voluntary associations, such as political action groups, support groups, and so on, are a common part of modern urban life, with its large population centers and the greater availability of critical masses of people with special interests or needs. Communities of place, centered around family-neighborhood-church-school are more likely, for urban dwellers, to be supplanted by other sorts of communities, resulting in what sociologist Melvin Webber calls "community without propinquity."[41] As the sociologist Claude Fischer states, in urban areas, "population concentration stimulates allegiances to subcultures based on more significant social traits" than common locality or neighborhood.[42] But most important for our purposes, these are still often genuine communities and not the

39. Fischer, *To Dwell Among Friends*, pp. 97–103.

40. Ibid., pp. 193–232. Urban communities of place vary widely along numerous dimensions, one of the most important and thorniest of which is socioeconomic status. High-income urban dwellers are more involved with those not their kin than are low-income urban dwellers (pp. 91–93). Obviously, very poor urban dwellers do not have access to anything like the range of voluntary communal urban opportunities that wealthy urban dwellers do. The generalized observations presented in the text are not intended to deny these differences, but rather to emphasize features of urban community that contrast most strongly with communitarian models.

41. "Order in Diversity: Community without Propinquity," in R. Gutman and D. Popenoe, eds., *Neighborhood, City, and Metropolis* (New York: Random House, 1970), pp. 792–811.

42. Fischer, *To Dwell among Friends*, p. 273.

cesspools of Rum, Romanism, and Rebellion sometimes depicted by antiurbanists.

Literature reveals that women writers have been both repelled and inspired by urban communities. The city, as a concentrated center of male political and economic power, seems to exclude women altogether.[43] The city, however, can provide women with jobs, education, and the cultural tools with which to escape imposed gender roles, familial demands, and domestic servitude. The city can also bring women together, in work or in leisure, and lay the basis for bonds of sisterhood.[44] The quests of women who journey to cities leaving behind men, home, and family are subversive, writes literary critic Blanche Gelfant, and may well be perceived by others "as assaults upon society."[45] Cities open up for women possibilities of supplanting communities of place with relationships and communities of choice. Thus, urban communities of choice can provide the resources for women to surmount those moral particularities of family and place that define and limit their moral starting points.

Social theorists have long decried the interpersonal estrangement of urban life, an observation that seems predominantly inspired by the public world of conflict between various subcultural groups. Urbanism does not create interpersonal estrangement within subcultures but, rather, tends to promote social involvement.[46] This is especially true for people with special backgrounds and interests, for people who are members of small minorities, and for ethnic groups. Fischer has found that social relationships in urban centers are more "culturally specialized: urbanites were rel-

43. See the essays in Catharine Stimpson et al., eds., *Women and the American City* (Chicago: University of Chicago Press, 1980, 1981); and the special issue on "Women in the City," *Urban Resources* 3 (Winter 1986).

44. This is pointed out in Susan Merrill Squier, ed., *Women Writers and the City* (Knoxville: University of Tennessee Press, 1984), "Introduction," esp. pp. 3–10.

45. Blanche Gelfant, "Sister to Faust: The City's 'Hungry' Woman as Heroine," in ibid., p. 267.

46. Fischer, *To Dwell among Friends*, pp. 247–48.

atively involved with associates in the social world they considered most important and relatively uninvolved with associates, if any, in other worlds."[47] As Fischer summarizes it, "Urbanism . . . fosters social involvement in the subculture(s) of *choice*, rather than the subculture(s) of circumstances."[48] This is doubtless reinforced by the historically recent, and sometimes militant, expression of group values and demands for rights and respect by urban subcultural minorities.

We might describe urban relationships as being characteristically "modern" to signal their relatively greater voluntary basis. We find in these relationships and the social networks formed of them, not a necessary loss of community, but often an increase in importance of community of a different sort from that of family-neighborhood-church-school complexes. Yet these more voluntary communities may be as deeply constitutive of the identities and particulars of the individuals who participate in them as the communities of place so warmly invoked by communitarians.

Perhaps it is more illuminating to say that communities of choice foster not so much the constitution of subjects as their reconstitution. We seek out such communities as contexts in which to relocate and renegotiate the various constituents of our identities, as Adrienne Rich sought out the Jewish community in her college years. While people in a community of choice may not share a common history, their shared values or interests are likely to manifest backgrounds of similar experiences, as, for example, among the members of a lesbian community. The modern self may seek new communities whose norms and relationships stimulate and develop her identity and self-understanding more adequately than her unchosen community of origin, her original community of place.

In case it is chosen communities that help us to define ourselves, the project of self-definition would not arise from communities in which we merely found or discovered our immersion. It is likely that chosen communities, lesbian communities, for example, attract us in the first place because they appeal to features

47. Ibid., p. 230.
48. Ibid.

of ourselves which, though perhaps merely found or discovered, were inadequately or ambivalently sustained by our *un*chosen families, neighborhoods, schools, or churches. Unchosen communities of origin can provide us with deeply troubled identities, perhaps severely lacking in self-esteem or basic self-respect. Thus, unchosen communities are sometimes communities we can and should leave, to search elsewhere for the resources to help us discern who we really are. Such a search is not a quest for a timeless essence but, rather, for a vital and potentially evolving self-concept that one currently affirms.

A community of choice may be a community of people who share a common oppression. This is particularly critical in those cases in which the shared oppression is not concentrated within certain communities of place, as with ethnic minorities, but, rather, is focused on people who are distributed throughout social and ethnic groupings and who do not themselves comprise a traditional community of place. Unlike the communities of ethnic minorities, women are a paradigm example of such a distributed group and do not comprise a traditional community of place. Women's communities are seldom the original, nonvoluntary, found communities of their members.

To be sure, communities of choice range widely, from benign associations of hobbyists, gardening clubs, for example, to more hateful and deadly associations such as the Ku Klux Klan. Regrettably, these treacherous communities of choice may define the personal identities of their members as decisively and as profoundly as do the most virtuous of affiliations. In this respect, even the most loathsome of voluntary associations exemplifies the communitarian's metaphysical conception of social selfhood. Such communities serve to remind us of my earlier call to conjoin the communitarian metaphysical account of the origins of moral identity with a critical perspective on communal traditions and practices. I contended that the normative traditions of communities of place should not be regarded unquestioningly as morally authoritative. That caution must obviously extend as well to communities of choice.

It must also be remembered that nonvoluntary communities of

place are not without value. Most lives contain mixtures of relationships and communities, some given/found/discovered and some chosen/created. Most people probably are ineradicably constituted, to some extent, by their communities of place, their original families, neighborhoods, schools, churches, and nations. It is crucial that dependent children, elderly persons, and all other individuals whose lives and well-being are at great risk be supported by communities or social relationships whose other members do not or cannot choose arbitrarily to leave. Recent philosophical reflection on communities and relationships not founded or sustained by choice has brought out the importance of these social networks for the constitution of social life.[49] But these insights should not obscure the additional need for communities of choice to counter oppressive and abusive relational structures in those nonvoluntary communities by providing models of alternative social relationships and standpoints for critical reflection on self and community.

If one has already attained a critically reflective stance toward one's communities of origin, one's community of place, toward family, neighborhood, church, school, and nation, then one has probably at the same time already begun to question and distance oneself from aspects of one's identity in that community and, therefore, to have embarked on the path of personal redefinition. From such a perspective, the uncritical invocation of communities of place by communitarians appears deeply problematic. We can concede the influence of those communities without needing unreflectively to endorse it. We must develop communitarian thought beyond its complacent regard for the communities in which we merely find ourselves toward (and beyond) an awareness of the crucial importance of "dislocated" communities, communities of choice.

In this chapter, I have drawn together some important themes raised earlier in the book. I have suggested that the social self, however deeply rooted in her found communities, may neverthe-

49. See Baier, "Trust and Antitrust"; Held, "Non-Contractual Society"; and Pateman, *Problem of Political Obligation*.

less branch out toward chosen communal relationships with those who share her interests and concerns. These communities of choice can afford her new perspectives from which to redefine herself and reconsider the moral authority of her communal origins. Such personal growth, in community with those who share her aspirations and her dreams, can provide new social and moral conditions out of which to forge a liberated future.

SELECTED BIBLIOGRAPHY

The various literatures in the areas of partiality and impartiality, care and justice, and friendship and other personal relationships are vast, the more so if fields outside philosophy are counted. The list below is not intended to provide comprehensive coverage of the relevant areas. It contains mainly citations of works to which I make explicit reference in my discussions, either in the text or in the notes.

Abel, Elizabeth. "(E)merging Identities: The Dynamics of Female Friendship in Contemporary Fiction by Women," *Signs* 6, no. 3 (1981): 413–35.

Ackelsberg, Martha. " 'Sisters' or 'Comrades'? The Politics of Friends or Families." In *Families, Politics, and Public Policy*. Ed. Irene Diamond. New York: Longman, 1983.

Ackerman, Bruce. "Why Dialogue?" *Journal of Philosophy* 86 (January 1989): 5–22.

Addelson, Kathryn Pyne. *Impure Thoughts: Essays on Philosophy, Feminism, and Ethics*. Philadelphia: Temple University Press, 1991.

Allen, Jeffner. *Lesbian Philosophy*. Palo Alto, Calif.: Institute for Lesbian Studies, 1986.

Annas, David. "The Meaning, Value, and Duties of Friendship," *American Philosophical Quarterly* 24 no. 4 (1987): 349–56.

Aristotle. *Nichomachean Ethics*. Trans. W. D. Ross. In *The Basic Works of Aristotle*. Ed. Richard McKeon. Pp. 927–1112. New York: Random House, 1941.

Avineri, Shlomo, and Avner de-Shallit, eds. *Individualism and Community*. Oxford: Oxford University Press, 1992.

Badhwar, Neera K., ed. *Friendship: A Philosophical Reader*. Ithaca, N.Y.: Cornell University Press, 1993.

——. "Friendship, Justice, and Supererogation," *American Philosophical Quarterly* 22 (April 1985): 123–31.

———. "Why It Is Wrong to Be Always Guided by the Best: Consequentialism and Friendship," *Ethics* 101 (1991): 483–504.

Baier, Annette. "Hume, The Women's Moral Theorist?" In *Women and Moral Theory.* Ed. Eva Feder Kittay and Diana T. Meyers. Pp. 37–55. Totowa, N.J.: Rowman & Littlefield, 1987.

———. "The Need for More than Justice." In *Science, Morality, and Feminist Theory.* Ed. Marsha Hanen and Kai Nielsen. *Canadian Journal of Philosophy* suppl. vol. 13 (1987): 41–56.

———. *Postures of the Mind: Essays on Mind and Morals.* Minneapolis: University of Minnesota Press, 1985.

———. "Trust and Antitrust," *Ethics* 96 (January 1986): 231–60.

Baron, Marcia. "The Alleged Moral Repugnance of Acting from Duty," *Journal of Philosophy* 81 (April 1984): 197–220.

———. "Impartiality and Friendship," *Ethics* 101 (July 1991): 836–57.

———. *The Moral Status of Loyalty.* Dubuque, Iowa: Kendall Hunt, 1984.

Bartky, Sandra. *Femininity and Domination.* New York: Routledge, 1990.

Baumrind, Diana. "Sex Differences in Moral Reasoning: Response to Walker's (1984) Conclusion That There Are None," *Child Development* 57 (1986): 511–21.

Becker, Lawrence C. *Reciprocity.* London: Routledge & Kegan Paul, 1986.

Benhabib, Seyla. "The Generalized and the Concrete Other: The Kohlberg-Gilligan Controversy and Moral Theory." In *Women and Moral Theory.* Ed. Eva Feder Kittay and Diana T. Meyers. Pp. 154–77. Totowa, N.J.: Rowman & Littlefield, 1987.

Bienen, Leigh. "Rape III—National Developments in Rape Reform Legislation," *Women's Rights Law Reporter* 6 (Spring 1980): 170–213.

Blum, Larry, Marcia Homiak, Judy Housman, and Naomi Scheman. "Altruism and Women's Oppression." In *Philosophy and Women.* Ed. Sharon Bishop and Marjorie Weinzweig. Pp. 190–200. Belmont, Calif.: Wadsworth, 1979. Reprinted from *Philosophical Forum* 5 (1975).

Blum, Lawrence. *Friendship, Altruism, and Morality.* London: Routledge & Kegan Paul, 1980.

———. "Gilligan and Kohlberg: Implications for Moral Theory," *Ethics* 98 (April 1988): 472–91.

———. "Moral Exemplars: Reflections on Schindler, the Trocmes, and Others," *Midwest Studies in Philosophy* 13 (1988): 196–221.

Blustein, Jeffrey. *Care and Commitment.* New York: Oxford University Press, 1991.

Brink, David O. "Utilitarianism and the Personal Point of View," *Journal of Philosophy* 83 (August 1986): 417–38.

Broughton, John. "Women's Rationality and Men's Virtues: A Critique of Gender Dualism in Gilligan's Theory of Moral Development," *Social Research* 50 (Autumn 1983): 597–642.

Bunch, Charlotte. *Bringing the Global Home*. Denver: Antelope, 1985.

Butler, Judith. *Gender Trouble*. New York: Routledge, 1990.

Calhoun, Cheshire. "Justice, Care, Gender Bias," *Journal of Philosophy* 85 (1988): 451–63.

Cancian, Francesca. "The Feminization of Love," *Signs* 11, no. 4 (1986): 692–709.

Card, Claudia. "Gender and Moral Luck." In *Identity, Character, and Morality*. Ed. Owen Flanagan and Amélie Oksenberg Rorty. Pp. 199–218. Cambridge, Mass.: MIT Press, 1990.

———, ed. *Feminist Ethics*. Lawrence: University Press of Kansas, 1991.

Chodorow, Nancy. *The Reproduction of Mothering*. Berkeley: University of California Press, 1978.

Cohen, Joshua. "Olin on Justice, Gender, and the Family," *Canadian Journal of Philosophy* 22 (June 1992): 263–86.

Cole, Eve Browning, and Susan Coultrap-McQuin, eds. *Explorations in Feminist Ethics*. Bloomington: Indiana University Press, 1992.

Collins, Patricia Hill. *Black Feminist Thought: Knowledge, Consciousness, and the Politics of Empowerment*. New York: Routledge, 1990.

Cooper, John. "Aristotle on Friendship." In *Essays on Aristotle's Ethics*. Ed. Amélie O. Rorty. Pp. 301–40. Berkeley: University of California Press, 1980.

———. "Aristotle on the Forms of Friendship," *Review of Metaphysics* 30 (June 1977): 619–48.

———. "Friendship and the Good in Aristotle," *Philosophical Review* 86 (July 1977): 290–315.

Cornell, Drucilla. "Toward a Modern/Postmodern Reconstruction of Ethics," *University of Pennsylvania Law Review* 133 (January 1985): 291–380.

Cottingham, John. "Ethics and Impartiality," *Philosophical Studies* 43 (1983): 83–99.

———. "The Ethics of Self-Concern," *Ethics* 101 (July 1991): 798–817.

———. "Partiality, Favouritism, and Morality," *Philosophical Quarterly* 36 no. 144 (1986): 357–73.

Daniels, Norman, ed. *Reading Rawls*. New York: Basic Books, 1976.

Darwall, Stephen. *Impartial Reason*. Ithaca, N.Y.: Cornell University Press, 1984.

Deigh, John. "Love, Guilt, and the Sense of Justice," *Inquiry* 25 (1982): 391–416.

————. "Morality and Personal Relations." In *Person to Person*. Ed. George Graham and Hugh LaFollette. Pp. 106–23. Philadelphia: Temple University Press, 1989.

Diamond, Irene, ed. *Families, Politics, and Public Policy*. New York: Longman, 1983.

Dietz, Mary. "Citizenship with a Feminist Face: The Problem with Maternal Thinking," *Political Theory* 13 (February 1985): 19–37.

Dillon, Robin. "Care and Respect." In *Explorations in Feminist Ethics*. Ed. Eve Browning Cole and Susan Coultrap-McQuin. Pp. 69–81. Bloomington: Indiana University Press, 1992.

Dinnerstein, Dorothy. *The Mermaid and the Minotaur: Sexual Arrangements and Human Malaise*. New York: Harper & Row, 1976.

Donner, Wendy. *The Liberal Self*. Ithaca, N.Y.: Cornell University Press, 1991.

Eagly, Alice. *Sex Differences in Social Behavior: A Social Role Interpretation*. Hillsdale, N.J.: Erlbaum, 1987.

Eagly, Alice H., and Valerie J. Steffen. "Gender Stereotypes Stem from the Distribution of Women and Men into Social Roles," *Journal of Personality and Social Psychology* 46 (1984): 735–54.

Edman, Irwin, ed. *The Works of Plato*. New York: Modern Library, 1928.

Ehrenreich, Barbara. *The Hearts of Men: American Dreams and the Flight from Commitment*. New York: Anchor Press/Doubleday, 1983.

Ehrenreich, Barbara, and Deirdre English. *For Her Own Good: 150 Years of the Experts' Advice to Women*. Garden City, N.Y.: Anchor, 1978.

Eisenberg, Nancy, and Roger Lennon. "Sex Differences in Empathy and Related Capacities," *Psychological Bulletin* 94 (1983): 100–131.

Eisenstein, Hester, and Alice Jardine, eds. *The Future of Difference*. New Brunswick: Rutgers University Press, 1980.

Eisenstein, Zillah. *The Radical Future of Liberal Feminism*. New York: Longman, 1981.

Elshtain, Jean Bethke, ed. *The Family in Political Thought*. Amherst: University of Massachusetts Press, 1982.

English, Jane. "What Do Grown Children Owe Their Parents?" In *Having Children*. Ed. Onora O'Neill and William Ruddick. Pp. 351–56. New York: Oxford University Press, 1979.

Ewin, R. E. *Liberty, Community, and Justice*. Totowa, N.J.: Rowman & Littlefield, 1987.

Faludi, Susan. *Backlash: The Undeclared War against American Women*. New York: Crown, 1991.

Feinberg, Joel. *Harmless Wrongdoing*, vol. 4 of *The Moral Limits of the Criminal Law*. Oxford: Oxford University Press, 1988.

"Feminism and Political Theory." Symposium in *Ethics* 99 (January 1989): 219–406.

Ferguson, Ann. *Blood at the Root: Motherhood, Sexuality, and Male Dominance.* London: Pandora, 1989.

Fetterley, Judith. *The Resisting Reader: A Feminist Approach to American Fiction.* Bloomington: Indiana University Press, 1978.

Finifter, Ada W. "The Friendship Group as a Protective Environment for Political Deviants," *American Political Science Review* 68 (June 1974): 607–25.

Firth, Roderick. "Ethical Absolutism and the Ideal Observer," *Philosophy and Phenomenological Research* 12 (March 1952): 317–45.

Fischer, Claude. *To Dwell among Friends.* Chicago: University of Chicago Press, 1982.

Flanagan, Owen. "Virtue, Sex, and Gender: Some Philosophical Reflections on the Moral Psychology Debate," *Ethics* 92 (April 1982): 499–512.

Flanagan, Owen, and Kathryn Jackson. "Justice, Care, and Gender: The Kohlberg-Gilligan Debate Revisited," *Ethics* 97 no. 3 (1987): 622–37.

Flanagan, Owen, and Amélie Oksenberg Rorty, eds. *Identity, Character, and Morality.* Cambridge, Mass.: MIT Press, 1990.

Flax, Jane. "Political Philosophy and the Patriarchal Unconscious: A Psychoanalytic Perspective on Epistemology and Metaphysics." In *Discovering Reality.* Ed. Sandra Harding and Merrill Hintikka. Pp. 245–81. Dordrecht: D. Reidel, 1983.

Frazer, Elizabeth, Jennifer Hornsby, and Sabina Lovibond, eds. *Ethics: A Feminist Reader.* Oxford: Blackwell, 1992.

Fried, Charles. *An Anatomy of Values.* Cambridge: Harvard University Press, 1970.

——. *Right and Wrong.* Cambridge: Harvard University Press, 1978.

Friedman, Marilyn. "Autonomy and the Split-Level Self," *Southern Journal of Philosophy* 24 no. 1 (1986): 19–35.

——. "Autonomy in Social Context." In *Freedom, Equality, and Social Change.* Ed. James Sterba and Creighton Peden. Pp. 158–69. Lewiston, N.Y.: Edwin Mellen, 1989.

——. "Going Nowhere: Nagel on Normative Objectivity," *Philosophy* 65 (October 1990): 501–9.

——. "Moral Integrity and the Deferential Wife," *Philosophical Studies* 47 (January 1985): 141–50.

———. " 'They Lived Happily Ever After': Sommers on Women and Marriage," *Journal of Social Philosophy* 21 (Fall/Winter 1990): 57–65.

Friedman, Marilyn, and Larry May. "Harming Women as a Group," *Social Theory and Practice* 11 (Summer 1985): 207–34.

Frye, Marilyn. *The Politics of Reality*. Trumansburg, N.Y.: Crossing Press, 1983.

———. *Willful Virgin: Essays in Feminism 1976–1992*. Freedom, Calif.: Crossing Press, 1992.

Gauthier, David. *Morals by Agreement*. Oxford: Oxford University Press, 1986.

Gelfant, Blanche. "Sister to Faust: The City's 'Hungry' Woman as Heroine." In *Women Writers and the City*. Ed. Susan Merrill Squier. Pp. 265–87. Knoxville: University of Tennessee Press, 1984.

Gewirth, Alan. "Ethical Universalism and Particularism," *Journal of Philosophy* 85, no. 6 (1988): 283–302.

———. *Reason and Morality*. Chicago: University of Chicago Press, 1978.

Gilligan, Carol. "Do the Social Sciences Have an Adequate Theory of Moral Development?" In *Social Science as Moral Inquiry*. Ed. Norma Haan, Robert N. Bellah, Raul Rabinow, and William M. Sullivan. Pp. 33–51. New York: Columbia University Press, 1983.

———. *In a Different Voice*. Cambridge: Harvard University Press, 1982.

———. "Moral Orientation and Moral Development." In *Women and Moral Theory*. Ed. Eva Feder Kittay and Diana T. Meyers. Pp. 19–33. Totowa, N.J.: Rowman & Littlefield, 1987.

———. "Remapping the Moral Domain: New Images of the Self in Relationship." In *Reconstructing Individualism*. Ed. Thomas C. Heller, Morton Sosna, and David E. Wellbery. Pp. 237–52. Stanford: Stanford University Press, 1986.

———. "Reply," *Signs* 11 (1986): 324–33.

Gilligan, Carol, Janie Victoria Ward, Jill McLean Taylor, with Betty Bardige, eds. *Mapping the Moral Domain*. Cambridge: Harvard Center for the Study of Gender, Education, and Human Development, 1988.

Godwin, William. *Enquiry Concerning Political Justice*. Ed. K. Codell Carter. Oxford: Clarendon House, 1971.

Goodin, Robert E. *Protecting the Vulnerable*. Chicago: University of Chicago Press, 1985.

———. "What Is So Special about Our Fellow Countrymen?" *Ethics* 98 (July 1988): 663–86.

Gould, Carol, ed. *Beyond Domination*. Totowa, N.J.: Rowman & Allanheld, 1984.

Graham, George, and Hugh LaFollette, eds. *Person to Person.* Philadelphia: Temple University Press, 1989.

Greeno, Catherine G., and Eleanor E. Maccoby. "How Different Is the 'Different Voice'?" *Signs* 11 (Winter 1986): 310–16.

Gutmann, Amy. "Communitarian Critics of Liberalism," *Philosophy and Public Affairs* 14 (Summer 1985): 308–22.

Haan, Norma. "Hypothetical and Actual Moral Reasoning in a Situation of Civil Disobedience," *Journal of Personality and Social Psychology* 32 (1975): 255–70.

——. "Two Moralities in Action Contexts," *Journal of Personality and Social Psychology* 36 (1978): 286–305.

Haan, Norma, Robert N. Bellah, Paul Rabinow, and William M. Sullivan, eds. *Social Science as Moral Inquiry.* New York: Columbia University Press, 1983.

Habermas, Jürgen. *Communication and the Evolution of Society.* Trans. Thomas McCarthy. Boston: Beacon Press, 1979.

Hallie, Philip. *Lest Innocent Blood Be Shed.* New York: Harper & Row, 1979.

Hampton, Jean. *Hobbes and the Social Contract Tradition.* Cambridge: Cambridge University Press, 1986.

Hanen, Marsha, and Kai Nielsen, eds. *Science, Morality, and Feminist Theory. Canadian Journal of Philosophy* suppl. vol. 13 (1987).

Harding, Sandra and Merrill Hintikka, eds. *Discovering Reality.* Dordrecht: D. Reidel, 1983.

Hardwig, John. "In Search of an Ethics of Personal Relationships." In *Person to Person.* Ed. George Graham and Hugh LaFollette. Pp. 63–81. Philadelphia: Temple University Press, 1989.

——. "Should Women Think in Terms of Rights?" *Ethics* 94 (April 1984): 441–55.

Hare, R. M. *Moral Thinking.* Oxford: Clarendon Press, 1981.

Hartsock, Nancy. *Money, Sex, and Power.* Boston: Northeastern University Press, 1983.

Haug, Frigga. "Morals Also Have Two Genders." Trans. Rodney Livingstone. *New Left Review* 143 (1984): 51–67.

Held, Virginia. "Feminism and Moral Theory." In *Women and Moral Theory.* Ed. Eva Feder Kittay and Diana T. Meyers. Pp. 111–28. Totowa, N.J.: Rowman & Littlefield, 1987.

——. "Non-Contractual Society: A Feminist View." In *Science, Morality, and Feminist Theory.* Ed. Marsha Hanen and Kai Nielsen. *Canadian Journal of Philosophy* suppl. vol. 13 (1987): 111–38.

——. "The Obligations of Mothers and Fathers." In *Mothering: Essays in*

Feminist Theory. Ed. Joyce Trebilcot. Pp. 7–20. Totowa, N.J.: Rowman & Allanheld, 1983.

——. *Rights and Goods.* New York: Free Press, 1984.

Heller, Thomas C., Morton Sosna, and David E. Wellbery, eds. *Reconstructing Individualism.* Stanford: Stanford University Press, 1986.

Herman, Barbara. "On the Value of Acting from the Motive of Duty," *Philosophical Review* 67 (July 1981): 233–50.

Heyd, David. "Ethical Universalism, Justice, and Favouritism," *Australasian Journal of Philosophy* 56 (May 1978): 25–31.

Hill, Thomas E., Jr. "The Importance of Autonomy." In *Women and Moral Theory.* Ed. Eva Feder Kittay and Diana T. Meyers. Pp. 129–38. Totowa, N.J.: Rowman & Littlefield, 1987.

Hoagland, Sarah. *Lesbian Ethics.* Palo Alto, Calif.: Institute of Lesbian Studies, 1988.

——. "Some Thoughts about 'Caring.' " In *Feminist Ethics.* Ed. Claudia Card. Pp. 246–63. Lawrence: University Press of Kansas, 1991.

Hobbes, Thomas. *Leviathan.* Ed. C. B. McPherson. Harmondsworth, U.K.: Penguin, 1968.

Hochschild, Arlie. *The Managed Heart: The Commercialization of Human Feeling.* Berkeley: University of California Press, 1983.

hooks, bell. *Ain't I a Woman: Black Women and Feminism.* Boston: South End Press, 1981.

——. *Feminist Theory: From Margin to Center.* Boston: South End Press, 1984.

Houston, Barbara. "Rescuing Womanly Virtues: Some Dangers of Moral Reclamation." In *Science, Morality, and Feminist Theory.* Ed. Marsha Hanen and Kai Nielsen. *Canadian Journal of Philosophy* suppl. vol. 13 (1987): 237–62.

Hutter, Horst. *Politics as Friendship.* Waterloo, Ont.: Wilfrid Laurier University Press, 1978).

"Impartiality and Ethical Theory." Symposium in *Ethics* 101 (July 1991): 698–864.

Jaggar, Alison M. "Feminist Ethics: Some Issues for the Nineties," *Journal of Social Philosophy* 20 (Spring/Fall 1989): 91–107.

——. *Feminist Politics and Human Nature.* Totowa, N.J.: Rowman & Allanheld, 1983.

Joseph, Gloria I., and Jill Lewis. *Common Differences: Conflicts in Black and White Feminist Perspectives.* Boston: South End Press, 1981.

Kamler, Howard. "Strong Feelings," *Journal of Value Inquiry* 19 (1985): 3–12.

Kant, Immanuel. *Groundwork of the Metaphysics of Morals*. Trans. Lewis White Beck. Indianapolis: Bobbs-Merrill, 1959.

Kekes, John. "Morality and Impartiality," *American Philosophical Quarterly* 18 (October 1981): 295–303.

Kerber, Linda, Catherine G. Greeno, and Eleanor E. Maccoby, Zella Luria, Carol B. Stack, and Carol Gilligan. "On *In a Different Voice*: An Interdisciplinary Forum," *Signs* 11 (Winter 1986): 304–33.

Ketchum, Sara Ann. "Liberalism and Marriage Law." In *Feminism and Philosophy*. Ed. Mary Vetterling-Braggin, Frederick A. Elliston, and Jane English. Pp. 264–76. Totowa, N.J.: Littlefield, Adams, 1977.

Kierkegaard, Søren. *Fear and Trembling*. Trans. Walter Lowrie. Princeton: Princeton University Press, 1941.

Kittay, Eva Feder. "Woman as Metaphor," *Hypatia* 3 (September 1988): 63–86.

Kittay, Eva Feder, and Diana T. Meyers, eds. *Women and Moral Theory*. Totowa, N.J.: Rowman & Littlefield, 1987.

Klein, Dorie. "The Dark Side of Marriage: Battered Wives and the Domination of Women." In *Judge, Lawyer, Victim, Thief: Gender Roles and Criminal Justice*. Ed. Nicole Hahn Rafter and Elizabeth A. Stanko. Pp. 83–107. Boston: Northeastern University Press, 1982.

Kohlberg, Lawrence. *The Philosophy of Moral Development: Moral Stages and the Idea of Justice*. San Francisco: Harper & Row, 1981.

——. "A Reply to Owen Flanagan and Some Comments on the Puka-Goodpastor Exchange," *Ethics* 92 (April 1982): 513–28.

——. "Stage and Sequence: The Cognitive-Developmental Approach to Socialization." In *Handbook of Socialization Theory and Research*. Ed. D. A. Goslin. Pp. 347–480. Chicago: Rand McNally, 1969.

Kohlberg, Lawrence, Charles Levine, and Alexandra Hewar. *Moral Stages: A Current Reformulation and Response to Critics*. Basel: S. Karger, 1983.

Kymlicka, Will. "Rethinking the Family," *Philosophy and Public Affairs* 20 (Winter 1991): 77–97.

Larrabee, Mary Jeanne, ed. *An Ethic of Care*. New York: Routledge, 1993.

Le Pichon, Yann. *Gauguin: Life, Art, Inspiration*. New York: Harry N. Abrams, 1987.

MacIntyre, Alasdair. *After Virtue*. Notre Dame, Ind.: University of Notre Dame Press, 1981.

Mackie, J. L. *Ethics*. Harmondsworth, U.K.: Penguin, 1977.

Manning, Rita C. *Speaking from the Heart: A Feminist Perspective on Ethics*. Lanham, Md.: Rowman & Littlefield, 1992.

Mansbridge, Jane. "The Limits of Friendship." In *Participation in Politics* (Nomos XVI). Ed. J. Roland Pennock and John W. Chapman. Pp. 246–75. New York: Lieber-Atherton, 1975.

May, Larry. *The Morality of Groups*. Notre Dame, Ind.: University of Notre Dame Press, 1987.

———. *Sharing Responsibility*. Chicago: University of Chicago Press, 1993.

May, Larry, and Stacey Hoffman, eds. *Collective Responsibility*. Savage, Md.: Rowman & Littlefield, 1991.

Meilander, Gilbert. *Friendship: A Study in Theological Ethics*. Notre Dame, Ind.: University of Notre Dame Press, 1981.

Meyers, Diana T. *Self, Society, and Personal Choice*. New York: Columbia University Press, 1989.

Milgram, Stanley. "The Experience of Living in Cities," *Science* 167 (1970): 1461–68.

Mill, John Stuart, and Harriet Taylor. *Essays on Sex Equality*. Ed. Alice S. Rossi. Chicago: University of Chicago Press, 1970.

Mohanty, Chandra Talpade, Ann Russo, and Lourdes Torres, eds. *Third World Women and the Politics of Feminism*. Bloomington: Indiana University Press, 1991.

Moody-Adams, Michele. "Gender and the Complexity of Moral Voices." In *Feminist Ethics*. Ed. Claudia Card. Pp. 195–212. Lawrence: University Press of Kansas, 1991.

Moravcsik, J. M. E. "The Perils of Friendship and Conceptions of the Self." In *Human Agency: Language, Duty, and Value*. Ed. Jonathan Dancy, J. M. E. Moravcsik, and C. C. W. Taylor. Pp. 133–51. Stanford: Standford University Press, 1988.

Nagel, Thomas. *The View from Nowhere*. New York: Oxford University Press, 1986.

Nicholson, Linda. *Gender and History: The Limits of Social Theory in the Age of the Family*. New York: Columbia University Press, 1986.

———. "Women, Morality, and History," *Social Research* 50 (1983): 514–36.

Nochlin, Linda. *Women, Art, and Power*. New York: Harper & Row, 1988.

Noddings, Nel. *Caring: A Feminine Approach to Ethics and Moral Education*. Berkeley: University of California Press, 1984.

———. "A Response," *Hypatia* 5 (Spring 1990): 120–26.

Nunner-Winkler, Gertrude. "Two Moralities? A Critical Discussion of an Ethic of Care and Responsibility versus an Ethic of Rights and Justice." In *Morality, Moral Behavior, and Moral Development*. Ed. William M. Kurtines and Jacob L. Gewirtz. Pp. 348–61. New York: John Wiley & Sons, 1984.

Okin, Susan Moller. "Justice and Gender," *Philosophy and Public Affairs* 16 (1987): 42–72.

——. *Justice, Gender, and the Family*. New York: Basic Books, 1989.

——. "Reason and Feeling in Thinking about Justice," *Ethics* 99 (January 1989): 229–49.

Oldenquist, Andrew. "Loyalties," *Journal of Philosophy* 79 (April 1982): 173–93.

Parfit, Derek. *Reasons and Persons*. Oxford: Clarendon Press, 1984.

Pateman, Carole. " 'The Disorder of Women': Women, Love, and the Sense of Justice," *Ethics* 91 (1980): 20–34.

——. *The Problem of Political Obligation: A Critique of Liberal Theory*. Berkeley: University of California Press, 1979.

——. *The Sexual Contract*. Stanford: Stanford University Press, 1988.

——. "Women and Consent," *Political Theory* 8 (May 1980): 149–68.

Paul, Jeffrey. "Substantive Social Contracts and the Legitimate Basis of Political Authority," *Monist* 66, no. 4 (1983): 513–28.

"Philosophy and Feminism." Special issue of *Journal of Social Philosophy* 21 (Fall/Winter 1990).

Piper, Adrian M. S. "Moral Theory and Moral Alienation," *Journal of Philosophy* 84 (February 1987): 102–18.

Pitkin, Hanna. "Obligation and Consent." In *Philosophy, Politics, and Society*. 4th ser. Ed. P. Laslett, W. G. Runciman, and Q. Skinner. Oxford: Blackwell, 1972.

Plato. *Euthyphro*. Trans. Benjamin Jowett. In *The Works of Plato*. Ed. Irwin Edman. New York: Modern Library, 1928.

Rachels, James. "Morality, Parents, and Children." In *Person to Person*. Ed. George Graham and Hugh LaFollette. Philadelphia: Temple University Press, 1989.

Railton, Peter. "Alienation, Consequentialism, and the Demands of Morality," *Philosophy and Public Affairs* 13 (Spring 1984): 134–71.

Rawls, John. "The Basic Structure as Subject," *American Philosophical Quarterly* 14 (1977): 159–65.

——. "Justice as Fairness: Political Not Metaphysical," *Philosophy and Public Affairs* 14 (Summer 1985): 223–51.

——. "Kantian Constructivism in Moral Theory," *Journal of Philosophy* 77 (1980): 515–72.

——. *A Theory of Justice*. Cambridge: Harvard University Press, 1971.

——. "Two Concepts of Rules," *Philosophical Review* 64 (1955): 3–32.

Raymond, Janice. *A Passion for Friends*. Boston: Beacon Press, 1986.

Reisman, John. *Anatomy of Friendship*. New York: Irvington 1979.

Rhode, Deborah L. *Justice and Gender*. Cambridge: Harvard University Press, 1989.

Rich, Adrienne. "Compulsory Heterosexuality and Lesbian Existence," *Signs* 5 (Summer 1980): 631–60.

——. "Split at the Root: An Essay on Jewish Identity." In *Blood, Bread, and Poetry*. New York: W. W. Norton, 1986.

Richards, David A. J. *A Theory of Reasons for Action*. Oxford: Clarendon Press, 1971.

Ringelheim, Joan. "Women and the Holocaust: A Reconsideration of Research," *Signs* 10, no. 4 (1985): 741–61.

Rosenberg, Carroll Smith. "The Female World of Love and Ritual: Relations between Women in Nineteenth Century America," *Signs* 1, no. 1 (1975): 1–29.

Royko, Mike. *Boss: Richard J. Daley of Chicago*. New York: New American Library, 1971.

Rubin, Lillian. *Just Friends*. New York: Harper & Row, 1985.

Ruddick, Sara. *Maternal Thinking: Towards a Politics of Peace*. New York: Ballantine Books 1989.

Sandel, Michael, ed. *Liberalism and Its Critics*. New York: New York University Press, 1984.

——. *Liberalism and the Limits of Justice*. Cambridge: Cambridge University Press, 1982.

Scheffler, Samuel. *The Rejection of Consequentialism*. Oxford: Clarendon Press, 1982.

Scheman, Naomi. "Individualism and the Objects of Psychology." In *Discovering Reality*. Ed. Sandra Harding and Merrill B. Hintikka. Pp. 225–44. Dordrecht: D. Reidel, 1983.

Schoeman, Ferdinand. "Friendship and Testimonial Privilege." In *Ethics, Public Policy, and Criminal Justice*. Ed. Frederick Elliston and Norman Bowie. Pp. 257–73. Cambridge, Mass.: Oelgeschlager, Gunn & Hain, 1982.

Schrag, Francis. "Justice and the Family," *Inquiry* 19 (Summer 1976): 193–208.

Seiden, Anne M., and Pauline B. Bart. "Woman to Woman: Is Sisterhood Powerful?" In *Old Family/New Family: Interpersonal Relationships*. Ed. Nona Glazer-Malbin. Pp. 189–228. New York: D. Van Nostrand, 1975.

Sennett, Richard, ed. *Classic Essays on the Culture of Cities*. New York: Appleton-Century-Crofts, 1969.

Shanley, Mary Lyndon. "Marital Slavery and Friendship: John Stuart Mill's *The Subjection of Women*," *Political Theory* 9, no. 2 (1981): 238–44.

Sherman, Claire. *Sex Discrimination in a Nutshell.* St. Paul, Minn.: West, 1982.

Simmons, A. John. *Moral Principles and Political Obligation.* Princeton: Princeton University Press, 1979.

Singer, Marcus. *Generalization in Ethics.* New York: Alfred A. Knopf, 1961.

Singer, Peter. "Famine, Affluence, and Morality," *Philosophy and Public Affairs* 1 (Spring 1972).

——. *Practical Ethics.* Cambridge: Cambridge University Press, 1979.

Slote, Michael. "Morality Not a System of Imperatives," *American Philosophical Quarterly* 19 (October 1982): 331–40.

Smart, Carol. *Feminism and the Power of Law.* London: Routledge, 1989.

Smart, J. J. C., and Bernard Williams. *Utilitarianism: For and Against.* Cambridge: Cambridge University Press, 1973.

Spelman, Elizabeth. *Inessential Woman: Problems of Exclusion in Feminist Thought.* Boston: Beacon Press, 1988.

Squier, Susan Merrill, ed. *Women Writers and the City.* Knoxville: University of Tennessee Press, 1984.

Stack, Carol B. "The Culture of Gender: Women and Men of Color," *Signs* 11 (Winter 1986): 321–24.

Stimpson, Catharine, et al., eds. *Women and the American City.* Chicago: University of Chicago Press, 1980, 1981.

Stocker, Michael. "The Schizophrenia of Modern Ethical Theories," *Journal of Philosophy* 63 (August 12, 1976): 453–66.

——. "Values and Purposes: The Limits of Teleology and the Ends of Friendship," *Journal of Philosophy* 78 (December 1981): 747–65.

Sumner, L. W. *The Moral Foundation of Rights.* Oxford: Clarendon Press, 1987.

Taylor, Paul. "On Taking the Moral Point of View," *Midwest Studies in Philosophy* 3 (1978): 35–61.

Telfer, Elizabeth. "Friendship," *Proceedings of the Aristotelian Society,* 1970–71, pp. 223–41.

Thomas, Laurence. "Friendship," *Synthese* 72 (1987): 217–36.

——. *Living Morally: A Psychology of Moral Character.* Philadelphia: Temple University Press, 1989.

Thorne, Barrie, with Marilyn Yalom, eds. *Rethinking the Family: Some Feminist Questions.* New York: Longman, 1982.

Tong, Rosemarie. *Feminine and Feminist Ethics.* Belmont, Calif.: Wadsworth, 1993.

Trebilcot, Joyce, ed. *Mothering: Essays in Feminist Theory.* Totowa, N.J.: Rowman & Allanheld, 1983.

Tronto, Joan. "Beyond Gender Difference to a Theory of Care," *Signs* 12, no. 4 (1987): 644–61.

Verbrugge, Lois. "The Structure of Adult Friendship Choices," *Social Forces* 56 no. 2 (1977): 576–97.

Walker, Lawrence J. "Sex Differences in the Development of Moral Reasoning," *Child Development* 55 no. 3 (1984): 677–91.

Walker, Margaret. "Moral Particularism," *Metaphilosophy* 18 (1987): 171–85.

———. "Partial Consideration," *Ethics* 101 (July 1991): 758–74.

Webber, Melvin. "Order in Diversity: Community without Propinquity." In *Neighborhood, City, and Metropolis*. Ed. R. Gutman and D. Popenoe. Pp. 792–811. New York: Random House, 1970.

Wellman, Carl. "Doing Justice to Rights," *Hypatia* 3 (Winter 1989): 153–58.

———. *A Theory of Rights: Persons under Laws, Institutions, and Morals*. Totowa, N.J.: Rowman & Allanheld, 1985.

Whitbeck, Caroline. "A Different Reality: Feminist Ontology." In *Beyond Domination*. Ed. Carol Gould. Pp. 64–88. Totowa, N.J.: Rowman & Allanheld, 1984.

Williams, Bernard. *Moral Luck*. Cambridge: Cambridge University Press, 1981.

Williams, Patricia. *The Alchemy of Race and Rights*. Cambridge: Harvard University Press, 1991.

Wolgast, Elizabeth. *The Grammar of Justice*. Ithaca, N.Y.: Cornell University Press, 1987.

"Women and Morality." Special issue of *Social Research* 50 (Fall 1983).

"Women in the City." Special issue of *Urban Resources* 3 (Winter 1986).

Young, Iris Marion. "The Ideal of Community and the Politics of Difference," *Social Theory and Practice* 12 (Spring 1986): 1–26.

———. "Impartiality and the Civic Public: Some Implications of Feminist Critiques of Moral and Political Theory," *Praxis International* 5 (January 1986): 381–401.

———. "Polity and Group Difference: A Critique of the Ideal of Universal Citizenship," *Ethics* 99 (January 1989): 250–74.

Young-Bruehl, Elizabeth. "The Education of Women as Philosophers," *Signs* 12 (Winter 1987): 207–21.

INDEX

abuse, 41n23, 74–75, 78, 160–61
  See also violence toward women
Ackelsberg, Martha, 187n1, 248n34
Ackerman, Bruce, 18n23
affirmative action, 41n22
Allen, Jeffner, 146
Annas, David, 207n1
Aristotle, 189n2, 192n7, 196n9, 199,
    220
  on equality in friendship, 210n5,
    210n6
art history, 168–69
autonomy, 78–79n32, 202, 235, 238

Baier, Annette, 143n3, 148n21, 232n6,
    254n49
  on trust, 204n15, 211n9
Baron, Marcia, 48n39, 126n19, 188n1,
    204n15
  on partiality, 38, 39n18
Bartky, Sandra, 146n14, 204n16
Baumrind, Diana, 98n23, 121n7
Becker, Lawrence C., 44n27
Benhabib, Seyla
  criticism of liberalism, 222n29, 231n1
  on impartiality, 17n20, 18n22
Berkowitz, M., 120n5
bias
  defined, 11–12
  elimination of, 31–34
  and equal consideration of all
    persons, 9
  See also partiality
Bienen, Leigh, 223n30
Block, Jeanne, 119–20n4
Blum, Lawrence, 53n47, 86n48,
    109n40, 146n15

on duties in public office, 81n39,
    213n14
on friendship, 187n1, 196
on impartiality, 13n11, 36
on partiality, 35n1, 35n3, 39n18, 66,
    191n6
Bonheur, Rosa, 169
Brabeck, Mary, 120n5
Brewster-Smith, M., 119–20n4
Broughton, John, 121, 131–32n28
*Brown v. Board of Education of Topeka,
  Kansas*, 96n14
Bunch, Charlotte, 83n44
Butler, Judith, 78n31

Calhoun, Cheshire, 148
Cancian, Francesca M., 132n29, 175–79
Card, Claudia, 133n32, 134n34, 170–71,
    187n1, 193n8
  on care ethics, 145–46, 155
  on moral luck, 70n21, 163n58
care ethics, 94–110, 118, 135–36, 147–
    55
  contrast with justice ethics, 109, 119,
    135
  and distributive justice, 107–8
  and esteem for women, 148–49
  feminist overview of, 145–55
  forms of care, 156–62, 173–84
  and gender, 169–74
  and individualism, 162
  integration with justice ethics, 108,
    128, 142–43
  and oppression, 146, 149–55
  See also justice ethics; love
care-justice dichotomy, 4, 67, 91–92,
    95, 119, 143–44

care-justice dichotomy (*cont.*)
  implausibility of, 126–34
  See also care ethics; justice ethics
charity. *See* global moral concern
Chodorow, Nancy, 172n79, 176, 237
commitments to particular persons,
  134–41, 188–95
  and affection, 193, 194–95
  and integration with abstract moral
    commitments, 138–41
  and respect, 137, 193–94
  risks of, 203–6
  See also friendship; relationships,
    close personal
communal traits, 124, 233
communitarianism, 71–72, 73
  community as constitutive of
    identity, 242–47
  feminist criticism of, 233–34, 237–39,
    241–42, 253
  and the social self, 234–47
communities
  of choice, 244–50, 252–53, 255
  lesbian, 252–53
  norms and traditions of, 239–42
  as oppressive, 217–18, 239–40, 253
  of place, 242–47, 253–54
  political, 242–43
  and self-identity, 235–37, 241, 243–
    47, 252–53
  urban, 247, 249–52
  women's, 153–54, 248–49, 253
context sensitivity, 110–16
contextual relativism, 93, 114
contractarianism, 103, 221–30
Cooper, John, 189n2, 196n9
Cornell, Drucilla, 232n5, 242n23
Cottingham, John, 103n33
  criticism of impartiality, 36, 55–57
  fulfillment defense of partiality,
    35n2, 59, 60
  on global moral concern, 79n33, 81–
    82
  on unjustified forms of partiality,
    39n18, 72n25
critical moral thinking, 9–10, 23, 140

Darwall, Stephen, 11n2
  on requirements for impartiality, 24,
    27, 28–29, 30
Diamond, Irene, 74n28

Dickens, Charles, 85
Dietz, Mary, 187n1, 196
Dillon, Robin, 40n20, 137n37
Dinnerstein, Dorothy, 237
discrimination, 30n39
  See also oppression of women

Eagly, Alice H., 124n15, 125n17,
  125n18, 233n9
egoism, 69
Ehrenreich, Barbara, 149n23, 169
Eisenberg, Nancy, 124n14
Eisenstein, Zillah, 231n1
empathy, 87–88, 124
empowerment, 176–77, 179–80, 182
  See also oppression of women
English, Deirdre, 149n23
English, Jane, 188n1
ethic of care. *See* care ethics
Ewin, R. E., 211n9
exploitation of women, 129–30, 160n54
  See also abuse; oppression of women;
    violence toward women

Faludi, Susan, 174n82
family, 47–48, 49–50, 240, 242, 244–46
feminism, 145n10, 148n21
  and friendship, 187–88
  and global moral concern, 83–87
  and individualism, 231–33, 238–39
  and liberalism, 222–23
  and partiality, 66–67
  and rights, 67, 150n27
  See also care ethics
Ferguson, Ann, 160n54
Fetterley, Judith, 169n73
Firth, Roderick, 11n5, 64
Fischer, Claude, 249n36, 250, 251–52
Fishkin, James, 86n49, 120n4
Flanagan, Owen, 99, 143n3, 232n6
Flax, Jane, 231n1
Fried, Charles, 69, 80n34
  on partiality, 35n3, 59n55, 66, 191n6
Friedman, Marilyn, 146n14, 204n16
friendship
  equality in, 189–90, 210n5, 210n6
  feminist approach to, 187–88n1
  and moral growth, 196–203
  and moral witnessing, 197–99, 204–5
  and potential for social change, 207,
    217, 219–21, 248

quasi-voluntarist account of, 212–30
and trust, 195, 204–5, 211
value of, 195–96, 217–21, 248–49
virtue-theoretic approach to, 187–88
voluntary nature of, 207–21, 227–28,
247–49
See also commitments to particular
persons; relationships, close
personal
Frye, Marilyn, 129–30
fulfillment defense of partiality, 35, 58–
61

Gauguin, Paul, 164–66, 170
Gauthier, David, 229n42
on the social contract, 223n32,
225n33
on utility maximizers, 225n36, 232n2
Gelfant, Blanche, 251
gender
asymmetries in philosophy writing,
70–71, 170
and care ethics, 171–73
and moral luck, 167–71
stereotypes, 105–6, 124–26, 151
gender differences in moral reasoning
(gender difference hypothesis), 1–
2, 91–93, 99, 117–25, 126n19, 131–
32n28, 233n10
division of moral labor, 118, 122–25
empirical studies of, 119–21
as myth, 124–25
gender differences in responsibilities,
169–73
gendered morality. *See* gender
differences in moral reasoning
Gewirth, Alan, 14n13, 38
on unjustified forms of partiality,
39n18, 72n25
Gilder, George, 51–52n43
Gilligan, Carol, 110–11, 147n19, 150,
152, 176, 237
on care ethics, 135–36, 153–54, 159
on care-justice dichotomy, 4, 67, 91–
92, 95, 119, 143–44
on context, 93, 113, 114
on gender differences in moral
reasoning, 1–2, 91–93, 99, 117,
119–25, 233n10
integration of care and justice, 128,
142–43

on justice ethics, 124n16, 132–33
global moral concern, 79–88
See also impartiality
Godwin, William, 80–81
Goodin, Robert E., 44, 45–46, 74n28
Greeno, Catherine G., 122n10
group loyalty, 71–72
Gutmann, Amy, 233

Haan, Norma, 119–20n4, 120, 121n7
Habermas, Jürgen, 17, 18n22
Hallie, Philip, 109n40
Hampton, Jean, 229
Hardwig, John, 53n46, 67n13
Hare, R. M., 10n1, 55n50
on impartiality, 11n2, 12n8, 14–15,
18–23, 25n27, 64–65
on universalizability, 14–23
Hartsock, Nancy C. M., 231n1, 232n7
Haug, Frigga, 91n2
health care, 113–14
Heinz dilemma, 96, 104–12
Held, Virginia, 68, 87–88, 118n2,
131n26, 155n40
on the mother-child relationship,
222n26, 232n7
on the social contract, 103n34,
222n27, 222n28
Herman, Barbara, 38
Hill, Thomas E., Jr., 38
Hoagland, Sarah, 146, 152, 157–58
Hobbes, Thomas, 221–22, 229
Hochschild, Arlie, 173n80
Holstein, Constance, 120n4, 120n5
Homans, George, 232n3
Homiak, Marcia, 146n15
hooks, bell, 182–83n95
Housman, Judy, 146n15
Houston, Barbara, 133n32, 145–46,
147n20
Hume, David, 148n21
Hutter, Horst, 127n20, 219

impartiality
achieving, 15
archangel image of, 64–65
contractual approach to, 14–16, 18–
20, 24–27
criticisms of, 10, 17n20, 18–27, 35–
39, 65–69
defined, 11–13, 36n4

impartiality (*cont.*)
  dialogical approach to, 18n23, 23–24
  elimination of recognizable biases,
    31–34
  as encompassing partiality, 37–38, 82
  and feminism, 66–67
  ideal-observer image of, 11n5, 64
  and impersonality, 11–13
  "love thy neighbor as thyself," 55–
    57
  as a matter of degree, 31
  monological approach to, 17–18
  and neutrality, 27–31
  not always morally obligatory, 13–14
  and objectivity, 12
  of reasons, 28–31
  required for critical moral thinking,
    9–10
  reversibility approach to, 15
  rhetorical uses of, 37, 64n3
  as a specific duty, 13
  universalization approach to, 14–15,
    16, 18–23, 27
  veil of ignorance, 17n20, 25n27, 26,
    128
  view from nowhere, 65
  See also bias; global moral concern;
    partiality
impersonality, 12–13
  See also impartiality
individualism, 124n16, 162, 229, 234–35
  feminist criticism of, 231–33, 238–39

Jackson, Kathryn, 143n3, 232n6
Jagger, Alison M., 71n32, 222n29,
  231n1
justice ethics, 109, 143
  and care, 95–99, 100–102, 106–7, 132
  and context sensitivity, 110
  distributive vs. corrective justice,
    130, 133
  life vs. property, 112
  and relationships, 101–2, 127–34
  See also care ethics

Kamler, Howard, 191n5, 192n7
Kant, Immanuel, 37, 48, 138
Kekes, John, 35n1, 66n7, 81n38
Keniston, Kenneth, 120n4
Ketchum, Sara Ann, 43n25
Kierkegaard, Søren, 100

Kittay, Eva Feder, 123n13
Klein, Dorie, 43n26
Kohlberg, Lawrence, 15, 95–97,
  159n51, 160n53
  on context sensitivity, 114, 115
  on moral development, 92–94, 98,
    100, 102–4, 108, 115

Langdale, Sharry, 120n4
Lasch, Christopher, 47n36
Lennon, Roger, 124n14
Le Pichon, Yann, 164n60, 166n64
lesbianism, 252–53
Levin, Margarita, 24n26
liberalism, 231n1, 234–35, 241
  liberal contractarianism, 103, 221–30
  libertarian defense of partiality, 59n55
love, 132n29
  expressive vs. instrumental, 174–79
  feminization of, 174–76, 178
  See also care ethics

Maccoby, Eleanor E., 122n10
MacIntyre, Alasdair, 71–72, 217–21
  on community, 239, 242–43
  on friendship, 217–21
  impartiality as impossible, 37n11,
    67–68
  on the social self, 67–68, 236–37
Mackie, J. L., 69
MacKinnon, Catherine, 120n4
Mansbridge, Jane, 196
marriage and divorce, 43n25, 43n26,
  46–47, 51–52, 189n3
May, Larry, 29n38, 87n51, 162n57
Meyers, Diana T., 78–79n32, 202n13
Milgram, Stanley, 249n38
Mill, John Stuart, 148n21, 189n3,
  241n22
Moody-Adams, Michele, 147, 150n28
moral development, 92–94, 98, 100,
  102–4, 108, 115, 121n7
moral luck, 163–68
moral witnessing, 33, 197–205
mutuality, 53, 158–61

Nagel, Thomas, 25n27, 28–29
  on impersonal standpoint, 12–13, 65
  on objectivity, 11n4, 12, 26–27
neutrality condition for impartiality,
  28–29

Nicholson, Linda, 123n12, 222n29
Nochlin, Linda, 165n61, 168
Noddings, Nel, 83n43, 143, 152n34
  on care ethics, 67n12, 153–54, 157–61
Nunner-Winkler, Gertrude, 120n6

objectivity, 11–12
  See also impartiality
Okin, Susan Moller, 16n20, 130n25,
  143n3, 144n8
  on marriage, 46–47, 52
Oldenquist, Andrew, 37, 72n24
oppression of women, 144, 148–49,
  151, 240, 243
  and care ethics, 145–46, 152
  and caretaking practices, 146, 182–83
  See also abuse; exploitation of
  women; violence toward women

Parfit, Derek, 28, 54
  on aim of partiality, 52–53, 59
partiality
  aim of, 52–53, 59
  as a duty in relationships, 40, 44–45,
  73, 212
  as encompassed by impartiality, 37–
  38, 82
  and familiarity, 58
  and feminism, 66–67
  fulfillment defense of, 35, 59, 60, 66,
  70
  and group loyalty, 71–72
  and inadequate resources, 52–61, 75,
  191n6
  intrinsic value of, 35, 66
  and Kantian deontology, 48
  libertarian defense of, 59n55
  paradigms of, 73
  practices and exemplifying actions,
  60n58
  required for integrity and the good
  life, 35, 58–61, 84
  required for relationships, 35, 36,
  65–66
  unjustified forms of, 39n18, 41, 72
  and value of relationships, 39–52, 66
  See also bias; impartiality
Pateman, Carole, 132n28, 222n28,
  222n29, 223n30, 225n35, 231n1
Paul, Jeffrey, 226n37
personhood, 138, 161–62

Piaget, Jean, 97
Piper, Adrian M. S., 29
Pitkin, Hanna, 225n35
Plato, 101–2, 127
prejudice, 12

Rachels, James, 58n54
Railton, Peter, 38
Rawls, John, 11n2, 60n58, 67n11, 195,
  198n10, 223n32, 225n36
  contractual model for determining
  principles of justice, 15–16, 17n20
  on impartiality, 12, 15–20, 24–27
  on original position, 15–17, 24–27
  on veil of ignorance, 17n20, 25n27,
  26, 128
Raymond, Janice, 187n1, 249n35
reasons, impartiality of, 28–31
reciprocity, 53, 158–61
Reisman, John, 210n5
relationships, close personal
  abandonment, 169–70
  conventions surrounding, 45–46, 49–
  50, 54–55, 73–75, 77–78, 217–21
  and duty, 44–45, 48–49, 106, 212–14
  family relationships, 47–48, 49–50
  irreplaceability in, 53–54, 138
  and justice, 67, 101–2, 127–34
  moral assessment of, 42–44, 49–50
  morally wrong relationships, 41–42
  partiality required for, 35n1, 36, 44,
  65–66
  and the social contract, 103
  uniqueness of, 40n20, 53–54, 190–91
  unreflective opinions about, 50–51
  and urban life, 249–52
  value of, 35, 39–52, 66
  See also abuse; commitments to
  particular persons; friendship;
  marriage and divorce
respect, 137, 193–94, 215
Rhode, Deborah L., 41n23, 149n24,
  149n26, 160n55
Rich, Adrienne, 149n25, 154n39, 245–
  46, 252
Richards, David A. J., 11n4
rights. *See* justice ethics
Ringelheim, Joan, 145n10
Rosenberg, Carroll Smith, 153n38
Royko, Mike, 132n30
Rubin, Lillian, 209n3, 209n4

Ruddick, Sara, 66, 131n26
on care ethics, 151, 153, 155n40

Sandel, Michael J., 67–68, 229n40
on community, 71–72, 235–36, 242–46
Scheman, Naomi, 146n15, 231n1
Schoeman, Ferdinand, 192n7, 195
self as individual, 69
self as partial, 67
self as social. See social self
Sennett, Richard, 249n37
Shanley, Mary Lyndon, 189n3
Sherman, Claire, 30n39
Simmons, A. John, 228n39
Singer, Marcus, 14n13
Singer, Peter, 80
Slote, Michael, 187n1
Smart, Carol, 67n13, 150n27
social contract
contractarianism, 103, 221–30
contractual approach to impartiality, 14–18, 24–27
social self, 67–70, 72–79, 232
and care ethics, 161
communitarian view of, 234–47
complexity of, 76–79
and global moral concern, 87–88
and natural drives, 79n32
and social criticism and resistance, 76–79
socioeconomic conditions, 57, 58
effects on relationships, 55, 140
Solomon, David, 200–201n12
Sommers, Christina Hoff, 50n40, 85
antifeminism in, 51, 172n78, 174n83
Spelman, Elizabeth V., 157n44
Squier, Susan Merrill, 251n44
Stack, Carol B., 147
Steffen, Valerie J., 124n15, 125n18, 233n9
stereotypes, 105–6, 124–26, 151
Stocker, Michael, 37
on friendship, 187n1, 214n15
subordination. See oppression of women

Taylor, Harriet, 148n21
Taylor, Paul, 65

Telfer, Elizabeth, 191n4, 192n7
on friendship, 188n1, 195
Thomas, Laurence
on friendship, 188n1, 207n1, 209n3, 210n8
on trust, 211n9, 211n11
traditions surrounding relationships, 45–46, 49–50, 54–55, 73–75, 77–78, 217–21
Tronto, Joan, 145, 146–47
Turiel E., 120n5

unbiased standpoint. See impartiality
universalizability
contrasted with contractual method, 16–17
and impartiality, 14–15, 18–23, 27
and personal relationships, 102–3
and primacy of justice ethics, 97
logical properties of moral concepts, 14
test for, 14–15
urban life, 249–52
utilitarianism, 37

Verbrugge, Lois, 202n14, 227n38
violence toward women, 149–51
See also abuse; oppression of women
voluntarism, 212–30, 231

Walker, Lawrence J., 98n23, 120–21
Walker, Margaret, 141n39
on rhetorical uses of impartiality, 37n12, 64n3
Webber, Melvin, 250
Wellman, Carl, 150n27
Whitbeck, Caroline, 68
Williams, Bernard, 37, 53n46, 70–71
fulfillment defense of partiality, 35, 59, 60, 66, 70
on moral luck, 163–70
Wolgast, Elizabeth, 67
women's movement, 157

Young, Iris Marion, 34n42
on community, 239n21, 242n24
on impartiality, 18n22, 37, 67–68
Young-Bruehl, Elizabeth, 77n30

Library of Congress Cataloging-in-Publication Data

Friedman, Marilyn, 1945–
    What are Friends for? : feminist perspectives on personal
relationships and moral theory / Marilyn Friedman.
        p.   cm.
    Includes bibliographical references and index.
    ISBN 0-8014-2721-5.—ISBN 0-8014-8004-3 (pbk.)
    1. Friendship—Moral and ethical aspects.   2. Interpersonal
relations—Moral and ethical aspects.   3. Caring.   4. Feminist
ethics.   I. Title.
BJ1533.F8F75   1993
177'.6—dc20   93-25812